Praise for

all you need is love
AND OTHER LIES ABOUT MARRIAGE

"This terrific book reveals that it often takes 'embarrassingly little' to move a marriage out of a tough stalemate. Whether your ambitions for change are large or small, you'll find something helpful in these pages."   —Harriet Lerner, Ph.D., author of *The Dance of Anger*

"This sensational book outlines the things to do and not to do to make a marriage succeed. It will be so useful for everyone who is married, for every therapist, and for everyone who teaches about marriage."   —Betty Carter, author of *Love, Honor, and Negotiate*

"Without romanticizing or moralizing about the virtues of marriage, Dr. Jacobs prescribes realistic, sound advice for nurturing the fragile bonds of contemporary marriages. What this book offers is not a quick fix but a long-term fitness program for improving your marital health."   —Constance Ahrons, Ph.D., author of *We're Still Family*

"Dr. Phil, Harville Hendrix, and John Gray may have some great new company. John Jacobs' no-nonsense talk, incredible experience, and realistic suggestions will make a huge difference for people across America struggling to deal with the challenges of twenty-first century relationships. Some books announce a substantial new presence. Jacobs has the kind of clear, healing voice that needs to be heard."
     —Ron Taffle, author of *The Second Family: How Adolescent Power Is Challenging the American Family*

"John Jacobs has succeeded in soundly debunking many mistaken beliefs about modern marriage. He challenges the myths fostered by popular culture and outdated traditions and goes to the heart of what makes marriage work—and not work. Brought to life by many real-life stories of couples struggling to get it right, this entirely accessible volume provides sound advice for dealing with the inevitable disappointments of marriage. Highly recommended and state of the art, this book reflects years of refinement in marriage therapy techniques and is definitely a must-read."

—Elliott J. Rosen, Ed.D., L.M.F.T., Director,
Family Institute of Westchester

"This particularly thoughtful and articulate volume marks the arrival of a major new voice in couples psychology. Jacobs' tone is friendly and impartial, and he makes no false promises. He teaches readers how to overcome anger and resentment without sacrificing their needs. Even happily married couples may find it useful." —*Publishers Weekly*

"Enlightening . . . puts the conflicts of modern married couples into historical and cultural perspective. [Jacobs'] recommendations for change focus on helping readers adjust their expectations and make the first move toward breaking the cycle of negativity in their relationships. Astute observations, authentic anecdotes, and brutal honesty make this a book worth reading." —*Cleveland Plain Dealer*

© Joe Orecchio

About the Author

JOHN W. JACOBS, M.D., is a psychiatrist in private practice in Manhattan. He is a psychiatric supervisor and associate clinical psychiatrist at North Shore University Hospital and a Clinical Associate Professor of Psychiatry at New York University Medical College. Dr. Jacobs is the author of *Divorce and Fatherhood* (American Psychiatric Press), and numerous scholarly articles. He lectures frequently on divorce and has appeared on national television.

all you need is love

AND OTHER LIES ABOUT MARRIAGE

How to Save
Your Marriage Before
It's Too Late

John W. Jacobs, M.D.

Perennial Currents
An Imprint of HarperCollins*Publishers*

A hardcover edition of this book was published in 2004 by HarperCollins Publishers.

HarperCollins books may be purchased for educational, business, or sales promotional use. For information please write: Special Markets Department, HarperCollins Publishers Inc., 10 East 53rd Street, New York, NY 10022.

First Perennial Currents edition published in 2005.

Designed by Nancy B. Field

The Library of Congress has catalogued the hardcover as follows:

Jacobs, John W.
    All you need is love and other lies about marriage : a proven strategy to make your marriage work, from a leading couples therapist / John W. Jacobs.
        p. cm.
    Includes index.
    ISBN 0-06-050930-9 (cloth)
    1. Marriage. 2. Marital conflict. 3. Marriage counseling. I. Title.
    HQ734.J324 2004
    306.81-dc21   2003056582

ISBN 0-06-050931-7 (pbk.)

05 06 07 08 09   ❖/RRD   10 9 8 7 6 5 4 3 2

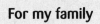

For my family

Contents

Contents

Preface

And when the event, the big change in your life, is simply an insight—isn't that a strange thing? That absolutely nothing changes except that you see things differently and you're less fearful and less anxious and stronger as a result. . . . You see things more clearly and you know that you're seeing them more clearly. And it comes to you that this is what it means to love life, this is all anybody who talks seriously about God is ever talking about. Moments like this.

—Jonathan Franzen, *The Corrections*

Laura is crying tears of outrage and disbelief. When she and Keith took their vows five years ago, she really meant the "for-better-or-worse" part. She never thought she'd end up in the office of a couples therapist trying to explain why she wants a divorce. "I just can't stand the fighting anymore."

Keith is fed up, too. They can't go a day without locking horns; last night they even argued about where to take their vacation. "She's just not the woman I married," he says.

Laura shakes her head. "Maybe the problem is that I'm exactly the woman you married. Maybe the problem is that you just don't love *me* anymore."

"That's completely not true," Keith says. "I do love you. I just don't understand why we're always fighting if we love each other so much."

• • •

"I feel completely taken advantage of," Marissa tells me. "Don and I agreed when we got married that we'd split all the household stuff fifty/fifty. I work ten-hour days, I drag myself home, and then I find that Don has done virtually nothing."

"That's not fair," protests Don, "I keep telling her, 'Just tell me what to do and I'll do it.' She doesn't give a damn that I'm just as tired as she is when I get home from work, too."

• • •

"I'm here, but I'm here under protest," Carlos informs me, his arms folded tightly across his chest. "What's the point of shelling out money for all this quote-unquote therapy when nothing is going to change how Kate acts anyway?"

"Can you believe him?" Kate turns to me in exasperation. "Like he's one to talk. There's plenty he should change. Why should I be the only one? But maybe he's right; maybe there's no point."

• • •

Married only two years, Ann and Larry have begun to feel that their relationship is more like a prison than the wonderful life they imagined for themselves and promised each other. "I don't think he loves me," says Ann tearfully. "He's always angry and critical of me. Everything I do seems wrong."

"Nonsense," replies Larry, "I do love you, but you're always so depressed and unhappy, and you're never interested in sex anymore."

"All he cares about is sex," says Ann. Larry throws up his hands.

"She treats me like I'm a sex maniac who only sniffs around her when I want some," he tells me. "Why is it always me who seems to want sex? She just pushes me away and tells me she feels fat and she's too tired anyway. It's humiliating to be sexually rejected by someone you love. I want to be with someone who wants me."

Ann just rolls her eyes. "How am I supposed to want you when you seem more interested in the women in the *Victoria's Secret* catalog, the *Sports Illustrated* swimsuit issue, and goddamn *Playboy*? I can't compete with that. Even the women's magazines never show any model who's bigger than a size two. Besides, sometimes I'd just like to be held without having to have sex all the time."

"You wouldn't have said that two years ago," says Larry, "Maybe we never should have gotten married."

• • •

Sally is furious at Greg for being so irresponsible with money. She's just learned that he hasn't paid many of their monthly bills for a long time, and she can't understand where all the money Greg earns is going. "It all goes to pay our bills," he says, "yours and mine. I don't buy anything you don't know about."

"It just doesn't add up," says Sally, "but whenever we try to discuss it, he just gets angry at me and threatens to get a divorce. I don't think he's committed to the relationship anymore. I don't trust him."

"How much of your salary do you contribute to your joint expenses?" I ask Sally.

"Very little," she replies. "How can I give him my money when he says he's going to divorce me? I need that money for my future."

Virtually everyone has significant problems at some time in their marriage. The couples who come to my office certainly aren't in denial that they're having problems; neither are you if you're holding this book. However, every one of the couples I've described above—in fact, almost everyone I've counseled about marriage—was at one time in denial about the *seriousness* of their interpersonal struggles and the immense capacity of forces outside their relationship to cause their marital disruption and unhappiness. Every day people come to my office citing variations on the same themes: "My husband is out of control—fix him." "My wife is driving me crazy—can you make her stop?" "We fight all the time about the stupidest things—can you help us communicate better?"

We live in a society that worships the psychology of the individual. We have been taught to believe that individual psychopathology is the source of all our problems; if only we could fix our *partner's* emotional problems, we could fix our marriage. We are masters at blaming each other. However, the reality is that the problems of marriage are bigger than individuals, even bigger than the two of you put together. Marriage itself is under attack. That social institution, which for hundreds of generations has fostered enduring adult intimacy and companionship, is beginning to look frail. For many, it has already become obsolete.

If you want a better marriage and a lifelong relationship, you need to understand three crucial points. First, you need to become very aware of the powerful social, historical, and even biological forces that are undermining marriage, driving your relationship toward disengagement, alienation, or divorce. It is only after recognizing how vulnerable today's marriages really are that you'll be willing to learn the skills required for a successful relationship and put in the time needed to succeed. Second, you must truly appreciate the natural tendency for couples to channel stress and anxiety into interpersonal strife, creating a recurrent, negatively reinforcing spiral of conflict and alienation that hides reasonable and realistic solutions from view. Third, you need the willingness and ability to stop that negative spiral and to replace it with effective, supportive communication and real changes in your behavior. This book will show you how to do all three.

We live in a society that promotes so many powerful lies about marriage, so many misunderstandings, myths, and fairy tales that have become so deeply entrenched in our minds, that we are rarely able to approach marriage with reasonable expectations. These lies and our unreasonable expectations set us up for failure. Most of them have existed for generations; others are of a more recent vintage—but all of them are conspiring to ruin your chances for a successful marriage. This book will help you identify those lies, strewn like minefields along your matrimonial journey, so that you can either avoid them or disarm them before they blow up.

The Dangers of Denial

Most of us are naive when it comes to problems in our relationships, and most of us want to stay that way because it's just too scary and overwhelming to acknowledge what's really required to sustain a lifelong loving connection with another human being. The predicament is that if we avoid certain realities, we make ourselves unnecessarily vulnerable to the forces that undermine the very relationship we most desire—a happy marriage. Lies about the nature of marital bliss lure us into complacency. Complacency prevents us from putting in the amount of thought and effort required to create and sustain a gratifying relationship.

Almost everyone writing about relationships seems to assume—and wants you to believe—that if you're not in a successful relationship, it's your fault, your problem, and that you can and should be able to fix it. Even a lot of well-intentioned therapists begin therapy with this preposterous supposition. The truth is the opposite. Much of what ruins marriage is not initially caused by personal emotional problems, but by forces outside of us that we do not understand. When the problems begin, we blame each other for our discontent and assume that the other will change and make things better for us. Regrettably, we fail to recognize that the destructive forces are still affecting us and hurting our relationship. While you should never evade your responsibilities in marriage, one problem with taking on too much responsibility is that most of us don't really know enough about marriage to know how to constructively solve its problems. This is especially difficult to accept since most married people deem themselves experts at it. The fact is that you've been raised to buy into many beliefs about marriage that are simply untrue, and those conscious and unconscious beliefs are largely responsible for many of the problems you're having. As a result, you can rarely fix your marriage just thinking about it from the inside out. You must also understand the forces that have changed the very nature of the marital union. You must understand your marriage, as it were, from the outside in.

Most books on marriage focus only very briefly on the reasons behind the serious problems facing married couples and devote most of their effort to giving readers simple exercises to improve their relationships. These hopeful books promise that if you only work at it hard enough, you and your spouse can have a permanent, satisfying marriage. This is what most of us want to hear.

Unfortunately, working hard is not all we need to do. We must be able to accept that no amount of hard work will save a marriage that is too ungratifying, too destructive, or too empty, or one in which you married the wrong person for the wrong reasons. Those who promote unrealistic marital myths make marriage more difficult for all of us. No marriage is easy. If we expect that just by marrying we will live happily ever after—and many people do expect this—then we will continue to enter marriage without a strategy for dealing with the inevitable problems. We will feel defective, embarrassed, and unsure of what to do when trouble starts.

Nearly all books about marriage are written for and read by women. Women alone cannot solve relationship problems, and it's not fair to expect them to. Men have to be involved, and they have to help. Having counseled couples for over thirty years, I simply don't believe that men and women are from different planets, that only women "get" relationships, and that therefore they have to do all the heavy lifting in making a marriage work. In writing this book, I have made a concerted effort to represent both male and female points of view. My hope is that both women and men will find it informative, useful, and sympathetic. My message isn't sugarcoated, but reading this book is like having a good battle plan: knowing what you're up against and anticipating the adversary's strengths and weaknesses gives you a better chance to prevail.

With its strong dose of reality, this book may be painful to read. If that is the case for you, I apologize and ask your indulgence. However, if you'll bear with me and think about what I'm saying, though it may at times worry or frighten you, I am certain that in the end you'll be stronger and better prepared to deal with your marital issues. Working at a good marriage is like making the commitment to exercise regularly. You need to have a good fitness program, appreciate its importance for your life and your future, and keep doing it, even when you think it's unnecessary or don't feel like it. Never get lazy or complacent about your spouse. That is the kiss of death to a marriage. I'm counting on your bravery and willingness to face the facts that I will share with you, and then to do what has to be done to make your marriage stronger.

A Marital Therapist's Journey

Why do I put so much faith in my readers? The long and short of it is that the direct, clear, honest approach has served my patients and me well for thirty years. For the past three decades I have been in the private practice of psychiatry in New York City. When I began my psychiatric residency at the Albert Einstein College of Medicine in 1970, psychoanalysis was the dominant treatment paradigm. My most brilliant teachers had received psychoanalytic training, and many believed that even the mysteries of schizophrenia would one day yield to a purely psychoanalytic therapy.

Following my residency, I enrolled at the oldest, most conservative psychoanalytic institute in New York City. While in analytic training I became the director of Outpatient and Emergency Psychiatry at the Montefiore Medical Center in the Bronx; a few years later I was promoted to the position of director of Montefiore's Psychiatric Residency Training Program.

My life changed one day when the head of Montefiore's Department of Psychiatry's Family Training Division, Dr. Harry Mendelsohn, offered to give me a personal tutorial in family therapy in the hopes that I would then want to make it a bigger part of the residents' curriculum. Under his supervision, I began seeing couples instead of just individuals in my private practice.

Within only a year or two, I shifted my thinking from the purely psychoanalytic to the systemic, that is, from what goes on in the mind of one person to what goes on between people and how one person's behavior affects the behavior of all those around him. In psychoanalytic theory, you are what is in your mind; your conscious and unconscious beliefs, patterned on early childhood experiences, are the primary creators of your world. In family systems theory, what you think and feel is assumed to be strongly influenced by your interactions with everyone and everything around you, especially the "systems" of your biology, your family, your community, your society, your culture, and your religious affiliation. All these systems to which you belong not only influenced you in the past, but continue to affect you today, and have a profound effect on your most intense interpersonal system, your marriage. Likewise, you powerfully influence all the members of all the systems that interact with you, especially your spouse. The goal of a therapist is to help you become a successful, mature individual—someone who is both his own person, and a comfortable, connected member of the systems to which he belongs. As an emotionally mature individual living as part of many systems, you can be yourself when you're with others, agreeing with them without becoming a clone, disagreeing without being nasty or excessively fearful of rejection. Systems theory when applied to couples offers practical solutions to marital problems and helps people strengthen their individual sense of identity while fortifying their marital bond.

While I was discovering the advantages to my patients of thinking in these interpersonal terms, I was going through my own divorce, which reinforced my interest in understanding how we choose a spouse and what makes marriage successful. It also made me acutely and personally aware of the emotional anguish of divorce as well as its frequent inevitability. This confluence of experiences fostered a lifelong professional interest in relationships and marriage; in 1990, I decided to devote myself to full-time private practice, incorporating my psychoanalytic and family systems perspectives.

This book is the distillation of what I have learned from working with hundreds of couples and individuals. It is not a report on scientific marital research. Nonetheless, where possible, I have tried to comment on the relevant research findings reported by others in the field.

All my patients want to work on their relationships with the important people in their lives. I see single people who want to be in relationships and married people who want their relationships to either improve or end. All of the depressed people I see are upset about the quality of their relationships. Now, even when I see these people individually, I am thinking of their effect on the people around them and how others are affecting them. As a systems thinker, I am always thinking of two or more people when I do therapy, even if only one is in my office.

A New Blueprint for Marriage

All the families and individuals I have worked with over the last three decades have given me a particular perspective. I have come to accept that marital unhappiness, dissatisfaction, and divorce are part of the fabric of modern life. It will always be so. Though the rates of divorce and marriage may fluctuate over time, people will always want to marry and people will always have to divorce. The best we can do is to try to better educate and prepare for marriage those about to wed, help those who do wed to create more fulfilling relationships, and minimize the anguish and unhappy consequences for those who choose to divorce. Up to now, we are doing a poor job with all three. There will always be many sustained, fulfilling marriages, but there will also be many missed opportunities to join those ranks.

In 2001, the National Center for Health Statistics reported that 20 percent of all first marriages ended within five years, 33 percent within ten years, and 50 percent after twenty years.[1] The era of once-in-a-lifetime, stable marriage appears to be over.[2]

The outcome is even worse for second marriages. Two-thirds

of all second marriages ultimately end in divorce, and second marriages end faster than first marriages.[3] In truth, long-term marital relationships are probably in even worse shape than these straightforward divorce statistics suggest, since many married couples separate but never legally divorce. There are also marriages that are "emotionally terminated." In these "dead" marriages, spouses continue to live together but are emotionally estranged. Some of these couples openly agree to stay together for the sake of the children, for economic reasons, or even for the sake of appearances, while maintaining their own separate lives. Other couples live this way without overt agreements but with similar unspoken provisions, often with one or the other partner having an extramarital affair.

There are also emotionally lifeless marriages in which one spouse is secretly unhappy or seriously dissatisfied but doesn't let the other know. Eventually, many of these marriages implode when the discontented spouse announces suddenly and seemingly out of the blue, "I want a divorce!" For many of these marriages, one spouse has secretly gone, what I call, "over the cliff." This aphorism is based on a game I play with my children in which we all climb onto a bed and then try to push the others off. Though someone may be mostly off the bed, he or she can still be rescued if a partner gets to him or her in time. But if one is too late, gravity takes over and the fall to the floor is inevitable. It is the same with marriage. People hold on to their relationship for a long time, even when things are terrible for them. They remember their vows; they remember how much they originally loved their spouse. They want their marriage to get better, even if they do not know how to make it happen. However, when you have been pushed over the edge, there comes a point of no return.

It is amazing how long we will tenaciously hold on to a desperate situation trying not to let go. The good news is that if the marital partner is able to see that there is a problem, this holding on gives the couple extra time to work on their marriage. The bad news is that once your partner is "over the cliff," there is usually nothing you can do to get him or her back.

However, despite the dismal statistics on divorce and separation, between 85 and 90 percent of Americans will marry at least once. And despite the growing popularity of prenuptial agreements and cynical references to "starter marriages," almost all of us who do marry want and intend to be married forever. We long for "the relationship" that will bring us permanent satisfaction. We want to wake up every morning with our "soul mate" by our side. Most of us have been raised to believe that and behave as if this perfect relationship is out there waiting for us, that others in large numbers have found it, that we cannot be happy without it, and, finally, that if we do not find it or, worse, if we find it and lose it, we have failed as human beings.

As common as these feelings are, in light of these statistical realities, are they not foolish? And, if they are foolish, how are we to give them up and become more accepting of the realities of contemporary life? How are we to achieve stability in our marriage if we cannot first accept that marital relationships are, by their very nature, fraught with difficulty and vulnerability; that they are very often not as mutually satisfying as we intended them to be? Furthermore, if we do accept these relationship realities, how do we construct a blueprint of marriage that will help us to understand and better preserve marriage for the future? I am certain that there is much more we can do to improve the structure and outcome of our marriages. We need to create stronger, more satisfying relationships.

The essential challenge of marriage is that while you are discovering and learning how to live with the differences *between you and your spouse, you must simultaneously maintain a respectful and loving relationship.* Marital partners must navigate and negotiate all the pleasures and pitfalls of life while maintaining a loving, positive regard for each other. For many of us, this is not so easy to do.

I believe that the first step in making things better is to accept that we are living through a massive historical social transformation and that this transformation is dramatically affecting marriage. Each couple needs to understand fully the effects these changes are having on our ability to remain successfully married and to learn how to manage them. I realize there are some who disagree, who will claim, in full denial of the knowledge that is all around us, that our lives haven't changed, and that, if marriage is falling apart as an institution, it's because we have simply become selfish and irresponsible people. Those who think this way prefer to point fingers at, for example, working mothers as a prime reason for the downfall of marriage. They reason that people who behave irresponsibly cause marital instability. They believe that if such people are forced to change their bad behavior or are shielded from its consequences by making divorce very difficult, the institution of marriage can be saved. Such thinking is seriously misguided. In a free society, the *only* way to save marriage is to make it more satisfying for those involved.

The structure and process of marriage are changing, and we are seriously lagging behind in appreciating the consequences. I want you to understand why marriage has become so vulnerable. Once you're aware of the forces that have weakened your marital bond and shaped your misguided expectations of marriage, you'll be far more ready to learn how you can strengthen your relationship despite them.

How to Use This Book

In the introduction, I will review the very important historical, sociological, and biological forces that have radically transformed the process of marriage, making it far more vulnerable to dissolution than ever before. I'll explain how this cultural transformation has encouraged individuals to subscribe to what I call the seven lies of marriage. In the following seven chapters, I'll discuss each of these lies in greater detail and offer concrete steps you can take to forestall or reverse their pernicious influence. Throughout the book, I will draw heavily on the cases of couples who have come to me together or singly for help.

Becoming aware of the beliefs and behaviors that undermine our relationships is the powerful first step toward changing them.

Acknowledgments

I am a distillate of all those who have taught and mentored me. I owe this book to their influence.

Many physicians, perhaps a hundred psychiatrists, and dozens of psychoanalysts have trained me. Thanks go to all those teachers who sparked my inner vision and to the family therapists who first expanded my thinking beyond the intrapsychic: Harry Mendelsohn, M.D., and Ian Alger, M.D.

Most of the way I think and work today—the subject of this book—is the product of my affiliation with Betty Carter, a renowned feminist thinker, writer, teacher, and therapist in the field of family therapy. Thank you, Betty, especially for reading and rereading every page of this book. When Betty retired, she pawned me off on her friend and colleague, Monica McGoldrick. In her own special way, Monica has expanded my thinking and pushed me to greater therapeutic activity. Thank you, Monica, for all your help, support and guidance.

My deepest appreciation and love go to my family, who have inspired me and supported my seemingly endless efforts at writing this book. For the past twenty-two years, my wife, Vivian Diller, a clinical psychologist, has taught me a great deal about commitment and marriage. Our marriage also put to the test my ideas about how important the choice of a mate is to a successful relationship. Vivian is my partner, friend, and life's teacher. I have learned much from her, and what we have achieved together is incorporated into this book.

Likewise, I have also been greatly influenced by my parents' life-long marriage and their emotional and intellectual honesty and support. All my life I have felt supported, loved, and encouraged by my family. I have had wonderful traditions to follow and models of warmth, affection, hard work, and fun to emulate. When they handed out parents, I was truly blessed. Also, without the enthusiastic encouragement and forbearance of my children, Seth, Jordana, Gideon, and Gabriel, I would never have completed this book.

Special thanks go to Avraham Inlender and Milton Katselas, whose artistic visions inspired me to be fearless about putting my thoughts on the page. Kudos to my friends Ann and Gary Deane; Julie Newdow; my brother and sister-in-law, Jeffrey and Heidi Hayes Jacobs; and my brother-in-law, Dr. Lawrence Diller, all of whom offered me unbridled encouragement. Very special thanks also to my agent, Beth Vesel, who stuck by me when I got discouraged and repeatedly told me that I had something important to say. I am deeply grateful to Gail Winston, my editor at HarperCollins, for her courage, vision, and incisive editorial feedback. Utmost thanks especially to Elizabeth Rapoport, who took a lengthy manuscript and helped me fashion it into the readable work before you. You saved the day.

I also want to thank the many psychiatric residents I've been privileged to train. In teaching them, I have always ended up getting back more than I gave.

Finally, many thanks go to my patients. From them I have learned how to be the best therapist I can be. I will always be grateful for their courage and willingness to share their stories. Readers should note that I have changed their names and other identifying characteristics and in some instances created composite cases to further disguise their identities and protect their privacy. Also, to make the book more readable, when speaking of both spouses in a marriage, I have often dispensed with the simultaneous use of both personal pronouns and simply used either "he" or "she" interchangeably.

The Truth About Marriage Today: Exploring the Seven Lies

Marriage is a great institution, but I'm not ready for an institution yet.

—Mae West

The Historical Trends Destabilizing Marriage

It amazes me that we are perfectly willing to discuss how someone's individual psychology or character contributes to a marriage's dissolution, but rarely mention—and may even deny—the role that social and historical trends play in destabilizing marriage. Perhaps we think that we can more readily change people's characters than overcome the tsunami of social forces, so we're more willing to believe that individual character defects lie at the root of all marital problems. However, denying the influence of larger social forces leaves us excessively blaming each other for the problems in our relationship. Besides being misguided and unfair, this propensity makes it harder to fix those problems. It also limits our capacity to make informed choices before and during marriage based on a better understanding of our complex world. Making these choices can dramatically change the functioning of your relationship.

1

Learning more about how external forces are influencing your marriage does not excuse you from taking personal responsibility for your actions, but personal responsibility means little if your thinking is misguided or you lack the information to make reasoned, responsible choices. It is only by having a broader understanding of the social and historical forces threatening your marriage that you can fashion more effective steps to protect it.

Till Death Do Us Part

One of the biggest problems facing marriage is simply that because of advances in medical science and the vast increase in our standard of living, most of us are living far longer than our forebears did. Fewer than five hundred years ago, most people died before they reached their thirtieth birthday. The average human being rarely survived infections, wars, famines, pestilence, tyranny, and common everyday murder to live long enough to become an old man or woman of age forty. Women had even less hope than men for a long life. Writing of an era only six hundred years ago, historian William Manchester states, "The toll at childbirth was appalling. A young girl's life expectancy was twenty-four. On her wedding day, traditionally, her mother gave her a piece of fine cloth that could be made into a frock. Six or seven years later it would become her shroud."[1] When people married " 'til death do us part," they both meant it and *expected* it soon, for death was never that far away. *Even as recently as 1900, the life expectancy of most Americans was barely forty-seven years.*[2] One or the other spouse generally died within a few years of the couple's youngest child's birth.

Under these circumstances, with husbands and wives usually losing a young mate, marriage could be much more easily romanticized. Marriages often ended while the spouses were still deep in romantic love and/or desperately needed each other for survival. There was little general experience with longer-term marriage or the natural changes in the atmosphere of marriage that accompany thirty to sixty years of conjugal life.[3] Also, with the absence of modern birth control, families then were much larger. As a result, almost all of a couple's life together took place while raising children. The "empty nest" era, in which couples live together for decades after their children have grown up and left home, is a very recent phenomenon.

Historically, couples have had very little time and few role models from which to learn how to be together for a longer lifetime. We are generally unprepared for and unskilled in the art of long-term sustained relationships. Therefore, it should not be surprising to realize that many marriages today last about as long as those of a hundred years ago, only now they're terminated by divorce, not death.

Survival of the Fittest—Not the Happiest

How and why did marriage evolve in the first place? Thousands of years ago, human society developed a system that successfully fostered the capacity to protect its young. Newborns, infants, and small children are extraordinarily fragile creatures who will die without an extended period of parental nurturing. Thanks to evolution, normal children are born with the biological capacity to form deep attachments to their caregivers and, when well nurtured, grow up with the reinforced capacity to form further attachments to other human beings—friends, a spouse, and, ultimately, in one of nature's most basic cycles, their own children.

Millennia ago, social, biological, and evolutionary forces came together in many divergent human cultures to create units known today as families. We have to assume that for thousands of years, the family, a social unit consisting of parents and the children they rear, served the important purpose of having some group smaller than the larger tribe or clan take responsibility for the care of children. Along the way, the relationship between the adult partners of these units became formalized and then ritualized into the institution known as marriage. This didn't have to happen, for as we know, humans can be partners and even coparent children without being officially married. But marriage probably developed to add greater stability to the connection between adults and to ensure the paternity, care, and protection of children. It undoubtedly served some social advantage.

However, there is little evidence that early ideas about marriage had anything to do with notions of human happiness or, for that matter, love. For most of human history, marriage has been a means of survival, a way for men and women to protect each other and their children. Conflicts within marriage, disappointments with spouses, or unhappiness in general were of less consequence, far secondary in importance to the struggle for physical survival.

Marriages further evolved into economic partnerships.[4] Wealthier families married off children to consolidate power and property, and most other couples worked together to survive harsh economic realities. Children were valued in direct proportion to the degree to which they could help the family survive. Happiness, satisfaction, gratification, and good sex were not the purpose of marriage. *Men and women put up with limited gratification in their marriages because they had other more serious problems with which to contend.* (Where harsh living conditions still exist, so, apparently, does this perspective on marriage. I once saw a documentary on a tribe struggling to survive in the Kalahari Desert of Africa. The director of the film asked a woman who was busy washing clothes if she was happy in her marriage. Along with all the women around her, she began to laugh, totally astounded by such a foolish question.)

The seeds for radical change in marriage were sown by the social and political revolutions of the eighteenth century. When Thomas Jefferson wrote that people were entitled "to life, liberty and the pursuit of happiness," he set forth a radical idea that, to this day, continues to ripple through our community, causing all kinds of social transformations. Mr. Jefferson was thinking mostly about political happiness, that is, freedom, and probably had little concern about marriage when he wrote those famous words. But words are powerful, and appealing ideas have few limitations. Today, we have come to believe that we have a right to pursue not just political but individual, emotional happiness. We believe we are entitled to feel emotionally satisfied and fulfilled. By the latter part of the twentieth century, when Western society had progressed far enough to offer most of its citizens a life free of economic dread, personal happiness in marriage could become a primary goal.

Here is the problem we are facing today. When marriage first developed as a tradition, couples expected and were able to tolerate high amounts of dissatisfaction. Marriage wasn't burdened by the hope that it would provide significant gratification or contribute dramatically to personal or emotional happiness. Furthermore, factoring in life expectancy, if you didn't like your spouse, how many years did you have to live with that person anyway?

Today, no longer preoccupied by issues of economic and physical survival, we expect marriage to deliver a significant degree of happiness. We can scarcely tolerate the idea that marriage can *cause* unhappiness. Studies suggest that one of the leading precipitants of depression in America is marital unhappiness, and chronic depression is more common in married individuals than among singles.[5] Furthermore, if we are unhappily married, we can no longer accept the view that we should stay married "'til death do us part" because that could be a long, long time.

In my office, patients regularly tell me, "I've lived in this dreadful marriage for fifteen years; that's enough. I want something more for the rest of my life. Even if I have to live alone for the next forty years, it'll be better than this." Such declarations imply both the expectation of personal happiness and the assumption that the speaker will live so long that death can no longer be counted on to step in and end the misery.

Furthermore, very few people appear to have the innate skills required to maintain high levels of marital satisfaction for extended periods of time. This really should be no surprise to us. If marriage wasn't originally designed to be emotionally and physically satisfying, where and how would human beings learn to make long-term marriage an emotionally fulfilling experience? Why do any of us assume that we *innately* know how to make lengthy marriage into a lifelong, satisfying relationship? There is nothing to suggest that our ancestors possessed these skills.

The Pill and the Power: Beyond Women's Liberation

World War II brought another dramatic social change: It proved that women could be exceptionally productive in this country's industrial work force. The women's movement of the 1960s and 1970s shook the ground still further by setting out to bring equality of opportunity to American women. Like Jefferson before them, the leaders of the women's movement of this era were initially not primarily interested in "emotional happiness," but the *right* to pursue "political happiness," that is, the right of *economic equality* and, thus, *self-determination*. It was assumed that attaining these goals would secondarily create more opportunity for emotional happiness. And while the women's movement has radically changed the capacity of women to take care of themselves and has forever altered, for the better, the lives of women, it has also forever changed the very *meaning* of marriage.

While love and desire for companionship, as well as the need for attachment, have played their roles, for most of history, women have married essentially to produce and protect their children and to ensure their own physical and *economic* safety. Prior to the last few generations, the only way a woman could be economically stable was to live with her family of origin (assuming her father was economically secure), inherit wealth, or marry a man who had the ability to support her economically.[6]

Contemporary women's greater economic independence has forever changed the balance of power between the genders and has had profound consequences for marriage. *Indeed, it has exposed a universal truth: Historically, one of the most important glues keeping marriage together has been women's economic dependency on men.*

Today, a generation of women has married after or while developing job skills for an array of careers mostly denied to their mothers. This same generation of women has come to expect that they will find jobs that will allow them to be financially self-supporting. As a result, a woman's need for a man's absolute economic protection has waned,[7] leading to profound changes in the way we experience and envision male-female relationships both in and out of marriage.

The single most powerful effect on marriage of women's new economic power is women's greater willingness to divorce. Though almost every divorce is accompanied by terrible feelings of fear and failure, women who can make their own living no longer have to contend with the devastating scourge of poverty. Women may not do as well economically as their ex-husbands following divorce; in general, the opposite is the case. But more women than ever before are willing to seek divorce because they know that, when all else fails, they can support themselves and their children. This ability to tolerate divorce has also allowed women to openly risk asserting greater power within the marital bond.

Obviously, some women have always been able to leave intolerable marriages, but most were economically tethered to their husbands. Today, women initiate the majority of divorces. I've seen in my own practice how differently women think about divorce based on their economic situations.

Tina, a woman with three adolescent children, comes to see me alone to work on her marriage; her husband, Brian, refuses to discuss their relationship. Tina tells one disheartening story after another. Her husband has never been affectionate. He makes an ample living, enabling her to stay at home with the kids, but he makes her ask him for every penny she spends and justify everything she buys. Though she doesn't think of herself as a spendthrift, Brian regularly becomes angry every time he opens his credit card statements and discovers what she's spent of *his* "hard-earned money." He doesn't work at all around the house since, he tells her, he has to work all day—what, raising three small kids is play?—so the home is her responsibility. Furthermore, he's a poor lover, rarely showing any interest in her feelings or sexual fulfillment.

Despite this litany of complaints, Tina says she loves her husband deeply and wants to save her marriage. I work with her for three months, giving her all kinds of strategies for improving her marital relationship.[8] We discuss the possibility of her going back to work part-time or spending more time engaged in activities she might find fulfilling. Tina expertly blocks each suggestion with a rationalization; her children need her, her husband won't allow it, she can't stand up to him. I focus on her fears, passivity, and guilt, but at every opportunity she informs me that she cannot do anything to change the way she feels or behaves.

Finally, my menu of solutions exhausted, I inquire why she doesn't consider divorce an option. It comes out that Tina has been told by her husband that she wouldn't get much money in any divorce settlement. Besides, she reminds me, she loves her husband too much; divorce is out of the question. Then I ask, "If you knew that you'd be economically secure if you got divorced, let's say you could get $150,000 a year for the rest of your life, would you get divorced?"

"In a minute," she declares. What seems like love everlasting actually masks a strictly economic calculation.

The Golden Ruler

Increasingly, I am seeing couples where the woman earns at least as much money as her husband and is no longer intimidated by his attempts to control her economically.

The women's movement accurately assessed that in our culture, education and money confer power. As Betty Carter, a well-known family therapist, so aptly puts it, the Golden Rule in families is, "Whoever has the gold makes the rules."[9] The shift in gender roles that has more and more women making the gold and making the rules, or at least demanding that their wishes be taken equally into account, has forced complicated adjustments to time-honored marital roles. The difficulty we have in accommodating these changing economic and gender realities has contributed to the destabilization of marriage.

Many men aren't prepared for their loss of power in relationships and many women aren't yet skilled or comfortable with the complexities of having or sharing the power. Some women don't know how to help men with this change in authority, and many men have difficulty accepting direction and advice from their spouses. I've seen a few marriages where the woman is significantly financially better off than her husband is and *she* becomes as tyrannical and critical as the worst of the men of yore.

Connie makes twice as much as her husband, Jason. Their relationship is often damaged by her criticism of his spending habits. He resents her attempts to control his spending and feels that if he made more money, she would have much less to say about it. Though he is not a spendthrift, he likes to buy up-to-date male "toys" like stereo systems and large TVs. Though Connie chooses to spend money on things Jason doesn't care about, he doesn't criticize her spending habits. Nonetheless, she remains critical of the way he is spending *her* money, and this causes great tension in their marriage.

Marriages in which the woman outearns the man have another problem. Not only does the couple have to negotiate their own differences from a reversal of traditional economic power, but they also have to contend with centuries of social indoctrination that suggest that men who make less money than their wives are inferior beings. Both husband and wife often share the same undercurrent of disrespect for the man.

Even in marriages where women make little or no money,

women have become less tolerant of men's assumption that, because they make the money, they are the Golden Rulers. Fortified by their new economic strength and a political and social philosophy supporting a woman's right to equal authority, most women presume an equal voice and an equal division of labor in their marital relationship. The postfeminist world has thrown out the old, outdated traditional gender-orientated rules, but couples haven't yet fully established a new set of useful rules, let alone learned to live by them comfortably or successfully.

Few people seem to realize that women's newfound economic self-sufficiency has also radically changed men's assumptions about their obligation to financially support women. Many husbands now expect their partners to help with the economic burdens of a family and are resentful if their wives don't hold their own. Furthermore, unhappy husbands are now more prone to divorce because they no longer see it as their responsibility to provide financially for wives from whom they feel alienated. Thus, reciprocally to their female counterparts, contemporary men feel less bound to unsatisfying marriages because they no longer accept the duty of forever being the economic providers for their wives.

Furthermore, women's economic independence has had a destabilizing effect on traditionalist men who feel it is their job to support the family. I've had several male patients lose their jobs and been overcome by terrible feelings of failure, anxiety, and depression when they were forced to depend on their wives' income. Equally problematic is the opposite situation when the husband feels perfectly comfortable being supported by his wife over an extended period of time.

Living in a Material World

One of the most profound and unrecognized influences on our ability to be happily married is the stress of living in the "material world." Many couples make "getting and spending" a higher priority than marriage. They convince themselves that their chase after endless possessions is for their families when it's the chase itself—the economic privilege and social status it brings them—that they really love.

Steve came to my office to see if he could salvage his marriage after he'd begun an affair with a coworker. In discussing what in his marriage had led up to his having an affair, I found out that, as he had experienced growing material success, both he and his wife, April, had begun to focus their lives on material goods. They spent enormous amounts of money on things for which they had very little use. For example, April owned thirty designer handbags and rarely used any of them. She had boxes of new clothes unwrapped and unworn in her closets. Steve had bought every adult toy he could get his hands on: the latest-model luxury car, a Jet Ski, and a fancy customized motorcycle. While this materialistic orgy was going on, the couple drifted further and further apart, apparently never realizing how their interest in things was substituting for their interest in each other.

Initially, they both accused the other of excessive spending and saw their own purchases as reasonable. Both spouses were caught up in a frenzy of compulsive, competitive buying, fearing that if either unilaterally stopped, he or she would be left with the terrible feeling of being *cheated* by the other spouse, who would still be continuing to spend their money. They had been unable to address what the underlying feeling of being cheated was telling them about themselves and their relationship.

Despite their impressive income, Steve and April hadn't saved any money. It was never that they didn't have enough to put some away. They didn't save because, no matter how much money they had, they felt compelled to use it all to maintain an ever-expanding lifestyle. Every time they thought of cutting back on their expenses, they saw how well someone else lived and wanted the same for themselves. To stop spending would have meant changing their social context and their values. This was very hard to do. Although Steve and April were financially very well off, I've seen this same pattern in couples who make well under six figures a year. No matter how much some people make, they don't save because they don't want to feel left behind in our consumer society.

Now certainly there are individual "psychological" forces driving this kind of spending, but there are also powerful cultural sirens luring people onto the rocks of consumer excess. One overspent husband confided to me in couple's therapy that he knew that he was spending foolishly, but he feared that if he said no to his wife, she might think less of him and perhaps leave the marriage. Also, they wouldn't look as good to their friends. So he never dared restrain his or her spending until his earnings slowed dramatically. By then, it was too late. The resultant financial insecurity antagonized the couple and jeopardized their relationship anyway.

Magazines showcase celebrities' homes and run seductive ads touting conspicuous consumption. TV advertisements display the latest cars, vacation hot spots, and other items that serve as barometers of social status. Every day brings a few more pounds of catalogues looking to drain our wallets as they remind us that our lives could be full of so, so much more. This incessant materialistic pressure creates unrealistic goals for many marriages, making us believe that our relationships can't be good unless they come with all the right status and all the right toys.

A recent study showed that people who place a great deal of importance on money, celebrity, and possessions are more likely to suffer from depression than individuals who put greater importance on the more enduring values of humanitarianism and spirituality. However, no study needs to be done to show how these narcissistic values are adversely affecting our marriages. We must be far more thoughtful about the pernicious influence that money and the pursuit of "stuff" can have on our emotional bonds. The emotional connection between spouses, so crucial for marriage, can come undone when we emphasize the accumulation of wealth and material goods over the emotional needs of our partners. (This idea is expressed most eloquently in the title of Joe Dominguez and Vicki Robin's book on getting a handle on spending: *Your Money or Your Life*.)

Too Much, Too Fast

Another underappreciated pressure on modern marriage is our sped-up society. As if organizing a family with two working parents weren't difficult enough, we must now cope with the ever-increasing flow of information and the unbelievable stress this exerts on our lives. FedEx is now too slow; let's e-mail—better yet, let's instant-message. Why leave a message on your office voice mail when I can just call your cell phone?

These and a hundred other efficiencies were supposed to save us time, which could then be used to enjoy more leisure, preferably with our families. Instead, we now live in a world that has sped up so much that *no one* has enough time for anything. We've eliminated the interludes between one assignment and the next, time we used to spend doing something relaxing or less pressured. Can you image someone saying today, "Well, the document can't be delivered until Monday, so let's just take the weekend off and deal with it when it arrives"? Instead, the document is faxed or e-mailed immediately, and the weekend is spent working on it, perhaps with our spouse laboring away on another project in the next room.

Technology has brought us dramatic efficiencies and improved much in our lives, but by speeding up its pace, and by providing us with endless diversions from which we cannot escape (TVs, VCRs, TIVO, video games, computer games, the Internet), technology has actually *robbed* us of everyday leisure. It has quickened, not slowed our pace, and this ever-increasingly rapid movement of our lives is having a savage impact on marriages.

In my practice, it's extremely rare to see a couple who feels they have enough time to spend together. Usually by the time I see them, they've lived for years with very little time focused on each other or their relationship. When I ask patients to tell me how much time they spend alone together, I usually get some form of incredulous snicker as a response. This lack of mutual attention isn't because the partners don't want to spend time with each other, at least not initially. It's because the individuals chronically sacrifice themselves for some other important cause like work, children, extended family, or their social responsibilities. Eventually, the spouses no longer remember what it's like to take time for themselves as a couple. Interestingly, in this too-busy world, when we have a moment of free time, we often think first of our desire to do something exclusively for ourselves, perhaps take a solo jog or a trip to the gym, watch a football game, go shopping, or take a nap. Spending time as a couple seems to run far back in the pack of priorities.

The Destigmatized Divorce

Our culture has further destabilized marriage by destigmatizing the alternative: divorce. Simply put, we're used to divorce. All of us have friends or relatives who have been through divorce; we may have experienced it ourselves. We are all too familiar with the emotional and financial consequences of a failed marriage. Many men and women head for their lawyers' offices to sign a prenup before they head down the aisle. Today's Gen Xers and their even younger peers are very likely to be adult children of divorce, well versed in the impermanence of the marital bond. "Starter marriages" and "serial marriages" are popular talk-show fodder. We devour the delicious details of the divorce proceedings of the rich and famous on the society pages of newspapers. Etiquette books help readers gracefully handle the expected proliferation of exes at weddings, christenings, bar mitzvahs, dinner parties, and other social events. As the rate of divorce increased, it became legally more readily attainable and socially more permissible.

Couples a generation or two ago were far more likely to be

stigmatized if they divorced, particularly women. Today, a divorced man or woman simply joins the majority of people whose first marriage is behind them. Those who just two generations ago might have stayed in a difficult marriage and tried to work it out now find divorce easier to obtain and easier to accept. Yet divorce is still a very painful emotional and legal experience. Living in a society where divorce has become so common while its consequences are still so frightening has undermined our very belief in the long-term viability of marriage. Divorce itself has given marriage a bad name.

Cultural Canards: The Seven Lies of Marriage

These historical and sociological trends are putting great pressure on marriage and are undermining the viability of long-term unions. Most people do not yet appreciate how these changes have increased the emotional and social complexities of married life. They also cause us to make avoidable mistakes in our choice of a mate because we simply can't foresee the kind of partner we'll need to manage the demands of long-term marriage. The ensuing frustrations caused by these historical changes and pressures, and the unresolved marital unhappiness that they cause, all too often, lead to the decision to divorce instead of the decision to change oneself or the relationship. There is less willingness and ability to understand and solve matrimonial problems. Also, the greater prevalence of divorce has exposed marriage to greater scrutiny. For centuries, erroneous assumptions about marriage remained well hidden behind impermeable walls that were maintained because social needs and cultural proscriptions demanded their strict upkeep. We couldn't see through them and did not try. Marriage was never considered to be a proper subject for inquiry. Now, with the modern rate of divorce upon us, we have been forced to look into the heart of marital relationships and, for the first time in history, to examine what really goes on there. It turns out that many of us do not know how to have a fulfilling marriage because we rely too heavily on beliefs about marriage that are simply wrong. Furthermore, we have been very slow to give up our old ideas. Over and over, I see couples subscribing to the same incorrect beliefs, hoping that these beliefs will still hold them together, not realizing that, instead, they are contributing to their unhappiness. I call these beliefs the seven lies of marriage.

LIE #1: All you need is love.

The reality is that marital bliss is a myth. Unconditional love, necessary for babies and small children, doesn't—and shouldn't—exist between marital partners. We live in a culture that stresses a preoccupation with personal happiness above all. As long as we raise our children, especially girls, to believe that marriage is the solution to life's problems and essential for personal happiness, we will continue to have many couples marrying with little appreciation for the true difficulties and complexities of married life. Couples come to my office deeply shocked: "We love each other so much. Why are we so unhappy?" Myths that suggest that romantic love is sufficient to create marital bliss leave people unskilled in developing and unprepared to manage sustained intimate relationships. As wonderful as love is, love doesn't conquer all, and alone it certainly won't prevent or solve your marital problems. For that, you need to understand the nature of marriage, learn specific skills, and accept that regularly applying these skills requires diligence and hard work.

I'll discuss how you can look beyond these myths and reprioritize your marriage in chapter 1.

LIE #2: I talk all the time; my spouse just doesn't listen.

The reality is that most of us talk ourselves to death, but we actually communicate very poorly. We live in an era that encourages us to be open about our feelings but doesn't teach us how to differentiate between helpful and harmful feelings. Very few of us know how to speak or listen effectively. Television talk shows are filled with marital experts who advise us to "tell it like it is" and be "brutally honest" so our partners will know how we really feel and what we really need.

The truth is that brutal honesty too often encourages brutality more than honesty. Spouses use their *version* of the truth to bludgeon their partners into submission.

Books such as John Gray's *Men Are from Mars, Women Are from Venus* and Deborah Tannen's *You Just Don't Understand* do an excellent job of explaining how men and women's communication styles can differ. However, I have found that problems in communication go far beyond these stylistic differences. Communication problems often hide serious differences in values, interests, goals, and desires. Even when spouses learn how to "communicate" with each other effectively, they are often surprised to find that they have major differences that are difficult to resolve. So, improving communication alone is not the solution to most marital problems. It is only the first step. Nonetheless, in chapter 2 I'll explain how by following a few simple rules you can quickly and easily become a more effective communicator and dramatically improve your marital relationship.

LIE #3: People don't really change.

Of course, the couples who come to my office tell me they want to change. (More often, what they really want is for me to change their spouse, whom they see as the one really in the wrong.) However, many people today believe that deep down, people can't change all that much or that nothing in a marriage can change unless both partners change. These incorrect and pessimistic beliefs sabotage efforts to improve marriage. The truth is that most people go about trying to change their relationships in unproductive ways, get frustrated by the results, and then claim that this outcome proves that people don't change. Also, many of us are so fearful of real change that we run for the escape hatch rather than commit to the hard work involved in getting what we say we want. And even if one partner is adamantly set against change, there's a lot the other partner can do to foster change in the marriage anyway. Change is *always* possible.

I'll explain how to encourage lasting change in chapter 3.

LIE #4: When you marry, you create your own family legacy.

You may live far from your family of origin, but now that you have your own family, their grip on you is tighter than ever. When we become husbands, wives, and parents, the models we saw and leftover conflicts we experienced within our families of origin emerge from our psyches and take over our intimate relationships. Our grandparents were likely to live close to their parents (if not in the same house), see each other often, and stay personally involved in each other's day-to-day lives. Today, in our highly mobile society, we tend to live farther from our parents. Paradoxically, their influence may be greater than ever; because they're not around, we're less likely to be aware of how we unthinkingly act in line or in opposition to the way they raised us.

It's especially shocking to find that your family seriously influences you if you have consciously chosen to behave differently from them. Spouses who don't appreciate the power their original families exert on their values and styles tend to have particularly tenacious problems in their marriages.

In chapter 4, I'll explain how to reconsider the influence of your family of origin and recognize the roles you may be consciously or unconsciously reenacting in your marriage.

LIE #5: Egalitarian marriage is easier than traditional marriage.

In the newer, egalitarian model of marriage, the expectation is that while not every chore will be split fifty/fifty, family responsibilities should be divided fairly, and decision-making power will be shared. The husband in this model respects his wife's work and shares in family life, never insisting on being in control based on financial earnings or gender. Equality, in theory, is wonderful; in reality, spouses in trouble often are conflicted over gender role expectations and responsibilities.

Men tend to feel *unappreciated* for what they do well, that is, for working hard away from home and for any chores they *agree* to do in the house. Likewise, women who work away from the home and then return to care for their households and children often feel equally *unappreciated* for their extra work. In *The Second Shift*,[10] sociologist Arlie Hochschild makes the point that woman are caught in a "stalled revolution." Seventy percent of married women work outside the home and then return to huge responsibilities at home with minimal or no help from the average husband or from social institutions. Many working mothers are overworked and exhausted, and some ultimately become bitter about their overburdened lives. Hochschild believes that the stress on marriage caused by the pressures of this "stalled revolution" is central to women's dissatisfaction with modern marriage and will not be resolved until men fully accept their share of household responsibilities.[11]

The confusion over gender-role expectations, the mutual feeling of insufficient appreciation, and the unresolved resentment this fosters between spouses are killing many marriages. I'll explain more about the growing pains in egalitarian marriages and how to translate the theory of the fifty/fifty marriage into more practical realities in chapter 5.

LIE #6: Children solidify a marriage.

Let's speak the unspeakable: Children are an enormous threat to your marriage. It's very, very difficult to admit that the children you love so much can drive a wedge into your life as a couple, especially if one of the reasons you got married in the first place was to have a family. However, the reality is that in a world where married partners already work too hard and don't spend enough time with each other, the addition of children to your life usually eats up the remaining physical and emotional energy you had for each other.

Even when you love your children fiercely, even when you thought you were prepared for the tremendous dislocation they would cause (who hasn't heard a million stories about the sleepless nights with newborns, the perils of toddlers, the terrors of teens?), your natural devotion to your children will tear your marriage down to its bedrock. If you have a child with any kind of additional difficulty—a physical or mental disability, a challenging temperament, ADHD—you will have to fight that much harder to save your marriage.

Let's just say it: *If you want to preserve your marriage, your children cannot always come first.* As counterintuitive as it may sound, your marriage and your spouse must come first, not only for your sake but also so that your children can grow up within an intact family.

I'll explain how to reprioritize your marriage and reduce the stress of child rearing in chapter 6.

LIE #7: The sexual revolution has made great sex easier than ever.

The veil of secrecy surrounding sex has been ripped away. The bestseller list is plump with books on how to get and give great sexual pleasure. Magazines offer the latest tricks of the trade. Even the toniest literary journals sport ads touting instructional videotapes. Men and women regularly confess their sexual issues on talk shows; there isn't any problem too embarrassing to discuss. Television entertainment puts sex front and center; characters discuss their sex lives and add new partners as readily and casually as they change wardrobes. Thanks to the invasion of the media, from the most seemingly innocuous sitcom to the steamiest porn video, your life is saturated with images of beautiful people having great sex all the time.

So if sex is everywhere, and if information about how to have it is more readily available than ever, why aren't you having more fun in your own bed? It's because the two of you are never really alone there; those ubiquitous images of everyone else having great sex have paradoxically made it more difficult for you to relax and have a satisfying sex life. Even if you joke about these unrealistic portrayals of people who are never exhausted by the toll of work and children, whose waistlines are never threatened by the twin specters of Krispy Kreme and advancing age, and whose libido is never dimmed by a partner's bad breath or the mountain of unpaid bills on the dresser—you are still powerfully influenced by them. They make you feel that you or your partner can never measure up, that there's someone out there who's more attractive to you or will be more attracted by you, and that you are missing out because everyone else is having more fun than you are. They make you believe that the natural evolution of a relationship, from the dazzling fireworks of infatuation and early courtship to the steadier, calmer flame of a mature partnership, represents loss of pleasure and acceptance of the mundane.

I'll show you how to take a reality check of your sex life and enjoy a new appreciation of it in chapter 7.

Marriage from the Outside In

I hope this discussion has given you a deeper understanding of how profound changes in our society and culture have undermined marriage in general and imperiled your relationship in particular. It is much harder today for real people to sustain a satisfying marriage. Nothing you do to rescue your marriage will work until you stop denying the complexity of married life, focus your attention on how important your marriage is, and cease believing and promoting naive and dangerous lies that distort your expectations and understanding of married life.

Once you have accepted this, it's time to start dismantling the lies one by one.

CHAPTER **1**

Lie: All You Need Is Love
Truth: Marital Love Is Conditional—Love Is Not Enough for Successful Marriage

> Nearly all marriages, even happy ones, are mistakes: in the sense that almost certainly (in a more perfect world, or even with a little more care in this very imperfect one) both partners might be found more suitable mates. But the real soul-mate is the one you are actually married to.
>
> —J. R. R. Tolkien, letter to Michael Tolkien, March 1941

"Romance is dead," we moan, but we don't mean it for a second. We collectively keep the notion alive by cherishing the belief that "somewhere out there" a human being exists with whom we can fall in love and from whom we can get love back, no matter what. We expect to develop with this person a lifelong relationship that will nourish both of us as we build a family. Our relationship and our children will simultaneously thrive and grow, and our whole family will find fulfillment. We'll weather the years of child rearing and be brought closer together by the process, providing a loving model relationship for our children and later our grandchildren. Sure, there will be rough times, but love will keep us together. We'll love each other unconditionally, taking the good with the bad, until, still close and warm at the end of our days, we'll look back together and believe with conviction that it was all worth it.

It sounds great, and we all want it. But how do we really get

23

there? The songwriters tell us that "all you need is love" and "love will keep us together." Pardon me for disagreeing, but as any divorced person knows, love simply isn't all you need to keep your marriage happy or together. Nonetheless, many of us still have a belief in the absolute power of love to guide and preserve marriage. This belief is embodied in two dominant lies that strongly influence our thinking—the lies of romantic love (merging with a soul mate) and marital bliss. These lies are fed to us from earliest childhood, and we long to have them materialize as we grow into adulthood. Unfortunately, in spite of the fact that most marriages begin with love, they do not come with ready made "happily ever after" endings.

The story of *Cinderella* is a wonderful example of how these myths function in our collective psyche. Every one of us knows this story, and probably most of us have seen its modern-day equivalent, the movie *Pretty Woman*. The overriding message of romantic fairy tales is that in the end, against all odds, two people meant for each other will miraculously find each other, fall in love, and then live "happily ever after." We find fairy-tale endings so satisfying because the beginnings of such stories usually make us anxious about the grimness of "real life." Cinderella, for example, has lost her parents and is forced to live with a seriously overtaxed stepmother responsible for the well-being of three daughters. They live in a society in which a woman's success and security is measured only by the economic value of the marriage she makes. Beautiful people are given chances for success that ugly ones don't have. There are rich and poor, and the rich cleave to the rich. Though Cinderella comes from a well-to-do family, her stepmother, who controls Cinderella's father's estate, treats her badly. The stepmother wants the best for her biological children and sees Cinderella as just one more woman with whom her girls will have to compete.

The prince in the story is being pressured to marry by his parents, who seem to care little for his feelings. Instead, his buffoonish father and domineering mother are preoccupied with maintaining royal lineage, wealth, and strategic alliances. His life is presented as full of privilege, but it is clear that he exists for little more than the fulfillment of his parents' narcissistic goals.

Real life in *Cinderella* teems with envy, greed, pettiness, unhappiness, ambition, and vicious competition. But with the final union of the prince and Cinderella, all those problems are supposed to be conveniently erased by the triumph of romantic love and the presumed marital bliss that must inevitably follow. When Cinderella slides her foot into the glass slipper and then marries the prince, we breathe a sigh of relief because we believe that with the marriage sealed, her troubles are over.

Even though we know we're too old for fairy tales, we still hope that marriage will bring this same relief to our lives. We want to forget that married life is complicated and problematic, that couples regularly have to solve many serious problems, and that we live in a complex and sometimes difficult world. In real life, Cinderella would certainly have difficulties getting along with her calculating mother-in-law. She would probably have to deal with an entitled husband who might turn out to be a buffoon, like his father, or an arrogant brat, like his mother. Cinderella might end up with a child with learning problems or ADHD (attention deficit hyperactivity disorder). With no models or experience of good mothering, her children would be lucky to get even a modicum of care from a mother who is little more than a child herself.

In our romantic notion of marital bliss, the prince would never go off to war or to work, never come home too tired to play with the kids, and never bury his head in a newspaper or park himself in front of a television. He would never be too tired to have sex with his wife and never have erectile dysfunction or premature ejaculation. Cinderella, of course, even while taking care of a slew of children, would always have time for sex, which she would love; exhaustion or worry about losing her looks would never dim her libido. The royal family and Cinderella's family would get along just fine and share all major holidays as if they were the best of friends; there would never be any bickering over who gets to see more of the grandchildren. With eternal access to the royal coffers, the prince and Cinderella would never have to argue over how to spend limited resources or how to get the kids a good education in underfunded, overcrowded public schools. They would share the same values about everything, and have the same religious and political persuasions. Neither of them would ever drink too much, use drugs, get depressed, have PMS, experience a midlife crisis, or have the urge to hop into bed with the stable boy or housemaid.

We know that real life isn't a fairy tale, yet a part of us still wants to buy into the marital myths that underlie Cinderella. We want to believe that the act of marriage, spurred on by romantic love, will somehow insulate us from life's major problems. So many of us actually live our marital lives as if we're thinking, Now that I've found a secure relationship, I've made it. I can cross "Find the love of my life" off my checklist and put my marriage on the back burner while I devote my time and interest to other things. And yet couples deeply in love and just as deeply in trouble, often on the verge of divorce, regularly come to see me and often ask, "How could this be happening to us?" We just don't want to believe that marital conflict and stress can ruin *our* marriage. Though intellectually we're well aware that divorce is common, the lie of marital bliss, which assumes that everything will be all right as long as we love each other, keeps us from accepting that our marriage could be in serious trouble until it is either almost, or absolutely, too late to do anything about it.

In a recent lawsuit, a woman successfully sued her ex-husband's new wife for taking her husband away from her. She won a large financial award from the "other" woman for causing the alienation of her husband's affections and for her role in splitting up the original family. When an interviewer astutely asked the first wife if there had been any problems in the marriage before the affair, she responded that there had been nothing unusual, although, come to think of it, she and her husband hadn't had sex during the five years prior to the marital breakup. She never considered this a problem; she just figured that every marriage has its "dry spells" and that sexual relations between her and her husband would probably begin again some day. In other words, this woman just assumed that everything would be all right *because she was married*. She believed in marital bliss and the innate stability of the marital union.

In its essence, this extreme case represents a kind of dangerous thinking about marriage that is actually very common: I know I have a date every Saturday night, so why worry if my wife complains a little that she never gets to see me, or that she feels lonely? Or, So what if I have a terrible temper and stomp around the house irritable and critical? We're married now; I don't have to worry so much about his feelings. Few people consciously have these thoughts, but it's remarkable how many behave as if this is exactly what they are thinking, as though marriage is the haven about which poet Robert Frost famously wrote, "Home is where, when you go there, they have to take you in."

Also, because it lulls people into believing that love is sufficient, the lie of marital bliss impedes and seriously delays couples from asking for outside professional help to make their marriage more satisfying. One patient expressed this denial by saying, "I know there are problems, but we love each other, so shouldn't we be able to work this out ourselves?" Even people who are miserable in their marriage still staunchly hold on to their belief in marital bliss. They imagine that if they could just get divorced and marry someone else, find their real soul mate, *then* they could achieve happiness. Often when we give up on a marriage, it's not because we have discarded the myths of romantic love and marital bliss; usually we are just hoping to pursue our dream of the perfect union with some other partner. Paradoxically, if a better relationship or marriage does develop with a new person, it won't be because the lies of romantic love and marital bliss are true, but because we're using better judgment (less mythical thinking) and have learned enough about the difficulties of marriage and ourselves to be able to avoid past mistakes. If we have not emotionally grown up, the future relationship or marriage usually ends up being just as disappointing as the preceding one. This is one of the reasons that so many second marriages end poorly and why so many people marry serially without success.

Soul Mates and Unconditional Love

Probably as a reaction to our anxieties about the tensions and instability in relationships and marriage, our culture has become increasingly invested in foolish and dangerous notions about love. All of us want to be in love and experience being loved. However, the proliferation of the idea that there exists a form of perfect love, known as "unconditional love," and that this love is to be found in one's "soul mate," wreaks havoc on our intimate relationships.

Recently, a Gallup Poll sponsored by Rutgers University's National Marriage Project found that, among people in their twenties, 87 percent believe that they will find a "soul mate" when they are ready to do so.

The idea of "unconditional love" suggests that there are people who expect to be intensely loved under all conditions, no matter how they behave. Furthermore, people who extol the virtues of unconditional love expect to be able to offer this form of love to others. On its face, it's reasonable to expect someone to accept us unconditionally, if we're talking about being liked for the way we already are. However, it's preposterous to extend that belief to the idea that any one particular person should love us forever, *no matter what* we do and think. Therefore, unconditional love must represent some other emotional dynamic. *I believe the wish for unconditional love represents a new mythical solution to our common fears of abandonment.*

We all hope that we were loved "unconditionally" by our parents, and we all wish to return to a state of emotional security that reminds us of the earliest days of life, when all our needs were satisfied without question, whether we were good or bad, difficult or compliant, mean or kind. As most of us grow up, though, we learn to accept that the way we behave and who we've become influence how others feel about and respond to us, and that includes our parents. They no longer have to applaud our every act for fear of crushing our fledgling self-esteem; now even they can express disappointment, disapproval, or outrage with us. Even their regard for us has conditions. When this happens, we lose our original "soul mates"—our perfect, and perfectly adoring, parents. If we are fortunate, our parents make it known to us that they will love us whether or not we fulfill all of their expectations, while at the same time they help us set reasonable and responsible goals for ourselves. But as a consequence of this maturing relationship with our parents, most of us come to accept that there are no perfect people out there, our parents aren't perfect, we aren't perfect, and there is no perfect form of intimate love.

However, for many of us, these developmental experiences haven't gone smoothly. Some parents have always put conditions on their love—withdrawing it, using excessive criticism, resorting to violence, or all three—to coerce their children. As children with these experiences get older, they tend to worry about losing the love of the people they have come to count on. They become insecure about love and loving attachments and long for excessive reassurance from others, even if that's not a realistic prospect. Adults with this background, when threatened with the loss of love, become frightened and do whatever they think is necessary to stave off the threatened loss. Sometimes that means giving up on needing love altogether, or at least trying to convince themselves that they can do without it. They stop trying to please others because it's no longer worth it. They don't expect any joy or security from seeking the approval of others. They become so angry that they just don't care about relationships anymore.

Other adults who repeatedly experienced loss of love or the threat of it as children go to the other extreme, searching for "unconditional love" and a "soul mate"—that person who will ful-fill this previously broken promise of childhood. If they were seri-ously abused or neglected as children, they may harbor the belief that they are now *entitled* to the perfect love or the perfect life to make up for past iniquities.

Paradoxically, adults who as children were "worshipped" by their parents may end up the same way. In some families, parents end up being unable to tolerate any discomfort in their children. They can-not bear seeing their children sad or angry, and become deeply uncomfortable when their children look the least bit upset. They cannot let their children cry, and they feel frightened and desolate if their children get angry with them. These parents cannot set appro-priate limits on their children's behavior and let their children get away with all sorts of willful, rude, destructive, and self-destructive actions. Children brought up in this way may also expect that, as adults, they are *entitled* to unconditional love, to find someone who will continue to love them as they have been loved in the past, no matter how awful their behavior might be. Furthermore, spurred on by a culture that fosters parental excess, these people may unwit-tingly pass down this pattern of overindulgence to their children. In this way, patterns of behavior are transmitted from generation to generation.

At the heart of the lies of romantic love and marital bliss is this powerful desire to find the perfectly loving, supportive parent we thought we had in childhood or the one we *wish* we had. Romantic love is the belief that we have found such a person, our soul mate. The problem is that, just as all parents sooner or later show their imperfections, every object of romantic love eventually demonstrates his or her limitations, too. When this happens, we inevitably become profoundly disappointed. At this point, the capacity for sustaining a prolonged loving relationship depends on a balance of three critical variables: (1) how capable you are of tolerating those feelings of dis-appointment and putting them into reasonable perspective, (2) how truly limited the character and behavior of your loved one actually turns out to be, and finally, (3) how skilled you and your partner are at finding a way to comfortably live with those limitations. If any of these variables require more endurance than either of you can muster, then the relationship will crumble as the realities hidden behind "unconditional love" are exposed and the lie is transformed into painful disillusionment.

The reality is that, as understandable as the longing for "unconditional love" may be, unconditional love does not exist, except perhaps in the newborn infant's love for his or her caretakers and the ideal parent's love for his or her newborn baby. Most important, if you think you have it, it's probably going to get you into a lot of trouble. In my experience, most of those who claim they've found unconditional love are generally the very young or the very naive, or those who must dependently maintain a relationship with someone who is emotionally seriously troubled.

Everyone wants to be in love, and human beings looking for love suffer from the common, regrettable characteristic of becoming deeply emotionally attached to a new lover long before they know whether it is really wise for them to form such an attachment. Furthermore, once this attachment is made, it is often maintained in the face of extensive evidence that the attachment is unwise and self-destructive. This remarkable human propensity for rapid, sometimes instantaneous, attachment is among the most dangerous of human interpersonal emotional responses. George Bernard Shaw wrote that marriage is "when two people are under the influence of the most violent, most insane, most delusive, and most transient of passions. They are required to swear that they will remain in that excited, abnormal, and exhausting condition continuously until death do them part." Such intensity often leads us down a very long, frustrating, and disappointing path. Nonetheless, the excitement of this emotional fusion is a central feature in what many of us experience as love. Paradoxically, this same emotional hyperresponsiveness encourages us to have children and form families. If we add the belief in and expectation of unconditional love to this already powerful, binding, natural force of deep, rapid human attachment, we significantly increase the danger of making poor partnership choices and potentially consigning ourselves to many years of unrealistic, discouraging relationships.

Jerry and Samantha, both in their early thirties, came to see me because their engagement was in jeopardy. They'd known each other for almost two years and were very much in love. For both, the relationship was a dream come true. Samantha had dated many men, but she lost interest in most of them because she felt they weren't her intellectual or social equals. Jerry, likewise, had found most of the women he dated too superficial and was delighted by Samantha's intellect, seriousness, and intensity. All went blissfully until Jerry decided to start his own business. The couple gave a lot of thought to how disruptive this new opportunity could be to their private life, but they both felt it was what Jerry wanted and would be a good investment for their future. Neither of them expected the job to become as all consuming as it ultimately did.

Jerry's new position required him to work seven days a week, sixteen to eighteen hours a day. On top of that, his importance to the company made him responsible for the financial well-being of its many employees. He felt burdened and pressured by his huge responsibilities. When he got home, it was all he could do to recover emotionally and physically from his draining day, much less pay attention to Samantha. He withdrew, too overwhelmed to say much, too exhausted to spend time with her. Because he wanted to forget his troubles at work, the last thing he wanted to do was chew them over with Sam. No matter how much she asked to share in his struggles, he rejected her pleas and kept her at an emotional arm's length.

Seesawing between acceptance, depression, and rage, Samantha felt increasingly shut out of Jerry's life and began to feel a growing sense of hopelessness about their relationship. Jerry heard Samantha's complaints, but he did little to change. He remained preoccupied with his work and was rarely "in the moment" even when he was with Samantha. Eventually, he became disillusioned by and annoyed with

Samantha's unhappiness, and he began to worry that he couldn't satisfy her emotional neediness.

Samantha consulted me alone because Jerry was too busy with work to attend the session. We discussed ways that she could talk with Jerry about her dissatisfactions without complaining, attacking, or withdrawing from him. None of these strategies seemed to improve the relationship, and Samantha became despondent.

When I finally saw Samantha and Jerry together, they seemed the picture of connectedness, even as Samantha explained that she was on the verge of ending the relationship. They sat together on the couch, thighs touching, holding hands, clearly still in love. They both agreed that things had gotten better since their last fight, though Samantha wasn't sure the improvement would last. Jerry said that he was taking Samantha's unhappiness more seriously now because he had heard that her family and friends were encouraging her to end their engagement. He admitted that he had been shocked by the news. It had never occurred to him that the relationship and their forthcoming marriage could be in real peril, though Samantha had been voicing her intense distress for well over a year. When asked why he might have ignored that possibility, Jerry replied that once they had gotten engaged, he just assumed that they would be together forever, no matter what. He believed in "unconditional love," which meant to him that he would love Samantha under every circumstance. He just *expected* the same kind of commitment from her.

Jerry told me that his parents had remained married all their lives and had devoted themselves to making sure that he was given every advantage, even if they did go "overboard" in retrospect. He believed that once he and Samantha had found each other, she, too, would, and should, be totally and unconditionally devoted to him. He assumed that he and Samantha would weather these very difficult times together and that she would be there, however he behaved, whatever happened, when it was over. When I asked if he would consider the possibility that his belief in unconditional love might have given Samantha the feeling that she was being taken for granted, he acknowledged that he could see that she might feel that way but wasn't sure what to do about it.

I explained that it's essential to separate any notions of unconditional love from the practical problems couples have to deal with when they choose to live together or marry. Love alone, "unconditional" or otherwise, cannot be counted on to preserve a relationship. For that, you need the willingness to listen to each other and the capacity to make some changes in your behavior that take into account the sensitivities, beliefs, and desires of your partner. If the idea of unconditional love lulls you into believing that you'll be loved and lived with, no matter how frustrating or infuriating you are, then you could be in a lot of trouble. You'll take your spouse for granted and overlook opportunities for productive change.

On the other hand, when faced with a marriage with very limited chances for fulfillment, an unrealistic belief in the power of unconditional love can make you labor doggedly to rescue a damaged spouse or save an unworkable relationship. If you do have the good sense to get out of a grimly unfulfilling relationship, the conviction that you should have unconditional love for your partner can leave you haunted by the worry that, because you've left the relationship, you're somehow flawed in your capacity for this higher form of caring. This problem will be even worse if you have prematurely decided that your lover is your "soul mate" or if your partner tells you that he or she loves you unconditionally. Unconditional love is an unrealistic concept that promotes excessive attachment and control during relationships, and creates excessive guilt and a sense of failure when those relationships end.

Set Limits on Your Love

By all means, hold on to your ideal of unconditional love for your younger kids and puppies, but give it up when it comes to your marriage. Your spouse will not and should not accept everything you dish out, and neither should you. If you exceed your spouse's limits of tolerance, or vice versa, even if the marriage superficially survives, the emotional ties between the two of you will unravel. Your fantasy belief in unconditional love will fail you, and you will feel unnecessarily disillusioned and disappointed with your spouse, yourself, or with love itself.

Most of my clients cherish the belief that practicality is the death of love. They believe that love is expressed only with romantic gestures, the more spontaneous the better. I disagree. If you really want a loving relationship, the best chance you have is to be practical and to explain what in real life makes you feel loved, while you also, clearly and forthrightly, set out the limits of your tolerance. Speaking like this is a sign that you're willing to expose yourself and learn what is and isn't acceptable in your relationship. This helps avoid misunderstandings and creates more realistic expectations—even if sometimes these expectations will not be met and can lead to realistic disappointment. It also shows that you are open to working on your relationship.

STEP ONE: Know Thyself

The first conversation you need to have is with yourself. *Be honest about what you can live with, what you cannot live with, and what you cannot live without.* This may mean acknowledging truths about yourself that are less than flattering. Perhaps you're a neatnik who cannot tolerate the smallest mess, or someone who freaks out if your partner is a minute late to an engagement—you wish you weren't that rigid, but it's how you feel. Perhaps you don't like it when your spouse talks with someone of the opposite sex because you find it flirtatious—and you suspect you're being a little prudish. You may have certain expectations about how often your spouse should check in with you when you're apart, whether it's okay to take separate vacations, how you'll spend money, run the household, and so forth.

Separate your "wants" from your "needs." The truth is that you *need* food, oxygen, shelter, and one good friend. Just about everything else is a *want*. Own your own wants. Take responsibility for your wanting and the consequences of those desires. Acknowledge that different people want different things and prioritize their wants differently. One spouse wants home-cooked meals; the other wants take-out and restaurant meals every night. One spouse may want the latest fashions to feel confident and attractive; the other might find that a frivolous want. One spouse might want to lease the latest car; the other wants a minimal investment in a used car. Stop speaking of your wants as if they are needs—absolutes, unquestionable, beyond discussion. You are entitled to want what you want (although you're not necessarily always entitled to get it). You don't have to call it a need to justify it, to make it sound more reasonable or correct. Commit yourself to discussing your different wants openly without ridiculing your partner's wants.

Upon closer examination, you may find some of these desires, beliefs, and behaviors petty or ungenerous. Own up to them anyway. They exist whether or not you acknowledge them, and bringing them into the light gives you a fighting chance that your partner will accept those limits, become sensitive to them, or realize the work you have ahead of you to try to change them. As I tell my patients, "Put your wants on the table."

STEP TWO: Share Your Views

A helpful way to share your views about what you want is to write down on a piece of paper the three most important things your spouse can do that would make you feel loved. For example, "I feel loved when you spontaneously make me a home-cooked meal; when you hold my hand when we walk down the street; when you tell me that I look beautiful." Or, "I'd feel loved if I saw you playing baseball with the children; if you gave me oral sex; if you watched my favorite TV shows with me." Honesty is crucial here. Don't censor your list by excluding those items that seem petty, unworthy, or somehow "wrong"; or things you believe you're unlikely to get. Don't include items because they're things you "ought" to want or because you think you're likely to get them. If the fact that your spouse leaves the cap off the toothpaste drains your psychic energy and you'd feel loved if he changed that habit, put it on your list even if it sounds minor—it isn't minor to you. If you really want your spouse to call you every day from the office, and you know that in a million years she wouldn't do that, put it on your list anyway.

After each of you lists the three most important ways that your partner makes you or could make you feel loved, exchange the lists. Are there any surprises? Was either one of you unaware that something on the other's list could be so important? Then discuss if these requests can be fulfilled. Are they easy things for your spouse to do or very difficult? Are any of the ways either of you feel loved impossible to get from the other? If so, can you live with the frustration comfortably?

Now that you've started the process, talk about other aspects of your relationship. Share your dreams, goals, desires, and interests. Be sure your spouse understands you and takes you seriously. Let your partner know what behaviors you can handle and what you cannot deal with. You'll be tempted to avoid those topics that are typically radioactive in relationships: differences over money, sex, and children. But those are exactly the subjects that most often drive couples apart. You'll be tempted to avoid those topics that just seem too petty for words: the dirty socks dropped right next to the hamper but not in it; your partner's garlic breath after an Italian meal; the newspaper never turned back to the front page. If you avoid these topics, they don't go away; they just acquire more traction and wreak more subterranean havoc in your marriage. If you discuss them, you may be surprised to find out that some of them are easily changed.

STEP THREE: Negotiate

Talk about what you can accept, that is, what you can at best embrace and at worst tolerate with grace and understanding. Find out what your spouse is willing to accept about you. How many of each other's wants can you fulfill? Which of each other's behaviors can you live or not live with? Discuss what you're willing to change about yourself. Be honest; change is effective only if it can be done without too much reluctance or resentment. If you cannot change something, ask if your partner can live with this part of you the way it is. If you are already too resentful to consider change, realize that the two of you must first improve the atmosphere of your relationship before you can change how you interact. (For more on effective change, and why the atmosphere of a couple's relationship can block change, see chapters 2 and 3.)

Jeffrey and Heidi had been married for three years when it became clear that they had to renegotiate the limits of their love. Jeffrey began to drink more than Heidi could tolerate. Her father had been an alcoholic who deserted his family when Heidi was a young girl. Understandably, she was very sensitive to Jeff's drinking and usually became anxious and angry when he came home hours late, smelling of booze. Jeff, on the other hand, felt that going out for drinks with the guys after work was a way of promoting his business and making new contacts. Even though he knew that he also had a strong family history of alcoholism, he resisted Heidi's interference and stayed out even later to prove to her that he could not be controlled.

In therapy, after diminishing their need to fight about it, we put the issue squarely on the table for negotiation. Heidi said that she could handle Jeff's going out for drinks after work, if he would tell her when he was coming home, not lie about it, and then be on time. This would help her control her underlying fear of abandonment and her terror that something might happen to Jeff when he was drunk. Also, she said, she would be able to tolerate Jeff's drinking if he could stop after two drinks so he wouldn't come home plastered. She stated her limit: She would not be in a relationship with a person who lied or drank to excess.

Jeffrey said that he wanted to have the freedom to go out after work with his friends and business colleagues without Heidi's trying to control him. She agreed not to nag him about drinking and to let him be in charge of his own life. Some months after these successful negotiations, Jeff realized on his own that his drinking was out of control and he joined AA (Alcoholics Anonymous). In order to calm her own emotional reactivity down, Heidi decided to join the group ACOA (Adult Children of Alcoholics).

Ideally, you enter into negotiations such as these at the beginning of your relationship, before you marry. It is remarkable though how many of us marry never having had meaningful discussions about our wants, our likes and dislikes, our values, goals, dreams, and interests. We act as if it's all already understood. However, I suspect that people who don't have these critical discussions before marriage are afraid that they will stir up trouble, so they avoid them. Also, they may just be naive enough to assume that everything they want in life will be okay with their partner, that is, that they will experience unconditional love. For example, if you want three children, you assume that your partner will give you what you want and be happy about it out of sheer love.

The main reason that couples avoid these discussions before marriage is that they fear exposing serious differences between them, differences that they worry will be difficult or impossible to resolve comfortably. Talking about real differences always requires sensitive, thoughtful negotiations. It forces you to learn that you cannot always have your own way in a relationship. The earlier one learns this the better it is for the relationship. Though we all know this intellectually, it is a very difficult thing to accept when it involves something that you care about strongly. Whether or not you had these discussions before marriage, they are valuable at any stage. The limits of your love aren't carved in stone. Expect to review and renew your list of wants from time to time. The longer your marriage lasts, the more you'll find you have to negotiate and often renegotiate issues as you and your spouse grow and change your views.

Marcia, an eighty-three-year-old woman, came to see me because she was about to divorce her eighty-seven-year-old husband, Arthur, who was having an affair. Marcia was very insightful about her husband of sixty-five years. She felt he was afraid of dying and was looking for a last fling because, as she told me, "He wants to feel young again." She was used to this kind of behavior, for Arthur had had other affairs when he was younger. It turned out that what was really bothering her now was that they lived in a small retirement community in an isolated town in Vermont, and all Marcia's friends knew what Arthur was doing and with whom he was doing it. They were coming up to Marcia and asking her why she didn't put a stop to Arthur's carrying on. "The old crones, why don't they mind their own damned business," she told me. When she confronted Arthur, he refused to talk about it and continued his hurtful behavior.

It became clear that Marcia really didn't want to leave the marriage and could even tolerate Arthur's affair if he would only be more discreet about it. The problem was that Arthur was embarrassing Marcia in front of her friends. I suggested a negotiation in which Marcia would offer to live with Arthur and not sue him for divorce if he would stop flaunting his girlfriend in their small community. Arthur agreed to the plan, and the couple stayed together (to the relief of everyone, including their children).

Stories like this one raise the question, especially for older people, of what you do if you reach an impasse with your spouse but don't want to bail out. The real question is: How do you live in a relationship if you're not getting something you want, something that you deem is very important to you? Here is where the myths of romantic love, marital bliss, and unconditional love come in again. These myths suggests that such a thing will not happen, or when it does, your spouse will be the one who gives in, who changes to make *you* happy. But again, this is not real life. In real marriage, every couple reaches an impasse sooner or later in their relationship. *Each of us eventually has to learn to live with something about our marital partner that we don't like very much.* This happens because we cannot marry the person we see in the mirror. Once we accept this, we inevitably discover that there is something about the other person that is so different from us that it makes us uncomfortable and, at times, incredibly unhappy.

So, the real question, the one that is so difficult to deal with in so many different contexts, is: How do we deal with disappointment and resentment? First, realize that in your relationship, disappointment and resentment will lessen dramatically if you begin with or develop reasonable expectations of yourself and others. Much resentment in marriage is based on having unrealistic expectations of both the process of marriage and your spouse. Next, appreciate that you can lessen your resentment, even when there is an impasse, if you are able to discuss differences with your spouse fairly and without rancor, something that in my experience is all too rare. You also need to remember that your background has a profound influence on what you can and cannot tolerate. Understanding the role that your upbringing has on your beliefs and your reaction to events can dramatically affect your capacity to handle or modify your disappointment. For example, Heidi had a particular sensitivity to alcohol abuse and abandonment because of her experience with her father, which was why she couldn't tolerate Jeffrey's excessive drinking at all. There are other women in my practice, married to men who drink far more than Jeffrey, who would have much less concern about this issue. (For more on handling the influence of family, see chapter 4.)

Resentment is a defensive reaction to being disappointed. Because resentments inevitably destroy relationships, holding on to resentments is a dangerous course of action. You must directly confront your resentments to protect yourself and your marriage. How you do this is a personal choice. You can do it by analyzing your upbringing (controlling childhood reactions that are being stirred up in you), through cognitive therapy or refocusing (learning to focus on the good in your spouse rather than the bad), meditation (cleansing your mind of negative thoughts and distress), spirituality (turning it over to a Higher Power or God), or numerous other techniques. The point is that it must be done. If you don't succeed, if you fail to control and resolve your own resentments, your relationship will be in serious jeopardy.

Even in situations in which you reach an impasse, you can strengthen your relationship, for it is not the impasse itself that is so destructive, but how you as a couple deal with it. If you deal with differences, disappointments, and frustrations well, your relationship will grow and thrive. You've let your partner know that you are not perfect for him or her and can accept that he or she is not perfect for you either. Yet you will love, respect, and treat each other well anyway. This is an enormously maturing emotional step in a marriage. You've shown that you're willing to keep sharing your life with a spouse who has a different, altogether human, set of frailties. However, never forget that, for you and your spouse, tolerance has its limits, and some differences and some behaviors will, in time, destroy a marriage.

Make Your Marriage Your Priority

If you've bought into the lie of marital bliss, contrary to what you naturally think, you are probably a less-attentive spouse. Recall your courtship days: you were on your best behavior; you worked hard to find ways to make your partner happy; you hid your foibles to the best of your abilities, and you tried hard to overlook those of your partner. Now that you have safely "landed" your love, your motivation to present your best self has receded. You're not quite so vigilant about how you dress. You're more aware of and critical of your partner's faults, and more myopic about your own.

Many patients who come to my office tell me that their marriage is the most important thing in their lives, but they don't act like it. Think of how you'd describe yourself to a stranger: "I'm an accountant, the father of two, and I love to ski." Or, "I have three kids, I work in magazine publishing, and I volunteer for the school literacy program. My favorite hobbies are cooking and reading." Where is your spouse in all this? Do you ever start with "I'm an involved husband"? Or, "I spend most of my time working on my marriage"?

Marriage is hard work and a constant commitment. Your marriage will survive only if you make it your top priority. The simple truth is that it doesn't take that much to give your spouse the sense that he or she is very important to you. And yet, many of us don't even give that much. In my practice, I regularly see busy men and women who are struggling to maintain their marriages while balancing work and, usually, family. When they ask me what they could do to make their spouses feel more appreciated, I give them a list of suggestions: Go home tonight and tell her what a great job she's doing with your children. Or tell her how beautiful she looks and how great it is to be married to her. Bring her flowers and tell her that when you saw them they reminded you of what a fortunate guy you are. Tell your husband how much you appreciate how hard he works and the living that he provides for you and the kids. Tell your husband how attractive he looks. Tell him what a good father he is. The possibilities are endless. However, as easy as they are for me to suggest, they are much harder for couples to remember to do. It seems to be more natural for many of us to criticize and be angry than to compliment, praise, or reward our spouse, all of the things that are necessary to make him or her feel appreciated. Again, you cannot do any of this if you are sitting on a powder keg of resentment. You have to get rid of that first.

Put Your Job Second

The myth of marital bliss also tells us that we can sacrifice our marriage on the altar of work because our spouse will be willing to put up with it. According to the U.S. Census Bureau, for the first time, beginning in 1998, the majority of American families were couples

43

with two jobs and multiple children. More and more couples find themselves literally spending more time with their colleagues than with their spouses.

It's unreasonable to expect that your partner's love for you will be unaffected by your putting excessive time and effort into your job instead of your marriage. When I encourage couples to ease off a little on their work life so they can spend more time with their spouses, it's with the understanding that we don't live in an ideal world with obliging bosses and infinitely flexible hours. And yet easing off slightly at work seldom gets you fired. *The truth is that, though divorce is more common than unemployment, we're much more frightened about losing our jobs than losing our spouses.* Especially for men, but increasingly for women, too, our self-esteem is based more on how successful we appear in our profession than on how well we do in our marriage. It's time to be courageous and shift perspective. As one of my patients once told me, "If I put as much effort into my marriage as I put into my work, there would never be any problem in my marriage." The world of work can do very nicely without you more often than you allow yourself to believe. The institution and act of marriage does not come with any warranties like unconditional love. You have to work for and earn the continuing love of your partner and the success of your marriage. Unfortunately, many people see this vision of marriage as terribly unromantic. I see it as the opposite—ill informed. Naïve romanticism leads to disillusionment, dissatisfaction, and divorce. It eventually kills love. Well-informed marital romanticism, true love, accepts that problem solving, the maintenance of mutual respect and the development of new interpersonal skills create greater intimacy. This understanding of marriage both preserves love and fosters deeper bonds of affection. This is certainly the more truly romantic view of marriage. The only way you'll get to the "happily ever after" is to recognize that it's the learning of this new information, and persistence and diligence in its use that make for successful long-term relationships.

CHAPTER 2

Lie: I Talk All the Time; My Spouse Just Doesn't Listen

Truth: Good Communication Is Much More Than Honest Speech

It is better to have a cool head and a warm heart than a hot head and a cold heart.

—Anonymous

Often the difference between a successful marriage and a mediocre one consists of leaving about three or four things a day unsaid.

—Harlan Miller

We never talked in our family. We communicated by putting Ann Landers articles on the fridge.

—Judy Gold

Amanda and Roy have come to see me because they're at an impasse. Laid off from her job in finance, Amanda got a hefty severance check, but her self-image was devastated. She's been home for the last six months, pondering what she should do next. Meanwhile, Roy took a promotion as an entertainment lawyer and is working crazy hours. Increasingly, he's less available to Amanda. She feels marginalized—not just in her career but in her marriage. She doesn't know whether the stress over losing her job is to blame or whether her concerns about Roy are legitimate.

"You're always coming home late; then you expect me to drop everything and entertain you," Amanda says accusingly. "Or you say you'll be home early, then I don't see you until after midnight and you don't even bother to call. You don't care what I'm going through. You're being completely selfish."

"Here we go again." Roy rolls his eyes. "Here's the God's honest truth: You have no life of your own. You wouldn't care so much about how late I work if you had something meaningful to do in your life. I've told you until I'm blue in the face that you should get another job, but you never do anything about it. You just don't get it." Roy turns an entreating face to me. "See what I mean? We've talked this to death, but Amanda refuses to listen to me."

"The way I see it," I say, "you're both coming in loud and clear. That's exactly the problem."

Sound familiar? We live in a society that teaches us to be open about our feelings but doesn't properly differentiate between helpful and harmful feelings or between helpful and harmful forms of speech. Many of us have been taught to believe that we should share with our loved ones whatever we feel, however we feel it. Moreover, we're often told that being "brutally honest" is an act of helpful communication; telling our loved ones exactly how we feel will help them understand us and make the changes we believe are so essential. But the truth is that brutally honest people are usually being more brutal than honest. They are emotionally overreactive and are expressing their irritation, anger, or rage in the form of uncontrolled, hurtful statements disguised as honest, constructive criticism. They are telling you what they feel and how they feel it without any concern for the effect of their criticism or any real self-awareness.

The majority of spouses I counsel have no difficulty saying what's on their mind, but they do have enormous difficulty communicating in a way that gets them heard and produces the results they want.

The Physics of Emotions

In high school I had a wonderful physics teacher who demonstrated how sound is carried by waves transmitted through the air. To do this, he brought out two finely made rectangular wooden boxes, each a few inches high and about a foot long, open at one end. My teacher inserted tuning forks of the same pitch into little holes in the top of each box, then arranged the boxes so that the open ends faced each other from either end of his long laboratory desk. With a hard rubber mallet he struck one of the tuning forks and let it vibrate for a few seconds so that it produced a clear sound. Then he grabbed the vibrating tuning fork with his hand and stilled it. To our surprise, the second tuning fork, ten feet away, was now vibrating on its own, producing its own ringing tone without ever having been touched. I found this nothing short of amazing. My teacher then released the first tuning fork and, after a moment, grabbed the second one, stilling it. Now the first tuning fork was vibrating again, making a clear but somewhat softer sound, while its mate was silent. He explained to us that if the system were engineered sensitively enough, once the original tuning fork was struck with the rubber mallet, the sound waves could flow back and forth, exciting the other tuning fork *ad infinitum*.

In marriage, each individual acts like a very sensitive tuning fork that receives and transmits emotional impulses instead of sound waves. When one member of a couple has an emotional reaction, the "vibrations" from that reaction are unintentionally or purposely transmitted to the other member. The recipient then begins to vibrate emotionally in response. This response then cycles back and has a reinforcing effect on the original person, who then responds to it. It turns out that *a central critical variable determining the comfort and outcome of marriage is the quality of this emotional vibratory cycle between marital partners.*

In physics, the harder and more frequently the initiating tuning fork is hit by a mallet, the more powerful the signal it sends out and the greater the effect it has on the other tuning fork. This is also true of the system of marriage. Individuals who have intense and frequent emotional reactions will have a greater impact on the people around them will than those who have less intense and less frequent emotional reactions. Also, the more sensitively set one person's emotional system is, the greater the tendency to pick up arousing vibrations from others and to generate reactive emotional responses.

In the physical world, either tuning fork will eventually stop vibrating if it doesn't receive additional reinforcement from the other tuning fork. Likewise, it always takes two reactive people to engage in a cycle of emotional vibration. This has a very powerful implication for troubled couples who are commonly caught in damaging cycles of emotional hyperreactivity: *Since intense negative emotionality expressed as angry, rageful, vicious, or hurtful attacks can ruin effective communication and harm relationships, it is necessary to calm down and control excessive negative feelings to be able to communicate successfully with your spouse. As with tuning forks, individuals have the power to mute the emotional reactions of each other by simply containing and dampening their* own *emotional responses.*

Typically, we experience emotional vibrations in one of three ways: positively (as loving interactions), neutrally (as everyday interactions that help couples get practical things done), or negatively (as disappointing, hurtful, critical, or hostile experiences). For example, a husband can walk in the door from work, give his wife a heartily felt hug and kiss, sit down with the children, and ask how everyone's day has gone. Everything else being equal, he will be experienced as giving out positive vibrations and, more likely than not, will get some sort of warm signal back from his wife and children. The tone for the rest of the evening is set by this brief interaction.

But what if he comes home feeling irritable because he had a tough day at his job or is overtired? Or what if he's angry with his wife for some unresolved conflict? Now he may broadcast very different signals as he comes through the door, and the significant people in his environment will immediately pick up on them. His coming home in a bad mood and not kissing his wife as he walks in the door may irritate her. He may then detect her reactive irritation and begin to respond to it. Now, dimly aware that his wife is avoiding him, he'll begin to feel angry and ignore his children. Next, their emotional receptors sense the tensions between their parents and their dad's neglect of them. They begin to vibrate responsively by asking for his attention, perhaps in a negative way, by making loud noises. He'll hear the noise, find it exacerbating to his already frayed nerves, and respond to it by becoming more irritable, sending out further negative vibrations that will additionally set off his wife and children. This homecoming is more likely to end in bad feelings or a family argument.

In couples, intense emotional cycles, positive or negative, can persist indefinitely until one or the other adult in the system decides to dampen or change its direction. For example, if the vibrations are negative, the negative cycle rapidly diminishes when one spouse gets control of his angry feelings. In most couples, when one partner cannot or will not dampen the emotional response, the other spouse can *unilaterally* improve the situation. In the example above of the dad's homecoming, this could happen in any number of ways, some more useful than others.

The harmful cycle could be stopped or at least diminished if the dad could identify his own irritability and control it, or, alternatively, walk through the door saying to his children, "I've had a terrible day. I'm in a grumpy mood. Could you guys give me a half an hour to relax? Then I'll come play with you." In the absence of the father's ability to regulate his own emotional reactions, his wife might say, "Gosh, honey, you seem very tense tonight. Why don't you relax for a while until you feel better? I'll take care of the kids. . . . Hey kids, keep it quiet, Dad's had a tough day." Under most circumstances, any adult in a system is capable of reducing the cycle at any time. In the best of all possible worlds, this is exactly what happens: couples have moments or periods of negative interactions, but they learn how to terminate them before they get out of control.

Unfortunately, all too often, this is not the outcome. For many of us, the tendency to react negatively to our spouses' negative vibrations comes all too naturally. Once someone has spoken or behaved badly to us, we have a phenomenal capacity to respond in kind—reflexively and unconstructively. Whether the counterreaction is defensive or offensive, a cold withdrawal or a heated counterattack, once we feel "messed with," most of us are inclined to keep it going. *Our capacity for automatic, insensitive or hurtful emotional actions and equally damaging and thoughtlessly automatic counterreactions creates and then maintains the conflict cycle between spouses.* If a couple frequently engage in this form of unpleasant marital interaction without the ability to dampen it and find a satisfactory resolution, they will eventually experience the cycle as a habitual pattern and expect it whenever they approach the communication of emotional issues. After a while, they'll find that they can precipitate an intense, heated, painful interaction in a nanosecond with a remark, word of criticism, look, or other negative behavior. Many spouses have emotional tuning forks that are so sensitive to each other that they regularly, even unintentionally, precipitate bad feelings through common misunderstandings. When this happens, each spouse becomes incredulous at being so misconstrued, and usually begins to see his or her mate as "crazy."

The Downward Spiral

When couples recurrently get caught in this negative, mutually reinforcing, emotionally overreactive cycle, they inevitably enter a downward spiral. Even without an overt escalation of the conflict, the inability to break the negative cycle has the unfortunate consequence of naturally allowing the cycle to worsen. This is because *in loving relationships the absence of regularly reinforcing warm feelings automatically breeds disappointment and resentment as a by-product of frustrated expectations and desires.* When a once-loving relationship becomes a disappointment and then fails to improve, we become increasingly disenchanted with our spouse and begin to withdraw our emotional connection. Unable to get the negative interaction to stop, as we disconnect, we begin to feel distrustful of our spouse and eventually *expect* each significant interaction to be exasperating, unproductive, and, finally, hurtful. These hurtful experiences provoke in us a characteristic biological fight-or-flight response; we either display anger or withdraw further from emotional interactions. These responses make the already tense situation worse. As this negative cyclic reaction between spouses goes unchecked, escalating bad behavior leaves a growing residue of bitterness and doubt. Typically one or both spouses start thinking or saying something like, "I *love* my husband/wife but I don't *like* him/her very much anymore."

If you have had these feeling or thoughts, you are already caught in this downward emotional spiral. After these feelings emerge, unless the downward spiral is reversed, it is frequently only a matter of time before a marriage begins to come apart. When the destructive spiral has gone on too long, when neither member of the couple can trust the other to respond calmly and effectively to the issue at hand, when ceaseless disappointment and hurt have given way to hopelessness, distrust, outrage, or emotional shutdown, spouses can look as if they are suffering from a severe case of mutual paranoia.

Negative spirals cause special trouble to both the individuals involved and to anyone on the outside who is trying to be helpful. The more ingrained the cycle, the longer it has gone unchecked, the greater the unhappiness, bitterness, and reciprocal blaming it creates. Over time, *each member of the couple develops an increasingly higher stake in seeing his own pain as being the result of the attitudes and behaviors of the other spouse.* If this process is left unresolved, as disappointment, frustration, and resentment build, the vision of the spouse changes from that of a lover and friend to that of an adversary and/or enemy. It is impossible to help a troubled couple without interrupting and reversing this communication nightmare. Interestingly, even divorce does not automatically resolve the cyclic reactivity, which can continue to play out painfully within a separated couple for life.

If you really understand the power of cycles and spirals in marriage, then you will accept that *no matter how little you believe you are adding to the problem, that little bit is the part which you have to take responsibility for and change.*

Reversing the Spiral

The essential first step in improving or repairing any troubled marriage is short-circuiting the negative emotional spiral you are caught in and reversing the direction of the damaging feedback loop. Before anything else, *you need to change the emotional atmosphere of your relationship; reversing this downward spiral is the way to do it.* Learning and then consistently using positive communication skills accomplishes this task. *What* you say and *how* you say it are extremely important to all relationships, but they are absolutely crucial to the success of your marriage. The old saying "Sticks and stones may break my bones, but names will never harm me" turns out to be little more than childhood braggadocio. Not only are we badly harmed by names and words, but also by the intonation and manner of their delivery. This is particularly true when someone we love is speaking them, or when the words are being used as weapons in a marital battle.

On the other hand, we are comforted and reassured by speech that is loving, respectful, and thoughtful. It is remarkable how many couples dramatically benefit just from learning to speak to each other more thoughtfully and carefully.

I am *not* suggesting that you be less emotional or passive with your spouse. Intense feelings are part of the bond that holds couples together. But negative emotions and behaviors like excessive anger, rage, devaluation, or sarcasm, which *reflexively* cycle within troubled relationships, lead to hurt, withdrawal, distrust, bitterness, resentment, and counterattacks. These feelings always undermine a marriage, no matter what appears on the surface. They destroy the potential for mutuality and closeness, and interfere with more beneficial feelings that promote togetherness and intimacy. After a horrible fight, some couples delude themselves into thinking that their relationship is improving because they believe that they have finally gotten their point across to their spouse or because they feel relieved that they're still together after the fight is over. Many people find sex at this point to be particularly exciting because they are so comforted by the reassurance that they are still connected. However, these couples are ignoring the corrosive nature of the buildup of the hidden residual bitterness and distrust that accompanies intense, recurrent marital battles. The first step to improving a strained relationship is to master effective communication skills so that you can reverse any negative emotional spirals affecting your marriage.

Mastering "Self-Statements"

At the heart of better communication is the self-statement. *A self-statement puts the responsibility for your emotional experience squarely on your shoulders. It is the one single, easy-to-learn skill that can most dramatically improve the communication in your marriage.*

Self-statements always begin by using the subject "I" to discuss a problem. They exist in opposition to their nemesis, "you" statements. A *"you" statement puts the responsibility for your emotional discomfort on your partner, never on yourself.* "You" statements are communications of criticism, blame, and anger. In "you" statements, your emotional experiences and negative behaviors are always presented as being an appropriate response to the irresponsible or hurtful action of someone else. "I" statements decrease the emotional reactivity of the system. "You" statements increase emotional reactivity and interpersonal tension. Here is an example of the difference between the two.

Barbara is consulting me about her marriage to Gary, her husband of eighteen months. The marriage is going well, but she has one problem: She sees herself as more organized than Gary. She wants everything planned out ahead of time. Gary is more laid back. When they go out, she wants to arrive at their destination a few minutes early. She finds herself impatiently waiting for Gary to get ready and then becoming critical of him when he appears to get distracted or looks as if he won't be ready to go when she is.

On one occasion, Gary wanted to make weekend plans with another couple and waited until Thursday of the same week to set up the date. When he found out that the other couple had already made other plans, he took the situation in stride. But Barbara was furious. "Why did *you* wait until the last minute?" she demanded to know. "*You* always wait until the last minute to make plans. If *you* really cared about seeing your friends, *you* would have called them earlier in the week."

For many of us, this form of criticism sounds perfectly reasonable and familiar. However, Gary is often hurt by these common exchanges, and Barbara worries that she is being too critical and unhelpful, a legitimate concern since her statements don't lead to any meaningful change on Gary's part. She's worried that the way she's approaching the problem may be hurting the relationship. She senses that she shouldn't be so harsh, but doesn't *know* how else to tell Gary that she finds his behavior distressing and irritating.

These few sentences from Barbara illustrate both the dangers and lack of practical usefulness of the "you" statement. Barbara's discomfort with Gary's style causes her to be annoyed with him, and she displays her irritation by her choice of words and her tone of voice. Metaphorically, her index finger is jabbing toward Gary as the exclusive source of the problem. When she asks, "Why did *you* wait until the last minute?" she's really not asking a question at all; she's offering a criticism. It would have been more honest and straightforward if she'd simply said, "You shouldn't have waited until the last minute."

The "you" statement is always some form of other-directed criticism or lecture, though it may be hidden or subtle at times. As a result, it will naturally lead the receiver to defend him or herself, even if the response is unspoken. As this defense is taking place, the respondent can no longer focus calmly on the content of the original complaint. His or her psychic energy is mostly channeled into a defense or counterattack, not into a reasonable, empathetic response or cooperative solution to the problem being raised.

In this example, Barbara, after the opening assault, tells Gary that he "always" waits too long to make plans. This second "you" statement now magnifies the conflict by adding *exaggeration* to the already outerdirected criticism. In this way, Barbara raises the emotional ante. She escalates the issue at hand from an isolated incident to a broader defect in Gary's personality. Exaggerating another person's idiosyncrasies is one of the most common, interpersonally damaging strategies used by spouses to make a point in an argument. Now Barbara is not simply criticizing some small aspect of Gary's style, she is *amplifying* the problem to the level of an unpleasant truth about his very being. Finally, in suggesting that he didn't make the date in time because he really didn't care enough about seeing his friends, Barbara has extended her indictment to question, and therefore express doubt about, Gary's underlying capacity for attachment and friendship. By raising a suspicion about Gary's sincerity, Barbara, by extension, inadvertently questions the validity of her own relationship with him.

What Barbara needs to master is the use of the self-statement. An alternative response to Gary's behavior might have been, "Honey, *I* get very anxious when *I* don't have things planned in advance, and *I* worry that people will think *I* don't care about them if *I* wait until the last minute to make dates. *I* know these things don't concern you as much, but it would be a big help to me if we could plan things out more and make dates with friends as far ahead as possible." Rather than blaming Gary for her discomfort and demanding that he change, Barbara in this way could make it easier for Gary to change by labeling the issue not as his problem but as something that causes *her* discomfort. It's then easier for him to make the choice to help Barbara when he doesn't feel as if he's a problem that needs to be fixed.

When making a self-statement, frame the problem in terms of the way the other person's actions affect or bother you. "I feel X when Y happens." "It would be helpful to me if you could do Z. I would then feel more or less X." Many of my more clever patients immediately figure out how to sneak criticisms behind enemy lines by cloaking them as self-statements: "I feel that you're behaving like a child when you wrestle with the kids just before their bedtime." Or, "It makes me feel uncomfortable when you always forget to clear the dishes." These aren't feelings; they're thoughts and opinions—"you" statements in the disguise of "I" statements.

Another important aspect of self-statements is that they move contentious issues into a territory beyond petty dispute. By talking about what you feel inside, how and why you are affected, the conversation can no longer be confined to bickering about who is right and who is wrong. After all, you can't argue about whether a spouse has a feeling. If your spouse says he feels upset by something, you can't reasonably disagree by saying, "No you don't." Gary and Barbara might argue in circles about whose style—hyperorganized or laid back—is the better or "correct" one. But there can be no argument about Barbara's feelings when she says she gets upset when Gary doesn't plan ahead. The couple then has to focus on addressing Barbara's issue and finding a constructive solution rather than bickering over which style is better.

Always Discuss Hurts Before Anger

An equally vital component of initiating dialogue with your spouse is always to remember to speak first about your hurts, not your anger. If we initiate important conversations by attacking or angrily criticizing our spouse, we immediately set off in our partner the need for defense. If the listener feels attacked, she will immediately shut down emotionally and begin to focus on how to protect herself or withdraw from the fray. This can be avoided by beginning any conversation over an issue that has angered you by first explaining how the situation has hurt your feelings. This is sometimes difficult to explain, even to yourself. Many of us do not understand that we get angry in response to feeling hurt or threatened. It is also difficult for your partner to hear. However, it arouses less need for self-defense or counterattack. Much more often than not it will open the door to real dialogue or at least serious consideration of your feelings in the near future. Beginning dialogue with an angry critical attack usually precipitates a fight, shuts off real discussion of the issues, breeds resentment, and frequently stifles any real change. So, if you really want to change your marriage through better communication, always discuss what has hurt your feelings and why you are hurt rather than displaying your rage or anger.

Meeting the Challenge of Listening

Simply becoming skillful at making self-statements and discussing your hurts before your anger won't guarantee a couple good communication (though it does go a long way). There needs to be someone on the other end to answer the call. The receiver needs to listen, understand, and seriously consider what is being said. It is also the listener's responsibility to communicate this understanding to the initiator of the dialogue so that the speaker can be reassured that he or she is being heard. This *reassurance is critical, because it diminishes the anxiety and pressure experienced by the initiator of the discussion, who is always fearful of not getting through.*

Most of us tend to short-circuit this crucial feedback loop. Humorist Fran Lebowitz deftly analyzed the typical way we communicate when she said, "There's talking. And there's waiting to talk."

The two most common mistakes made on the receiving end of troubled dialogue are (1) the natural tendency to defend oneself from criticism by striking back and (2) the natural tendency to do too much to solve the other person's problems (this will be discussed in the next chapter). Remember, self-statements are valuable in large part because they make it easier for the receiver to listen to what is being said without having to take defensive measures. A well-designed self-statement simply informs the listener of the effect she is having on the speaker without holding the listener principally responsible for that effect.

However, there are times when the initiator of a dialogue does not do a good job. *The extremely difficult task of the listener is to control the natural tendency to withdraw, defend, or counterattack when feeling criticized and, instead, to respond in a concerned, empathetic way.* In other words, the listener must learn to control the tendency to automatically vibrate back. How can you respond this way when you're feeling criticized or attacked?

First, Do Nothing

Learn to wait. It's extremely difficult to listen silently without withdrawing or defending yourself when you're feeling criticized or attacked. The impulse to cut off your spouse is usually the first sign that your defenses have been aroused and that you are now more intent on constructing an excuse or a rejoinder than in paying attention to your partner. As Drs. Virginia and Redford Williams point out in their book *LifeSkills*, "You're not really listening unless you're prepared to be changed by what you've heard." If you're busy mounting your defense to a perceived affront, you cannot be truly listening to your spouse. Occasionally, the tendency to cut off a spouse is simply a sign of impatience, but whatever the motivation, if you interrupt, your spouse will feel unheard and you will have missed an opportunity for meaningful communication.

If you're able to absorb information without a defensive reaction, your spouse will begin to feel that he is getting your attention and automatically experience a sense of relief and diminished anxiety. However, if you constantly interrupt your spouse, he will simply become more anxious, frustrated, and agitated, reinforcing the belief that the same argument has to be made all over again, this time with the volume turned up higher.

I learned the dramatic benefits of silent listening from my first family therapy supervisor. We were working with a couple in deep marital distress. The wife was so anxious and defensive that no matter how or what the husband said, she couldn't stop interrupting him, making it impossible for him to feel heard. After numerous attempts to get her to just listen, my supervisor got up, sat next to the wife on the couch, held her hand and said, "Now, you and I are just going to listen to what your husband is saying and we're not going to make a sound." Every time the woman began to interrupt her husband, the supervisor simply held her hand more tightly, looked her right in the eye, smiled his friendliest smile and said, "I'm going to help you listen. We will listen together. Now remember, not a peep until your husband is finished, and then we will hear what you think, too." This maneuver was successful. For the first time, this woman began to listen without interrupting her husband, and this began a breakthrough for their relationship.

Learn to Check and Repeat

Once you've mastered receptive listening, your next step is to give your spouse the proper feedback. Learn how to ask questions and make statements that reassure the speaker that you've heard and understood what's being said. I call this checking and repeating. *Check* with the speaker by asking simple questions such as: "Could you explain more of what you mean when you say X?" Or, "When you say Y, do you mean . . . ?" Or, "I don't think I understood Z. Could you run it by me again?"

Then, *repeat* what you've heard by simply paraphrasing your understanding of what your spouse has said, concluding with, "Is that right?" Or, "Am I understanding correctly what you're saying?" Keep on checking and repeating until your spouse agrees that you have understood what is being said.[1]

Typically, when my patients begin to practice checking and repeating, they worry that they'll sound wooden or robotic. "She's going to think I sound like a moron when I repeat something she just said." Or, "I sound like a parrot." This is why it's important to paraphrase rather than just regurgitate what you've heard; rewording what your spouse said conveys that you're making the effort to understand and consider it. You may, in fact, feel a little awkward when you first check and repeat, but you'll quickly discover that your spouse's relief at being heard will trump any concerns that you're acting like a mindless tape recorder. Be sure that your spouse acknowledges that you've heard things correctly and truly understand what you've heard. This helps avoid the later accusation that "you never listen," though it often reveals that the real "communication" problem is that you have heard something very clearly but do not agree with it. Only comment on what your spouse said after there is an agreement that you have understood things correctly. Then remember to also respond by using self-statements.

This type of managed communication at first feels artificial, but it can quickly become natural with practice. It usually leads to a dramatic change in the atmosphere between spouses and a rapid resolution of hitherto insoluble problems. Paradoxically, it can also lead to a quicker appreciation of some serious differences of opinion or agenda that may not be so easily resolved. If you follow these guidelines, you'll find less temptation to resort to coercion to get your point across, and you'll be far less frustrated by communication problems. If you don't provoke bad feelings, instigating the negative spiral, you'll have a greater opportunity to find workable solutions for both the more easily solved issues and the thornier, more immutable differences between you.

Listen for Feelings First, Facts Second

The problem with life, of course, is that people commonly fail to follow the script. In your effort to be a good listener, you're bound to react in a less than Buddha-like way, despite your good intentions. In an argument, it may help you to stop responding in kind if you consider that *the critic is only a critic because that person feels hurt, frightened, frustrated, or ignored by you and doesn't know how to communicate that feeling to you in a more productive way. And, it is because you are a* very important person *in your spouse's life that you bother your partner at all.* Unfortunately, when most people get hurt or feel frustrated, they don't clearly say, "I feel hurt, frightened, frustrated, or ignored. Will you help me with my feelings?" Instead, nearly everyone gets irritable and angry, or withdrawn and sullen. Frequently, the frustrated speaker believes that he has made the same point to you many times in the past, only to be ignored. The speaker then becomes more demanding or more hopeless, pushing you even further away. This forces you to become ever more self-protective, which means you'll end up putting your energy into defensiveness rather than creative problem solving. This is how couples get themselves into trouble—a downward spiral, the communications nightmare.

How can you, the listener, hold your ground and see criticism or anger as the request for help that it really is? In order for you to help an angry or critical speaker, you must first be willing to give up your own anger.

If you are angry and resentful of a spouse who has been chronically hurtful to you, you may feel that giving up your anger is tantamount to becoming a defenseless saint. In a way, that is true. But accepting that your partner is a complex, feeling person who cannot always be counted on to behave in the most rational or reasonable manner does not mean that you need to become passive or let yourself be victimized. You should never be a doormat for your spouse's anger or unhappiness. However, there are many ways to show strength without counterattacking or being reactively hurtful. Simply telling a spouse that you will discuss any issue once he or she calms down, stops devaluing you, or stops using provocative, hurtful language is a message of great strength that also shows how deeply you care about your marriage.

In most situations, by setting limits and enforcing them, even if you have to withdraw from emotionally abusive behavior, your self-control will eventually work to calm your agitated partner. If you really listen to your partner, check and repeat what is being said, and then respond sympathetically and practically to his or her fears or hurts, your spouse will almost certainly become more agreeable.

Sometimes this happens very quickly. Sometimes it takes a while to regain trust. You have to have the courage to go first and then find the strength to hold on to your new position for a while. It will work. Remind yourself that one person acting alone to change the dance can reverse a negative spiral, sometimes very quickly. This can lead to rapid improvement in the atmosphere of even a much-deteriorated relationship. Once you have done the job of controlling *your* reactivity, as your relationship improves, you will be free to leave sainthood to join the ranks of the reasonably thoughtful, wise, and mature among us.

Don't Beat a Dead Horse

It is remarkable how many people will persist in a particular form of behavior even though they have seen, over a lengthy period of time, that it won't succeed in getting them the outcome they want.

Frequent criticism of a spouse commonly falls into this category of repetitive, ineffective action. Hoping to get what you want, do you persist in using the same failed tactic over and over again? For example, many of us act as if, by shouting the same thing louder and louder, we will ultimately be heard by someone we feel isn't listening. Unfortunately, the person we are yelling at (especially if it is our spouse) is almost always someone who doesn't like to be spoken to that way, and will refuse to listen or change anything until he or she is treated with respect. It's amazing how many of us behave as if we believe that we can get the marriage we want by badgering, criticizing, nagging, or intimidating our spouse into submission. Also, there are married people who won't talk to a partner until the partner agrees to apologize for something hurtful they have said or done. Extracting a coerced apology or admission of guilt from a spouse will never work, even if it does allow the partner receiving the apology to feel momentarily victorious in a marital battle. Getting what you want in a marriage by coercion is a Pyrrhic victory at best because it simultaneously creates resentment in your spouse that silently undermines your relationship.

This is where carefully crafted self-statements come in. They work. They increase the chance that you will get what you are asking for because they increase the chance that you will be heard and decrease your spouse's need to reflexively, defensively reject your wishes.

Stay in Your Own Zip Code

Your spouse arrives home twenty minutes late: "You're always late," you fume. Your spouse forgets to send a birthday card to your mother: "You never remember any of the little things," you say. In each case, you've taken a specific incident, then exaggerated and generalized it into a global indictment. Absolute words such as "always" and "never" are rarely accurate; when you apply them to your spouse's behavior, these exaggerations and amplifications have the effect of assassinating your spouse's character rather than focusing on and resolving a specific complaint. Banish these words from your vocabulary. Address your concerns to the specific, local incident; don't blow it up to global proportions.

No Piling On

"Piling on" is a close kin to global indictments. You and your spouse are arguing about an unpaid bill, and you take the opportunity to mention that he also forgot to pick up your son from soccer practice, and he didn't take the car in for inspection, and he should have made that appointment with the dentist . . . and you're off to the races. Address one issue at a time, and don't drag in past disappointments or old arguments to bolster your case.

Another very destructive form of piling on is invoking other people's opinions or experiences in making a point to your spouse. It is like inviting a jury into the room and telling your spouse that others have also indicted her for the crimes against you. "You know, the Buckners find you rude and irritable just like I do." Now your spouse has to defend herself from you and the Buckners at the same time. There are just too many people on your side. This will increase her hurt and require her to find more ammunition with which to fight back. Always leave the Buckners out of the discussion. Any problem between the two of you must be discussed between the two of you alone. You shouldn't need allies to make your point, and calling on them, furthermore, implies that you feel too weak to stand up for yourself. It is fairer and more powerful to be able to say for yourself, "It is very hurtful to me when you say those things and behave that way in front of other people. We have to do something about it because it makes me very unhappy." The rule always to follow is that all dialogue that has to do with marital issues must be bilateral, that is, kept just between the two of you.

Finally, never embarrass your partner or yourself in public. Wait until you get to the privacy of your home to have all personal discussions, fights, or disagreements. Once there you can say, "There is something that happened tonight that upset me. I want to discuss it with you to keep it from happening again."

Turn Your Demands into Requests

Many of us are conditioned to believe that making demands makes us seem clear, resolute, and firm, while asking questions makes us sound unclear, uncertain—wimpy. However, other people usually experience demands as a need to control. Most people respond poorly when they feel they are being controlled. On the other hand, many of us are afraid we'll lose ground if we request instead of insist, or that our partners will think we're pushovers. We also fear that if we ask for what we want we will be told no, more often than not. That no is very hard to bear. So we make demands, hit the inevitable brick wall, assume we were right to expect the no, and then make louder demands. You can reverse the negative spiral if you stop making *demands* in relationships and learn instead how to make *requests*, offering personal, comprehensible explanations for your desires.

Ask politely and clearly for what you want, and explain why you want it using self-statements:

- This is what *I* am feeling.
- This is what would make me happy.
- This is who *I* am.
- This is what *I* care about or want in a relationship.
- This is what is important to me. This is what *I* believe.

Put what you want in your relationship squarely on the table, and then negotiate it in good faith. You can still stick up for what you want when you make a request. Remember that you are entitled to *have* wants; you're just not entitled always to get things your way or to believe that you should.

Stop Being a Mind Reader

"You think I'm always taking sides against you." "I know what you want—you want to do all the planning yourself." "You say that running a business takes a lot of time, but I know you just want to stay away from home." "You just want me to shut up and go along with whatever you say." "You're only saying that because you're upset." "You wouldn't do that if you knew how I felt about it." "That's your mother talking, not you." Every one of these statements is an example of mind reading, a skill I can absolutely assure you that you do not possess. By all means, explain yourself. But *never* tell your spouse why he's doing what he's doing, or why she's saying what she's saying. *Never* take on the role of your spouse's psychoanalyst. *Never suggest that you know the conscious or unconscious motivation for your spouse's behavior, especially if you are hurt or angry.*

One of the cardinal mistakes made even by many psychotherapists is to assume that the *outcome* of an action is its *motivation*. This mistaken notion of absolute determinism has been adopted by our psychologically minded culture. An example of this is the assumption that if I say something that hurts your feelings, that was my intention in the first place. Much more often than not, this is not actually the case. Your hurt feelings are much more likely to be the by-product of my poor communication skills, a misunderstanding, my need to take care of myself, my need not to give in to you, or your own sensitivities and your need to get your own way. None of these imply my having a primary desire to hurt you. When we are hurt, we tend to criticize the person who causes the hurt and blame him for the outcome. This rarely helps the situation. Avoid assuming the worst about your spouse and then sharing this remarkable insight with him. If you think it will help, "interpret" your own motivations to your spouse, but never the reverse. Unless you have stated it explicitly, your spouse cannot know exactly what you're thinking or feeling, or why you act the way you do; the reverse is equally true.

Assume that you and you alone are the expert on your thoughts, feelings, and motivations, and that your spouse is the expert on his. By all means, ask for an explanation if you don't understand why your spouse is doing or saying something: "I'm not really sure what you mean; could you tell me more about your thinking?" "Why do you feel that way?" "I'm confused; could you please explain that more to me?" Then acknowledge the legitimacy of your spouse's point of view even if you don't agree with it.

Mind reading can be counterproductive even if you're doing it in the hopes of pleasing your spouse: "Let's go see that movie because I know how much you like romantic comedies." "I bet you're only saying that because you don't want me to be embarrassed." "I bought this because I knew you'd love it." Even with the best of intentions, your pseudo-psychic abilities can irritate your spouse because they will often be wrong and they don't acknowledge that your partner is the better judge of her own mind. At their worst, these false divinations turn good intentions into pointless misunderstandings as spouses guess at what their partners want and avoid clearly saying what they themselves prefer. Both parties end up feeling cheated. Much better to say something like, "I'd like to see that new Schwarzenegger flick; what are you up for?" Or, "What makes you say that? I'd like to understand." Or, "I bought this because I'd love for you to have it." Tell your spouse, "I will trust you to say what it is you really want, and you can count on me to do the same. When we're both clear, we'll figure it out from there."

A common pernicious outcome to excessive mind reading is an angry couple in which one or both spouses openly reject the explanations of behavior offered by the other. Legitimate simple or altruistic explanations of motivations are met with comments like, "I don't believe you." The usual reason for these rejections is that they don't match the preconceived cynical assumption of the hurt spouse.

This is a particularly dangerous moment in the life of a couple trying to learn how to communicate better. If your spouse offers you a peek at her insides by telling you why she did what she did, or why she thinks or feels as she does and you reject it, or insist that she is not telling "the truth" because you know better, it is tantamount to telling your spouse that nothing she says is believable to you. This act of refusing to accept a spouse's (usually less malicious) explanation for behavior is equivalent to saying, "I do not have a relationship with you. I only have a relationship with the negative person I believe you to be, not with the person you think you are." The disavowed spouse caught in this predicament feels unrecognized, unloved, unseen—invisible.

All of this can be avoided by just controlling the impulse to be your spouse's therapist or mind reader. If you present your own point of view in a nonhostile, straightforward manner that accepts responsibility for yourself first, and welcome a similar presentation when offered by your spouse, the way is then open for further discussions about what's really important and what has to be resolved. Conversations about feelings, ideas, sensitivities, and wishes that don't take the form of criticism, demands, or attacks can bring partners emotionally closer and foster long-lasting intimacy and affection.

Agree to Disagree

Regrettably, not all conflicts between married people can be resolved. *Fortunately, not all differences, even extreme ones, have to be resolved to maintain a good marriage.* Sometimes, we just have to accept a draw and agree to disagree. Clearly, this lack of resolution to a problem can work only if both parties can live with the outcome. Everyone finds it hard to adjust to certain issues within a relationship or to specific characteristics of a spouse. But it is remarkable how often we *are* able to live with each other's idiosyncrasies. The important variable is whether you can live with the differences and the issues they create without chronic frustration and resentment. If so, you can then agree to stop talking about your disagreement and move on.

Hallie was extremely angry with her husband, Jon, for not defending her when her future in-laws treated her poorly shortly after the couple became engaged thirty years ago. Hallie was Episcopalian, and she never forgot how Jon's parents told her that they were disappointed that Jon wasn't marrying a "nice Jewish girl." They'd treated her very coolly while Jon did little more than wring his hands. Whenever the couple fought, Hallie's old hurts would reemerge, and she would once again accuse Jon of not having properly defended her. He explained his actions as being the best he could do at the time. He'd been a young man, caught in a loyalty conflict between his girlfriend and his parents. He felt both ashamed of his parents and guilty that he hadn't done more to shield his fiancée. Even so, any new fight led Hallie to the resurrection of this ancient hurt and the recurrence of her old, bitter feelings, even though Hallie now had a decent relationship with her in-laws and had long since been accepted into their family.

Recurrent arguments such as these, as foolish as they may seem, fulfill a purpose in a relationship. They can serve, albeit unfairly, as an example of when we were unimpeachably in the right and as an ongoing reminder that our spouse cannot claim to be wholly trustworthy in the future. Rather than build a fresh case for our position in the conflict at hand, we lazily brandish a weapon from skirmishes past, one so finely honed that it cuts with the slightest pressure. The only solution is a disarmament pact and a laying down of all past communication's weapons. Initially, this can be a scary prospect; without "old faithful" at the ready, we can feel disarmed.

Hallie and Jon couldn't move forward until they agreed to stop talking about the old conflict. By accepting this resolution, something profound occurred in this couple's life. Jon no longer lived in dread of his past failure being thrown in his face and Hallie accepted that she could no longer try to use this old mistake to make him feel guilty enough to win the current argument. If she was unhappy about something, she had to articulate the exact reasons for her present distress and ask clearly for what she wanted. The playing field of their relationship became fairer for both of them.

Sometimes couples can experience severely disruptive disagreements and still successfully move forward with their marriage. Susan and Jack lived in New York City when they married and had children. Susan loved the city and was excited by its cultural offerings. Jack appreciated the city but felt that, once they had children, they should move to the suburbs so that their children could enjoy a backyard and have all the good things he associated with his own suburban childhood. Susan thought an urban upbringing was more intellectually stimulating, plus she felt she'd be a much happier city mom. She envisioned the suburbs as a place where bored housewives spent their days driving children around in minivans, going to the mall as a cultural diversion, and cursing the day they moved out of Manhattan. Both wanted their dream lives, and only one could get it completely his or her way.

Unfortunately, as the conflict escalated, it became heated, bitter, and personal. Jack accused Susan of being selfish for wanting to stay in the city more for herself than for her children. He pointed out that even though living in the city dramatically shortened his commute to work, he wanted to move to the suburbs for the sake of their children. Susan admitted that she wanted to stay in New York mostly for herself, but she was deeply hurt by the vehemence of Jack's accusation of selfishness. She knew many children going to fine schools in New York and felt living there offered children many advantages over suburban life. She was further hurt by her feeling that Jack didn't seem to care how a move to the suburbs might affect her. No matter how strongly she fought for staying in New York City, Jack powerfully fought against her.

The struggle deepened and positions hardened. Jack was so

angry that he often thought of getting a divorce. Susan was so hurt that she, too, considered it. Finally, when there was no acceptable compromise attainable, Susan put her foot down, simply informing Jack that she refused to move out of the city in the near future. He would have to accept it or leave the marriage, but that no matter what, he would have to stop badgering her and accusing her of being selfish. She insisted that he stop devaluing her and cease talking about the conflict, saying that she and the marriage could not take it anymore.

Jack was disappointed and furious. I met alone with him to help him see that there was nothing more he could do for the time being. I pointed out that a divorce would only ensure that his kids would forever grow up in New York City, because it was certain that Susan would be awarded custody. Furthermore, if he continued to engage in conflict with Susan, it would only cause additional damage to his already tenuous marriage. Nothing good could be achieved from further discussions, even if they remained civil. For the time being, the only choice was to get a divorce or to agree to disagree and forget the differences between them as best he could. Jack reluctantly made this agreement, but he wanted Susan to agree that if he stopped pressuring her, she would at least consider moving as an option for the future. Under these conditions, she was willing to do just that.

It was very difficult for Jack to keep his word, and he continued to investigate promising suburban real estate listings; but the agreement quieted the fighting, and the couple began to live more comfortably with each other. Jack had the additional burden of learning how to deal with his resentment over Susan's getting her way, at least initially. By simply putting her foot down and refusing to move, Susan had forced an end to the issue, but they hadn't resolved the marital problem. She had the life she wanted, but at the cost of dangerously alienating her husband. Jack had to spend many hours working out what he was going to do with his anger and resentment over Susan's intransigent "victory," and Susan had to find ways to sympathize with and appreciate Jack's grief over the loss of his dream.

Nonetheless, in the end, the only solution was for both of them to accept that they were different people who had significantly different agendas and styles. Neither was completely right or wrong. They both had to accept that since they couldn't easily resolve their differences, they would have to figure out a way to live with them. Both of them had to get over their anger at each other for the manner in which they had pressured the other to change. They had to stop making their differences into a "communication" problem and repair the emotional distance their irresolvable conflict had created. Fortunately, with a great deal of help and support, they were able to accomplish this task and move on with their lives together. They had another child, and, within three years, Susan voluntarily suggested that they start looking for a primary home in the suburban community in which Jack longed to live.

As these two stories indicate, the greatest challenge when you agree to disagree is dealing with the leftover resentment. This is true even when your truce is completely mutual. When you agree to declare an old hurt or disagreement off-limits, you may resent that you can no longer resort to a convenient tool for gaining an advantage in an argument. When you're a party to a forced outcome, you'll resent either that you were forced into it or that your partner gave in without genuinely agreeing with your point of view. Your task then becomes acknowledging and monitoring your own resentment and learning how to let it go.

CHAPTER 3

Lie: People Don't Really Change
Truth: Change Is Always Possible, and Little Changes Produce Big Results

Why does a woman work ten years to change a man's habits and then complain that he's not the man she married?

—Barbra Streisand

You can't change a man, no-ways. By the time his Mummy turns him loose and he takes up with some innocent woman and marries her, he's what he is.

—Marjorie Kinnan Rawlings

By the time couples come to my office, they have often become terribly disillusioned with their marriages. After hearing them explain their views of the marriage's problems and getting a history of their relationship, I lay out the hard work they'll have to do to put their marriage back on track. At this point, they typically balk. Despite the fact that they know that their marriage is no fairy tale, they still half expect me to wave a magic wand over their spouse (never over themselves) and fix the problem effortlessly. They can't believe they'll have to put in so much effort to make their marriage work. And lurking in the back of their minds is the worry that they'll end up doing all this heavy labor and it won't make any difference anyway.

"Oh, please," groans Maya. "I can't even get Frank to change his socks. I've bought him a million new pairs, and he still wears the old ratty ones. He's such a creature of habit. How on earth am I going to get him to change the way he talks to me?"

"What's the use?" pleads Gus. "Emma is the world's most stubborn woman; she wouldn't change if I held a gun to her head. And to be honest, I'm just so pissed off at her that I'll be damned if I'll change anything to make her life easier."

"I don't think I should have to change," Cara says. "Manny's always been a bully. Whenever I try something he doesn't like he just steamrolls right over me. I don't think I can bear to get beaten down anymore."

"If I stop nagging Rachel, nothing will ever get done in our house," Dan tells me. "Bottom line: I don't think she can really change."

Sooner or later, in most couples therapy, one or the other spouse usually asks me if I think that people can really change. My answer, much to their surprise, is an unequivocal yes. I've seen it happen all the time. If no one ever changed, I'd be out of business in a second. The more useful and valuable questions to ask are: What *prevents* change; *what* can change; *how* does change take place; *what conditions* motivate and foster change; and *how much* change is necessary to make a real difference to your marriage?

Roadblock to Change: It's All Your Fault

The greatest impediment to change is the belief that *you* aren't the one who needs to change. It is very common for people to come to my office and claim that their spouse is entirely responsible for their marriage's problems. In fact, in twenty years of practice, I have *never* found one spouse to be the source of all the marital troubles, even when appearances suggest overwhelmingly to the contrary.

We're a culture that loves to play the blame game, and psychotherapists certainly aren't immune. Trained to recognize and treat individual pathology, many therapists still typically finger one member of a troubled couple as being more disturbed, and then assume that that person provokes most of the difficulty in the relationship. It is assumed that the "bad" spouse's problems are caused by faulty genes or neurotic reactions to disturbing past experiences. Many therapists believe that who we are is mostly set in stone by the time we are finished with our adolescence. Little or no responsibility is laid at the feet of events in the present, including reactions to powerful stresses impinging on the marriage from both inside and out. This pessimistic view of human behavior—hey, we can't change the past—is one of the reasons that couples are convinced that very little of what is currently going on between them can change for the better. We believe that our spouse's character and behaviors are set in historical cement.

This linear thinking about psychological problems retains its primacy even for *non*professionals because it resonates perfectly with the typical erroneous and destructive assumptions made by unhappy spouses caught in marital strife. Each spouse approaches therapy looking for a hanging judge who will indict the other spouse for that person's bad attitude or behavior. Many successful media therapists engage in this practice, publicly attacking an obviously poorly behaved spouse, while the studio audience and viewers at home vicariously thrill to the moral flogging, wishing the good doctor would pay them a virtual house call and berate their spouse as well. When I see this dynamic in my office, typically one spouse styles herself as the virtuous victim, while the other is the bad person or "mental case."

If we believe that the origin of all behavior is deep-seated, rooted in childhood, and thus impossible to change, we lose all motivation to try. Paradoxically, we also judge that the person who dares to make changes must be the one who caused the problems in the first place. These mistaken assumptions oblige one partner to either accept most of the blame for the marital problems or pass the blame onto the other spouse. They don't allow for a combination of reciprocal causes and effects, or symmetrical escalation of outrages.

Let's suppose that the husband genuinely (if mistakenly) accepts that he's the only disturbed one in the relationship. Curiously, the *relationship* is still not very likely to improve even if he shoulders the entire fault for its going off course. If he takes on all the responsibility for the couple's problems, especially if he goes into individual therapy, the other spouse will inevitably decide that she doesn't have to change at all for the relationship to improve. That belief leads to only a few possible outcomes. If the "healthy" spouse continues the old cyclic behavior, the spouse in therapy must decide whether or not to keep seeing himself as the "ill" member in the relationship. If he continues to see himself as defective and acts out the role of the symptomatic spouse, the "healthy" partner will end up feeling frustrated and take it out on him; she might even get fed up with having to take care of the "ill" spouse and leave the marriage.

On the other hand, if the "ill" spouse in seeking help finally decides that he isn't that disturbed or has gotten better, he is then faced with the difficult task of confronting the hitherto "healthy" spouse from that new position. If the couple is still having troubles, he will likely conclude, erroneously, that his wife was the "real" source of the problem all along. Or, more commonly, the "ill" partner will declare that he was once sick but now is well, and so it's time for the other spouse to accept her "illness" and go for individual therapy as well. However, there is usually very little chance that the "healthy" partner will be willing to reverse positions and become the identified "patient" with all the required burdens of responsibility, guilt, and mandatory individual treatment. At this point, the marriage frequently ends.

Harry, forty-five years old, was sent to me by a couples therapist who decided that, though the wife had some problems, Harry's difficulties needed to be addressed in individual therapy. Harry readily admitted that he was the source of all his marital tribulations. He believed this because his wife, Beth, had told him so; she'd delivered the ultimatum that if he didn't get his act together, she'd leave him. He told me in our first session that I had to "fix him fast" to save his marriage and prevent the impending dreaded divorce. Once I started seeing Harry alone, Beth precipitously ended their couples therapy as well as her individual therapy. After all, she wasn't the source of their marital problems.

In sessions with me, Harry listed all the "neurotic" flaws that made Beth so angry. He had difficulty spending money; she spent it freely. He wanted to have sex with her, but she pronounced him "oversexed." She blamed her lack of physical interest in him on his faulty character. Harry was so afraid of confrontation that he frequently withheld information that he thought might make Beth angry. When she found out about these hidden things anyway, she'd fly into a rage and accuse him of deliberately lying to hurt her. During these episodes, Harry became frightened and cowed as Beth castigated him for his weaknesses and failures. Harry would then feel guilty that he'd caused her so much distress. He racked his brains but couldn't remember a single time in their life together when Beth told him she loved or admired him.

I asked the couple to come in together to see me. Beth wasted no time informing me that, though she knew that she'd had some minor emotional issues, she'd handled them in her previous six-week therapy and no longer saw herself as the source of any difficulties; my job was to "fix" Harry. When I told her that it would be very helpful to her husband's therapy for her to explain her feelings about the marriage to me in future sessions, she replied she couldn't possibly make the forty-minute drive once a week. When I suggested we meet every other week, she gave the same excuse, adding that she didn't think that a male therapist could fully appreciate how hard it was to live with a person as difficult as her husband. I promised that I would continue to work with Harry alone and referred the couple to a well-known *female* therapist who practiced within a few minutes of their home.

This therapist asked Beth to think about the nature of her violent reactions to her husband and what she could do to modify them. After that session, Beth quit the therapy, saying that she couldn't trust this female therapist because the therapist was overweight, a sign that she had severe problems of her own and therefore couldn't be helpful. She made no further attempts to change her behavior and waited for her husband to solve all the marital problems alone.

If you've come to the conclusion that Beth was a terrorizing harpy, and that Harry's only fault was his willingness to accommodate her, think again. They had both damaged the marriage, not just Beth.

In therapy with me, Harry focused on his terror of Beth's outbursts. In the early days of their marriage, his wife had had a severe panic attack and he'd worried that she would turn out to be mentally ill. Since then, he'd been afraid to confront her, fearing that she'd have some sort of emotional breakdown. I pointed out to him that his fear of her emotional vulnerability had made it impossible for him to help her control her disturbing outbursts, and that, in this way, he had contributed to her becoming the frightening "monster" that he now perceived her to be. Furthermore, his inability to stand up firmly to her uncontrolled behavior had forced him to enact his resentment in passively aggressive ways that endlessly frustrated and further provoked in her the very behaviors that he most feared. He was an active participant in a cycle of mutually poor, reciprocally hurtful behaviors.

As Harry began to understand his role in the cycle, he unilaterally changed his behavior in the marriage. He held his own when Beth threw her tantrums, telling her that screaming at him didn't help solve their problems. As he improved, he went from seeing himself as the source of all the marital difficulties to recognizing that he was one of two people locked in a hurtful, sad dance.[1] He tried very hard to change his responses to his wife and became more honest and straightforward. As this happened, he began to feel that no matter what his contribution to the negative emotional spiral had been in the past, he couldn't live with Beth's cold, unloving rejection, punctuated by extreme rage. He asked her to make some changes, but she refused to take responsibility for her own actions.

Eventually, instead of fearing that his wife would leave him, Harry began to worry about Beth's vulnerability if *he* left her. He was amazed by how responsible he felt for her and what he now saw as her emotional limitations. Whom would she blame if he weren't around as a convenient explanation for all her discontent? For a year, she had emotionally stagnated while he had slowly grown. Eventually, he very reluctantly decided that his only chance for happiness was to get divorced.

In a way, what ended this marriage was Harry's individual therapy with me. As the other therapist involved in the process, I was unable to undo Beth's belief that Harry was the sole cause of the marriage's problems, a train of thought that the original therapist inadvertently reinforced when he referred Harry to me for individual therapy. Because it intersects so nicely with our own need to cast the blame for marital problems on our spouse, the "it's all your fault" defense presents a particularly dangerous roadblock to change.

Differentiation: Change as a Struggle Toward Maturity

The lie of unconditional love and the belief in the existence of soul mates expresses our hope that when we marry, we will unite with someone who shares our level of emotional maturity, who vibrates on our same wavelength. Indeed, Murray Bowen, one of the founding fathers of family therapy, declared that people of similar emotional maturity are frequently attracted to each other and tend to end up marrying. It was his contention that individuals achieve varying degrees of success in their quest for emotional development, depending on genetic/biological factors and especially on the functioning of the family in which they grew up. For Bowen, the most important variable in defining emotional maturity was the extent to which a person could *differentiate* himself from others, especially his family of origin. Differentiation refers to the human ability to acknowledge and *maintain* a separate sense of self while still remaining closely connected to others. One of the hallmarks of differentiation is the capacity to contain and manage our internal emotional states.

Bowen saw differentiation as existing on a sliding developmental scale. Very poorly differentiated people cannot generally function on their own away from their family or some other very supportive environment, and they frequently suffer from severe psychiatric symptoms. Somewhat better differentiated individuals can leave their families, but their judgment is usually hampered by the intensity of their emotional reactions. They are usually excessively needy and emotionally dependent.

On the highest end of Bowen's scale of differentiation are people who have a very clear sense of who they are and where they have come from. They can think through problems. They can use their feelings as information about themselves, as well as for intimate connections with others. *They take responsibility for themselves.* They are willing to work to change what they don't like about themselves or their circumstances. Though they have solid beliefs, they can also be flexible and modify their thinking and behavior when presented with new ideas or thoughtful arguments. They are attentive, empathetic, concerned people who are genuinely emotionally connected to others in their family and community.[2] In short, you know you have successfully differentiated when you can spend three days with your parents and still feel like your adult self.[3] (I'll talk more about families of origin and their effect on your marriage in chapter 5.)

Our task as individuals is to grow emotionally so that we achieve the highest level of differentiation possible for us. Our task as one-half of a couple is to continue this growth within the context of our marital relationship. Our task is to change for the better.

Polarization: The Unbalanced Seesaw

Bowen believed that for the most part, when it came to levels of differentiation, like married like. So, highly thoughtful, caring, empathic, goal-oriented people aren't likely to marry people with bizarre ideas or lives that seem mostly out of control. As often as this seems to be true, it is sometimes very hard to see how it works with a particular couple. This is because as couples live together, they usually create *complementary* emotional systems. In well-functioning couples, this balancing process works smoothly and is mutually useful. However, in marriages in which differences become exaggerated, they can become the focus of the conflict.

A common example of this is the couple who disagree about money. One spouse sees the other as a penny-pincher while the other spouse sees the first as a spendthrift. The spendthrift often responds to the penny-pincher by becoming even more profligate. The penny-pinching spouse sees this as dangerously wasteful and institutes even more drastic cost-cutting measures to undo the damage created by the free-spending spouse.

In this way, what were once potentially useful, complementary points of view turn into uncomfortable, exaggerated *polarizations*. As the couple remains conflicted and as the polarized positions diverge further, each spouse throws up emotional walls that drive the other spouse to become more solidified in his own stance. Each partner becomes more like what he is being accused of and less like what he is criticizing. Polarizations like this one are the reason that so many spouses who are basically functioning on a similar level of differentiation can, in the end, look so different from each other. To help change conflicted, polarized couples, each spouse has to move closer to the center.

Janice and her husband, Sonny, had been married for many years. She was unhappy with the marriage; he was fine with it. She wanted to talk about her marriage, but he felt there was nothing to say. After a few sessions Sonny dropped out of therapy altogether. Janice explained that the major problem was that she was a frightened, dependent woman who married a bright, goal-oriented, successful executive. She admired Sonny greatly for his emotional health, wealth, and intellect. The only problem was that she had little say in the way her family functioned. Sonny controlled the money and made most of the major family decisions. He was the Golden Ruler. If she complained, they would get into a fight, which usually led to his telling her that if she didn't like her life as it was, she was free to leave. This immediately ended all discussion, for it was clear to Janice that she needed her husband much more than he needed her.

Over the years she came to feel ever more dependent on him. Now, they were so polarized around the issue of dependency that Janice felt Sonny no longer needed her at all. At the same time, she felt increasingly miserable, powerless, and dependent on a man who didn't seem to love or admire her.

For a few months, we worked on the marriage from her side alone. I helped Janice begin to face her fears of rejection and abandonment and suggested ways that she could experience the more competent, calm side of herself. I addressed the polarization by suggesting that underneath all her husband's bravado, he probably was very attached to her, and that below all her anxiety, she was certainly a far more competent, independent woman than she had ever let herself or anyone else see. After a few months, she left therapy feeling much better about herself and her prospects for a better marriage.

Almost two years later she returned, announcing that she wanted my help with divorcing Sonny. She had come to regard him as a bully who couldn't control his temper or change his abusive treatment of her. She was completely fed up with him. Over a period of many months, I helped her examine her desire to divorce, feeling that she had many new skills that could be used to improve her life, even within the marriage. I wasn't certain that divorce was necessary. Nonetheless, she remained adamant and began to organize her life to support herself financially.

When Janice finally announced to her husband her intention

to separate, Sonny underwent a radical transformation. He began to cry and begged her not to leave him. He told her that he loved her and couldn't live without her. Seeing Sonny this way made her realize that she was, in fact, much stronger than she ever realized. She now felt sorry for her husband.

I pointed out that Janice's inclination to view herself as weak and excessively fearful of abandonment had given her husband license to do many of the emotionally abusive things he had done. If she had stood up to him earlier, she might have avoided decades of mistreatment and unhappiness. She might have glimpsed his needy, dependent side, and he might have been able to accept his vulnerability and be a better husband. She agreed that this was possible, but felt that she was too resentful now to give him another chance. Instead of reconciling, she proceeded to get the divorce.

In this example of polarization, the issue is dependency. Sonny enacted the role of the fiercely independent character (common for many men), while his wife enacted the role of the dependent spouse, which women are still socialized to believe and embrace. However, even in this unhappy marriage, there was a kind of balance, like that of a seesaw stuck in the position where one child is way up in the air and the other is pushed to the ground. The two children may be of equal weight and capable of balancing themselves evenly, but right now they've maneuvered themselves into positions of extreme opposition. These types of polarizations in couples make it very hard to see the way in which spouses are actually very similar in their levels of maturity or immaturity. The polarization forced Janice to behave and feel far more emotionally immature or more "disturbed" than Sonny. In many polarized couples, the spouse who appears to be functioning less well is actually doing so, without realizing it, to preserve the marriage.

Like moving up the scale of differentiation, reversing polarization is the kind of change that dramatically improves relationships. Finding the middle ground on the polarization seesaw is no longer child's play.

Understanding the Nature of Change

The first step on the road to change is the resetting of the emotional atmosphere of your marriage. Change rarely takes place in an atmosphere of mutual deprivation, frustration, or resentment. First of all, there is too much anger. In relationships where both spouses feel cheated or deprived, each partner believes that it is only fair that the other partner change first. If you feel deprived, it's very hard voluntarily to give more to the very person whom you perceive as the source of your deprivation. And yet to save your marriage, to make it more satisfying for yourself, this is exactly what you have to do. Start by changing your emotional attitude. To allow yourself to change, first recognize that changing—giving more or giving something different to your spouse—doesn't make you a fool or a victim. Breaking your marital stalemate makes you a hero, an adventurer. Going first means that you have the guts to try to make things better. If you fail to produce a more mutually satisfying relationship, at least you can be proud of yourself for trying. Don't focus on your anger, bitterness, or resentment; reset your emotional barometer to reflect your courage, daring, and sense of pride and purpose.

Many people are motivated to change by a desire to please their spouse. But before this can happen, you have to *like* your mate sufficiently to *want* to please that person. Paradoxically, and as so many of my patients have confirmed, you can still love someone very much and not like him or her anymore. *Most people change in relationships when they like the person they are changing for, feel cared for by the person requesting the change, understand why that person wants them to change, feel capable of the change being asked of them, and believe that the change does not imply a loss of power or position. Unfortunately, very stubborn people may only change when they are convinced that, by not changing, they are putting their critically important relationship in jeopardy.*

Change requires good communication. It does no good if your

spouse agrees that your requests are reasonable, but won't go along with them because she dislikes you for the way you ask for them. You have to offer the possibility of change in a manner that allows your spouse to feel comfortable and in control. Becoming a blowhard, critic, bully, nag, or lecturer rarely leads to change because your spouse will see compliance with requests made these ways as capitulation, implying a loss of power or position. Even when coercion does force change in another person, that change will most likely be accompanied by overt or hidden resentment, which, in the end, is certain to create distance between you and your spouse, silently devouring your connection. Changes conceded under duress also have the paradoxical effect of hiding serious flaws in a relationship until they unexpectedly emerge at a later date, sometimes shockingly uncontrolled. Effecting changes in this way is like applying new wallpaper to wet, cracking walls without repairing the walls first. For a while, the new wallpaper looks good, but eventually the cracks show through.

Before you attempt any of the following suggestions for encouraging change, make sure you have mastered the communication skills presented in the previous chapter.

Why Do People Change?

What motivates change? Why would anyone change when we all pretty much like ourselves the way we are? We'd like to believe that we'll feel motivated to change out of sheer love for our spouses and a desire to make them happy. However, when a marriage is in trouble, the motivation to change usually springs from negative emotions such as dissatisfaction, unhappiness, and fear of marital breakup. This is bleak but true; happy, satisfied people don't change their lives too much; if they do, they do it so easily that they barely notice the effort.

For conflicted or unhappy couples who want to remain

together, the ultimate motivator of change is often the fear of losing the spouse. What if a spouse comes to believe that no matter how bad his or her behavior, the other spouse will never leave? This belief opens the door to emotionally hurtful behaviors or abuse and leaves very little room for change. This is why spouses who are emotionally fused to their partner (codependent) and have no real capacity to get out of their relationship rarely can produce any meaningful change in their marriage, no matter how often or loudly they protest. Sadly, I have seen many bereft, desperate spouses agree to change only after being told by their partner that the marriage is over. These people admit that they never felt compelled to change until it was too late. They couldn't conceive of their spouses' ever having the nerve to leave them.

All significantly conflicted spouses *threaten* each other with divorce sooner or later. In some marriages, this trump card is played repetitively to pressure a spouse into capitulating on really important issues for which there has been insufficient resolution. The problem with such repeated threats is that the spouse being coerced knows that if he or she accedes to the threat, the next time there is a serious disagreement, the same tactic will be used. This causes an inadvertent accumulation of resentment. Because of this, acceding to ultimatums creates great risks in the marriage. If a spouse doesn't yield to the threat of divorce and refuses to make any concessions, the threatening partner is left without any further trump cards to play. Under these conditions, the one who delivers the ultimatum is exposed as ineffectual and impotent.

I see a lot of couples for which the repetitive threat of divorce has become toothless. Nevertheless, each time it is used, the ultimatum is powerfully hurtful and destructive to the relationship. The constant threat of divorce in a marriage drives a wedge of discomfort, fear, insecurity, resentment, and distance between partners, making it much less likely that one or both partners will change for the better.

As appalling as this may sound, resolution of marital problems sometimes comes from transforming the ineffective, manipulative *threat* of divorce into the thoughtful, *realistic option* to divorce. Sustained, meaningful change often comes, not in circumstances where fear of divorce or separation is generated by recurring ultimatums and intimidation, but instead when the apprehension is based on the reasonable and realistic assessment that divorce is the likely consequence if there is no solution to the marital difficulties. It is frequently at this moment of truth, when a couple must face the reality of coming apart or changing, that true marital growth takes place. *Marital transformation is created by the decision to change yourself for the sake of the relationship, making the relationship a higher priority than your individual desire to hold on to a particular behavior.* The alternative choice is that the relationship isn't worth the required change and you choose to end it.

Understanding this highlights two reasons why it's so important for conflicted spouses to break the downward negative spiral before it goes on too long. If a couple waits too long, when they arrive at this decisive moment in their relationship, the spouses may find that one of them is "over the cliff," no longer sufficiently invested in the marriage to make the changes necessary to preserve it. Also, if there has been long-standing conflict and/or frustration, the weight of the conflict may have so damaged the image of the spouse or the relationship that the marriage no longer appears worth saving. Many despairing spouses divorce without ever really knowing if they or their partners were capable of meaningful change.

It Takes Two to Tango, but Only One to Change the Steps: Unilateral Change

Ideally, both members of a couple consciously set out to change something that's not working in a marriage. However, sometimes your spouse isn't willing or able to work with you on this. This does not mean you have to give up. Amazingly, because of the nature of emotional cycles in marriage, those old vibrating tuning forks, you can change your marriage and often your spouse without your partner even being aware of what's happening. Quite often, people seem unaware of the changes they have made. When I ask a couple who is doing better why they think this is happening, each partner will typically tell me that the *spouse* has changed and this has made life easier for them. We are so overfocused on our spouse as the source of our problems that we even overcredit them as the source of marital improvements! Much more rarely I hear, "Well, I decided I would do such and such differently, and this has really helped the two of us get along better."

On one level, it doesn't matter what or who has initiated the change in your relationship. As long as the change is for the better, it's a big advance. But there *is* a danger in not realizing that alterations you've made have led to a positive outcome. When your marriage is in trouble again, having this knowledge could help you quickly to reverse the deterioration and get back on track. Without accepting your role, you'll be less willing to consider whether the new trouble has anything to do with your returning to *your* old behaviors. You're more prone to assume automatically that your partner has reverted to old patterns and is stirring up the negative cycle all over again.

Of course, change is easiest when there is a sense that each partner is trying to accommodate the other. However, if couples can't change themselves bilaterally, the need for unilateral change becomes even more important. Unilateral change is frightening for most of us because it raises the possibility of becoming vulnerable, feeling weak, or being blamed for the problems. It can feel like a one-sided disarmament, making you feel fearful and foolish, while leaving no outlet for your own angry feelings. It is a hard lesson to learn, but in intimate relationships unilateral change can rapidly lead to the resolution of emotional conflicts. This happens because unilateral change can bring a quick end to the negative cycle perpetuated by the spouses' emotional reactivity and counterreactivity. Change from *either* side brings an end to the need to fight to prove a point and the need to defend against it and, in doing so, makes it possible to start a constructive dialogue about significant issues. You must be able to stand firm in the belief that *figuring out how to be part of the solution does not mean that you are the sole cause of the problem.*

Unfortunately and paradoxically, unilateral change can also make you feel *too* strong, as the cases of Harry and Beth, and Janice and Sonny illustrate. An individual in a troubled relationship who decides to behave more maturely can experience a new sense of power that can be very frightening. In a conflicted marriage, as soon as one spouse grasps the idea of self-control as a method of changing the relationship, it sends shock waves through both spouses' emotional lives.

The decision to behave fairly and agreeably, no matter how you continue to be treated by your loved one, is terrifying because this kind of *self-control inevitably foretells greater maturity and differentiation of the self. It is self-empowerment.* The inherent danger of unbalanced, unilateral maturation is that the less mature spouse rapidly becomes undesirable to the maturing partner. Fearing an emotional and/or physical separation from your spouse, you may shy away from the very changes that might lead to your own emotional growth. This is a disastrous choice for your marriage because the alternative, the choice to remain caught in the negative spiral, leaves the marriage stagnant, conflicted, or dead. You and your spouse will be stuck in a noxious dance that both of you hate and neither of you has the courage to change.

However, if you can hold on to this stronger sense of yourself that comes from your moving toward greater maturity, your partner will be forced to deal with the more self-assured, clearheaded, less emotionally reactive person you are becoming. Your partner then has a choice: rise to the occasion, becoming more stable and mature, or remain incapable or too angry to grow into the new partnership with you. A partner who elects not to change will begin to look less and less desirable to you, the now more mature person. The two of you will no longer be able to count on intense conflict to serve as an adhesive for your relationship. Though you may feel racked by guilt over leaving your less emotionally developed spouse, you may eventually feel that you have no choice. This is what happened to the marriages of Harry and Janice.

Having read all this, if you are unhappy in your marriage or wish for it to improve, you may feel that you're damned if you do change and damned if you don't. In a narrow sense, this is true; but I still come down wholeheartedly on the side of encouraging change and embracing the risk involved. Not just because it gives you the opportunity to experience real emotional growth, but also because if you forgo changing yourself when it is the only viable choice, you'll also never have given your spouse the chance to show what he or she is capable of in return. Ironically, avoiding change allows you to maintain your negative, judgmental view of your spouse. If you give in to your fear of disappointment or believe that your spouse is hopeless, and then use this as an excuse to avoid doing your part to make things better, you will never have the chance to be pleasantly surprised by your spouse's newly realized capabilities. Remember, people caught in power struggles are usually locked into polarized positions that show them at their worst and make it very hard to see their underlying flexibility and potential. Finally, if you don't take the chance to change yourself, even unilaterally when necessary, you are dooming yourself and usually your marriage to either the acceptance of prolonged unhappiness or eventual divorce.

How Much Change? The 10 Percent Solution

How much change does it take to move a marriage out of a stagnant stalemate? Often, embarrassingly little.

More often than not, when one spouse suggests that the other spouse needs to change, the listening spouse hears the request as critical, radical, absolute, and therefore untenable. There's a simple way to avoid this reaction. *The secret to requesting change is to encourage the smallest possible change that will satisfy you while convincing your spouse that the change will not be toxic.* I call this the 10 percent solution.

Carol wants her executive husband to take the time to call her from work to say hello. She feels that this will allow her to feel connected to him during the day and to feel that he is thinking of her while she stays home with their newborn child. Todd says that it's very hard for him to remember to drop everything in the middle of his hectic day to make such a call and feels irritated by what he perceives as Carol's "selfish demand" for "endless attention." Todd hears Carol's request as requiring "enormous" amounts of his professional time. Right now his total phone time with Carol consists of the time it takes him to call her and report what train he'll be on so she can pick him up at the station.

I ask Todd to describe to me his typical day. The effect of going over his schedule is twofold. First, Carol gets to hear what his pressured day is like for him, and, second, he and I get to hear where he might be able to find time for a brief call home. As we discuss the issue, it becomes clear that Todd wouldn't mind calling Carol if he felt that she wouldn't try to keep him on the phone, telling him every last detail of her day because she's alone and wants company. I invoke the 10 percent solution, asking Todd if he could increase his telephone time with his wife by one call a week and asking Carol if she could limit her discussions with him to a quick connection so that he doesn't feel guilty when he has to stop talking and go back to work. To both of them, the change seems minimal and easy to accomplish. Every few weeks, Todd adds another successful phone call until he's calling Carol almost daily with neither of them feeling pressured by it. Both Todd and Carol were able to accept the change in their stalemated situation because *it is actually very hard to admit that you cannot make a very small change in your life. It is embarrassingly obvious that anyone can make* small *changes if he or she really wants to.*

Ruth says that she wants her husband to become "an affection-ate person." Ian replies, "I'm just not an affectionate person. It's not my nature. Don't try to change me. You knew this when you married me, so you should just learn to live with it." The line is drawn. I acknowledge to Ian that he's not naturally an effusive, ten-der person and probably never will become one, but for the sake of his marriage, would he be willing to act more affectionately on occasion, just once in a while? For example, once a week could he put his arm around Ruth while they're doing something together? Or, once a week could he come home and give his wife a kiss as he walks in the door? It is extremely difficult to reject such a small appeal. By reducing change to its smallest increment, and not demanding that people change "who they are," altering "the unal-terable" becomes much more feasible.

People will avoid even the smallest change when they see it as opening the floodgates to endless, excessive demands, the fear that "if you give 'em an inch, they'll take a mile." If you or your spouse is worried about the proverbial "slippery slope," you can make change more palatable by openly addressing this anxiety and constructing agreements that take them into account. People who fear excessive demands being made on them should discuss this fear and ask that reasonable limits be respected. Carol needed to respect Todd's time limit on telephone contact from his work. She needed to resist draw-ing him into lengthy chats. She also had to find more stimulation in her own life. Ruth had to respond to Ian's kiss without sighing because he didn't hug her, too.

Another reason that we resist even small changes in our behavior is that anger forces us to withhold change, even when the withhold-ing is foolish and self-destructive. Often we will not change ourselves until we first get what we want from our spouse. Sometimes we resist change because the requests for important change stir up the unpleasant fear that too much of us is unacceptable to the one we love. The assumption that I have to make a dramatic change in my *behavior* to please my partner quickly mutates into the thought that my partner doesn't like *me* very much. This is a very painful idea that can cause intense feelings of rejection. However, you can short-circuit hurt feelings and anger if you minimize your request for change so that your partner feels mostly lovable—except for that *little* part that's causing the problem. Put this way, your spouse is likely to be more open to honoring your requests.

Requests for small changes also work in unexpected ways because they end standoffs. They actually reverse negative spirals, opening the way for much larger changes. Frequently small changes are all that are really necessary in the first place. In intimate relationships, our desire to have something change and our frustration over not getting what we want commonly causes us to exaggerate our needs over time. We get so frustrated that we ask for more than we really must have in the hopes that we'll get at least something. Regrettably, this escalation of demand produces the opposite outcome. Also, instead of nicely requesting a small change early in a relationship, we let our wishes accumulate, get frustrated, and then demand larger changes later on. As our spouse resists these demands and our requests fail to produce results, our frustrations mount, and our relationship becomes more conflicted and polarized. As we polarize, we feel the need for greater and greater change while change simultaneously becomes less and less feasible.

Small changes have enormous effects on you as a couple. They provide hope where there was prior hopelessness and can transform a downward emotional spiral into an upward spiral literally within minutes. So, *if you want your spouse to make an adjustment, start small*. Later, you can request another equally small change.

Remember to have the courage to change yourself, even if you have to go first. Also remember that most of us believe that we should be able to get whatever we want in marriage. It is very difficult to accept that there is a lot in life that does not come to us in even a very good marriage. Your partner isn't there to give you everything you want in life any more than you are there to do that back. Marriage is a constant balance of getting some things and not getting others, giving some things and not giving others, all the while feeling that the relationship as a whole is worthwhile.

Instant Appreciation

If your spouse has responded to your request by changing for the better in any way large or small, it's crucial that you express your appreciation *immediately*. This is one area in life where people truly deserve instant gratification. Notice the change and show your appreciation with kind words and compliments:

- "It meant a lot to me that you . . ."
- "I noticed that you . . ."
- "I really appreciate the effort you made to . . ."
- "It was really nice of you to . . ."

Taking the time to notice a change is reinforcing. It motivates your spouse to change again, and in turn should motivate you to offer more compliments. This mutually gratifying request-change-appreciate-change cycle marks the shift of your relationship into a positive emotional spiral. This gives both of you a fresh chance to remember what it is you like about each other. You'll discover that change doesn't mean "losing" or "giving up."

This may sound self-evident, but, in fact, it can be extremely difficult for some people to offer appreciation or encouragement to a spouse who has made changes only after years of frustration. Many of my patients have a hard time shaking the attitude that "it's too little, too late," or "why should I reward him/her after all I've been through?" Once again, that's why it's so important to make changes in a relationship before either of you is "over the cliff" and to be aware of the emotional atmosphere of your relationship before you try to encourage change; entrenched bitterness or resentment has poisoned many an honest effort to change direction or recommit to a relationship.

Many well-intentioned people very rarely show any appreciation at all to their spouse. The other day a patient of mine asked me why she should thank her husband for doing what he was expected to do anyway. "Why not?" I answered. What could be wrong with thanking someone for doing a nice thing even when it's expected or routine? Wouldn't that make routine life more pleasant and fulfilling? If my wife always makes dinner for me when I come home late at night, does that mean that I shouldn't thank her and tell her how much I appreciate it? If she works and contributes to our financial well-being, does that mean that it wouldn't be nicer (and better for our marriage) if I said thanks for bringing in the money and making life easier for us? Shouldn't she be saying the same things regularly to me? I have had innumerable men and women tell me that they have never felt sufficiently appreciated for what they do in their marriage. There is no reason that you or your spouse should *ever* have to feel that way.

Compromise: Too Often a Lose/Lose Proposition

Many couples believe that the solutions to their problems lie in knowing how to *compromise* with each other. In the broadest sense this is true, but real compromise is often *not* the best solution to a disagreement. The problem with compromise is that frequently neither party gets what he or she really wants. Ryan wants to spend their winter vacation skiing in Vermont, and Gina wants to spend it on a beach in the Caribbean. They could *compromise* by going halfway between the two destinations to somewhere in South Carolina in February. This choice would leave both of them dissatisfied because it would be too warm for Ryan to go snow skiing and too cold for Gina to lie on a beach. They're both giving in and getting nothing.

Assuming that they have only one winter vacation a year, a better solution would be a quid pro quo: *Sometimes we do it my way and sometimes we do it yours.* But we do it fairly, evenly. This way, both partners get exactly what they want, only a little less of it. They take turns; first one spouse gets to pick the solution, the next time the other spouse gets to decide. Ryan and Gina might go skiing in Vermont one year and go to the Virgin Islands the next. However, in order for a quid pro quo to work, both spouses have to allow the person who gets his or her choice to enjoy it fully. Ryan cannot sit on the beach in St. John's complaining about how he has nothing to do and blaming his wife for all the good skiing he's missing. If they've gone to Vermont, Gina has to either take lessons and try to enjoy skiing, or find some other way to entertain herself. Sulking is absolutely not allowed. If you can't support each other in a fair quid pro quo, you're going to generate a lot of resentment in your relationship. The challenge here is to accept what is fair and to avoid feeling that you've "lost" when you cannot have it all your own way. At least half the time, you will have to accept your spouse's lead and find ways to make the most of a situation that by definition isn't your choice.

Morris was furious at Jean because every time he suggested that they go to a movie, she rejected his choices and substituted her own. When he objected, she argued vehemently that the movies he chose weren't well reviewed and pressured him into going along with her desires. Morris usually capitulated to Jean, feeling he could never win the intellectual argument, but he felt increasingly resentful of Jean's control of their lives.

When I questioned Jean about it, she admitted that there was nothing objectionable about Morris's choices; she just felt that her choices were better. She reluctantly realized that her insistence on getting her way was setting up an unfair situation, causing Morris to become increasingly bitter about their relationship. This was very perilous for their marriage. We negotiated a simple quid pro quo; they would alternate choosing which movie to see, and they agreed not to ruin the other's pleasure. After seeing any particular film, they could discuss the movie, but not criticize the choice or the person who made it.

Stopping the Complain/Fix-It Cycle

Another source of friction for couples attempting to promote change is the scenario called the "complain/fix-it cycle." In this form of communication, one spouse has a problem outside the marriage. The problem may be with a relative or a friend, a boss or an underling, a contractor or a nanny. The complainer wants to talk about the problem, often implying the need for advice. The listening spouse feels compelled to suggest a change to relieve the partner's distress. Occasionally the distressed speaker really does want direct help, but more often than not, the complainer just wants to vent, feel heard, and be reassured. The speaker often perceives the spouse who offers even well-intentioned suggestions as unhelpful, sometimes even interfering.

This happens because the listener's response usually doesn't address the complainer's discomfort, loneliness, and desire for *emotional* support. Furthermore, the complainer hears the suggestions as implying that she cannot handle the situation. The complainer often dismisses the suggestions or responds as if they are insults rather than assistance. ("You don't understand what's going on here." Or, "Don't you think I could have thought of that myself?") This kind of reply frustrates the putative helper, who is only trying to prove that he is listening and is concerned. The listener then becomes offended, even annoyed. ("If you don't want my help, why ask me what I think in the first place?") Now the complaining spouse not only has a problem outside the relationship, but one within it as well. The complain/fix-it cycle is in full spin.

The majority of people who complain to their spouse about issues outside their relationship just want someone with whom to share their experiences. Essentially, they're looking for some assurance that things will turn out okay—the verbal equivalent of a hug. *Except when specifically asked for your advice, train yourself to listen to your spouse for the purpose of providing support and reassurance, not to gather information for problem solving.*

Robin and Bill came for help because Robin felt no "passion" for her husband. She wanted him to talk to her and listen to her the way her father had listened to her and comforted her all her life. The problem was that Bill was going through his own struggles and was often depressed. As a doer, though, he helped Robin get through many of her own difficult times, often taking over the running of the household and the care of their newborn child when she was physically incapacitated. He thought he was supporting Robin by *doing* what was necessary to fix the situation. At other times, he was so exhausted or stressed out that he couldn't satisfy her need for prolonged verbal closeness. He felt Robin's need to talk out every problem was like a bottomless pit, and sooner or later he withdrew in frustration, failing Robin. Feeling hurt and disappointed, she in turn slowly withdrew her affection from him.

The dynamic was perfectly illustrated by what Bill called "the latest adventure of the Diaper Brigade." Robin was a dear friend of two other women, Jackie and Laurie. The three hung out together practically every day, infants and toddlers in tow, and bucked one another up over the burdens of child rearing. "I'd go stir-crazy without them," Robin told me. Over the preceding weekend, Jackie had become critical of the behavior of Laurie's child and had called Laurie to tell her about it. Robin knew the conversation had taken place, but she didn't know what exactly her two friends had discussed.

The next day Robin bumped into Laurie at a cocktail party. After a curt nod, Laurie froze her out for the rest of the evening. As the party went on, Robin felt increasingly anxious and depressed. She was afraid to discuss her feelings with Laurie directly, fearing that somehow she would get into a confrontation that she wouldn't be able to handle emotionally.

By the time she got home, Robin was in a state of agitated

despair. She was frightened that Laurie would sever their relationship even though she had no idea what she'd done to cause the catastrophe. She didn't know what she'd do without this critical lifeline that was the only thing pulling her through the long days of formula, diapers, and tantrums. Worse yet, Bill's response to her distress had made her even more upset. In our session, as Robin described what happened at home, she and Bill began to enact their difficulty right in front of me. While describing the conflict with Laurie, Robin began to weep copiously. She turned to Bill and said, "I don't understand what happened. I don't understand why she treated me that way." Bill, looking very concerned for his wife, then began a thoughtful and detailed analysis of Laurie's character and behavior, a sincere attempt to "understand" why Laurie had acted so coldly toward Robin at the party.

"That doesn't help me at all!" Robin sobbed. She turned to me and said, "You see? This leaves me feeling so alone." She never felt Bill really understood what she was talking about, and he never made her feel any better.

I asked Robin to tell us what she felt *would* be helpful to her, since Bill's hard work and careful analysis clearly wasn't what she was hoping for. Still crying, she said she didn't know. I pointed out that, if she didn't know what would make her feel better, it would also be very hard for Bill to figure it out. Was she expecting Bill to solve the problem between her and Laurie? No, she was not. Did she think Bill knew that she didn't expect him to solve that problem? This took her aback.

Bill was equally surprised. Since he saw Robin in great distress so often, he'd wrongly intuited that his role was to sweep in and help her fix everything. Then I again asked Robin, "If you don't expect him to fix the problem, if you know he can't do that, what do you really want of him when you're so upset?" Her only response was continued sobbing.

"How about a hug and his telling you that he knows how awful this is for you and how badly he feels that you are being put through this by Laurie, but that he's sure you'll work it out with her in your own way, in your own time?" Robin offered a little smile through her sobs and nodded approval.

Bill took Robin's hand and told her he felt terrible that Laurie was putting her through all this. He told her that he thought Laurie was crazy and added that, as awful as this was, he was sure that, in time, she would figure out how best to handle the situation. Robin started to laugh and wiped away her remaining tears. As she went from crying to laughing in a matter of seconds, she seemed transformed from a fragile, depressed little girl into a resourceful woman.

This was what she'd wanted from Bill all along, but she didn't know how to get it. Robin felt profoundly relieved, but she didn't fully understand why. I explained that when confronted with an emotionally frightening situation, she used the same phrase over and over again—"I don't understand. I don't understand"—to cover up a host of feelings like the hurt, fear, and anger she was experiencing with Laurie. Though her phrase was a way of hinting at her feeling about being treated unfairly, and though her crying was a way of expressing her hurt and fear, by not being more clear and direct, she was actually making it harder for Bill to know how to respond.

In a perfect world, we tell our spouses clearly what we're feeling and why. But in our imperfect world, we tend to transmit our messages in code: When I cry, it means I'm frustrated or I'm scared that you will be too angry with me. When I have a temper tantrum, it means I'm hurt or humiliated and feeling vulnerable. When I lose it after nine P.M., it means I'm just really tired and you shouldn't take anything I say seriously; I'll be all better in the morning. Another patient describes the coded dynamic between her and her husband this way: "When I'm upset, I walk around like I've got a broomstick up my backside. Then it's Paul's job to ask me what's wrong. Then it's my job to say, really coldly, 'Oh, nothing. I'm fine.' Then it's his job again to follow me around the house and figure out what the problem is." It would have been great if Robin had been able to tell Bill that Laurie's behavior had really hurt her, that she was angry at being treated that way, that she was frightened that her relationship with Laurie was in jeopardy, and that she knew it would pass and she could take care of it. With no code to break, it would probably have been easier for Bill to respond to her without feeling he had to fix the problem. What Laurie most needed from Bill was sympathy and reassurance that she had the courage to confront the situation herself.

Bill's role in this situation is more challenging than it seems. Many spouses feel inadequate if they do no more than offer emotional support. They feel they've failed their loved one by not offering a solution to the problem. However, when you leap in to solve your spouse's problems, not only do you short-circuit the emotional connection between the two of you, but also you lose the opportunity to give your spouse the reassurance that he or she can handle the job. Then your spouse feels unrecognized, weak, and misunderstood, and suddenly the attention turns from the problem on the table to dissatisfaction with your response. *You* become the new problem. Of course, then you'll feel unfairly criticized, and you'll be headed right toward a negative cycle. So no matter how poorly your spouse may ask for it, your job is to remember that, most of the time, all a spouse usually wants is to be listened to and responded to in a reassuring, supportive, and empathetic manner.

Know Your Goal

Robin and Bill's situation illustrates how important it is for both partners to have a sense of the goal they're trying to reach in resolving any problem. My patients often sound alarmingly vague when I ask them what changes they want to make in their relationship. "I don't know; I just want him to be nicer to me." "I just want things to be better." "I shouldn't even have to ask; she should just *get* it."

Once again, it's ridiculous to expect your spouse to be a mind reader. You need to have a very clear goal, and very clear ideas about the baby steps that will ultimately take you there. What is the 10 percent change your spouse could offer that would most satisfy you? What will the realization of your goal look like? If you can't put it into words, how on earth do you expect your spouse to help you reach it? Many of my patients actually resist this kind of articulation because they find it somehow unromantic that the person whom they've deemed their soul mate doesn't automatically know what they want. Soul mates are supposed to see into your soul. Once again, this is where the lie of unconditional love, the notion of soul mates, and the expectation of marital bliss pollute a couple's thinking and ability to effect true change. If you want a real marriage, you have to know what you want and know how to clearly and calmly ask for it.

Your Brain Is a *Biological* Organ

Often couples fail to make progress despite a lot of hard work and genuine good intentions. In many of these frustrating relationships, one or both partners turn out to be excessively emotionally reactive. For example, one partner always feels angry or cannot get over being resentful. One partner generally feels irritable or critical. Or, one or both partners feel anxious or depressed and cannot keep these feeling from burdening the marriage. These couples often feel especially hopeless because, in spite of knowing what to do to make their relationship better, they simply cannot control their emotions long enough to allow for the improvement. They are trapped in the negative spiral of their marriage because one or both spouses are too emotionally labile or volatile.

Couples like these who seriously want to improve their relationships and change their lives in general should be aware that their difficulties might stem from another source. For many of us, either predisposing vulnerabilities or the stress of the prolonged marital conflict itself may have caused an alteration in those parts of our brain that maintain emotional equilibrium. This change in biological functioning may make it impossible for us to calm down long enough to stop the vicious cycle and allow for improvement. The good news is that the problem is almost always reparable, thanks to major advances in the world of neurochemistry and psychopharmacology.

For many people, and especially for some family therapists, the idea of mixing pharmacology with couples therapy is still controversial. However, because there are now medications available that can actually help people caught in destructive emotional states, psychopharmacology has become a critical adjunct in the preservation of marriage. It goes without saying that serious psychiatric problems wreak havoc on a marriage. All studies of divorced populations support the commonsense assumption that almost every form of mental illness contributes to marital instability and divorce. There is little doubt that staying married to a person with a serious mental condition usually requires the support of some type of medical intervention. But for our purposes, I will not focus here on the problems that severe mental illnesses pose to marriage.[4] They are beyond the scope of this book. Instead, I would like to address the effects on marriage of temperament and its role in "normal" personality.

Temperament refers to the biologically assigned proclivities with which each of us is born. Newborn infants are behaviorally different from one another right from birth and perhaps from conception. As we grow older, who we become is modified by experience, but our essential temperament doesn't change much, except perhaps under conditions of enormous stress. Most of us recognize that each of us has this inbred tendency toward a particular temperamental style, and early in life it becomes part of the bedrock of our personality. However, in marriage, it is surprising how often we fail to appreciate that many of our own and our spouse's personality characteristics, so crucial to the fit and success of our relationship, are temperamentally determined by our biogenetic inheritance.

For some psychiatrists, all of human emotional and behavioral experience can be reduced to biology. Many of today's psychiatric training programs put so much emphasis on brain chemistry and the use of medication that psychiatric residents are no longer being adequately trained in, or even being made aware of, the extraordinary power of nonmedical interventions.[5] These areas of expertise are now relegated almost exclusively to nonpsychiatric practitioners, mostly social workers and some psychologists.

My position, which I hope is shared by the majority of therapists, is that *the problems generated by the human condition are fashioned both by human biology and by human experience and that the two are inextricably dynamically entwined.* When I see a spouse who is *stuck* in an intensely dysphoric (irritable, depressed, anxious, enraged, frightened, panicked, desperate, overwhelmed, exhausted) emotional, overreactive, out-of-control state, I often suggest he or she take some medication to feel better. It is remarkable how quickly a seriously distressed spouse can gain control when treated with the appropriate medication. It is equally remarkable how quickly the marital conflict can subside once the emotional discomfort becomes more manageable.

Individuals coming for help with their marriage have special problems with the use of medication. They tend to fall into three categories. Some come to therapy strongly hoping that their problems can quickly and effectively be helped by medication. Others are totally opposed to any use of medication, even when it is clear that medication would offer significant relief and make both the therapy and the marriage more successful. Somewhere in between fall the majority of people who would prefer not to take medication but are open to its usefulness, even if they are wary of side effects and longer-term consequences. One major hurdle to the use of medication is that the spouse who takes it is often labeled as the one with the problem, the source of the marital difficulty. If this vision of the conflict cannot be overcome, the person for whom medication might offer the greatest benefit may refuse treatment because he or she won't accept the role of defective spouse in the marriage. In the long run this is detrimental to both spouses. It is also important to remember that severe marital conflicts can stir up so much extreme feeling that people who would otherwise be able to remain calm can be driven into a state of emotional disequilibrium by their unhappy relationships. These people may also benefit from a short course of a medication, allowing them to calm down long enough to explore new ways to solve their interpersonal problems.

Here is an example of how the treatment of a vulnerable temperament with medication dramatically affected the outcome of a marriage. Ralph and Alice came to see me at the urging of their adult children, who felt that their parent's thirty-year marriage was deteriorating. The couple told me that constant bickering had always marred their life together, but that they had expected their relationship to "mellow" as they got older and had fewer responsibilities. It had not.

Ralph saw Alice as a superficial, materialistic compulsive shopper. He was irritated by her need endlessly to decorate and redecorate their home. Her desire for extensive social contacts put pressure on him to be friendly toward people whom he did not like and with whom he did not want to spend his "precious time." He had hated his job for a long time and couldn't wait to retire. Alice claimed that Ralph was "a grouch," always irritable, critical of her, and unfriendly to others—just no fun. Though she admired his competence, she was often embarrassed by his rude public behavior. Though the couple wanted to spend time alone together, they rarely enjoyed it because it usually precipitated talk of one or the other's marital discontent. This always led to recriminations and further unhappiness. They rarely had sex, and both criticized the other for being sexually inept.

There was every reason to be hopeful about this couple's chances of improving their marriage through couples therapy. Both seemed motivated to make their lives better. Their children were grown and out of the house, and they didn't have any serious economic concerns. Both of them were intelligent, well educated, and seriously engaged in the process of therapy. Yet the treatment turned out to be very frustrating. Just when they seemed to make some small progress, they would backtrack into their time-honored irritable backstabbing. Soon we arrived at a stalemate.

Then I suggested Ralph try Prozac. Although he wasn't overtly depressed, I believed that there was good evidence that Prozac and other SSRIs (selective serotonin reuptake inhibitors) helped modify many different forms of emotional overreactivity. I thought that an SSRI might diminish Ralph's general level of irritability and dissatisfaction, which, in turn, might break the logjam in his endless conflicts with his wife. He agreed to give it a try.

Four weeks later Ralph reported that he felt like "a new man." He was less critical of his wife and disclosed that he also found it actually *enjoyable* to go out to dinner with other couples. Most remarkably, he now loved his work and couldn't wait to go to the office in the morning. He was shocked by the transformation in the way he felt and wondered if he could get used to it. Alice was dumbfounded. She likewise saw Ralph as "a new man"—the man to whom she had always wanted to be married.

After several weeks of living in this more content, less irritable state, Ralph wondered if he had been somewhat depressed all his life without realizing it. How much of his life had been wasted not enjoying the many things that could have brought him great pleasure? My experience with Ralph and other depressed, irritable, or anxious patients who have tried Prozac or some other SSRI is that many benefit even in the absence of an obvious psychiatric diagnosis. The ability of SSRIs to soothe "difficult" personalities or to calm people reacting intensely to "difficult" circumstances, like severe marital stress, begs the question of what is going on in the brains of people whom we used to think of as simply "difficult or impossible to live with." People helped by these medications do not become drugged or passive in their marriages. Along with achieving greater control of their emotions, they become more focused, cooperative in improving the marriage, and able to exercise good judgment.

Having witnessed the profound change in her husband, Alice began to wonder whether Prozac might be useful to her. Though she traveled often, she hated flying and was in a panic before each flight. She was often depressed about struggles with her family of origin. She asked to try Prozac, too. Weeks later, her general level of anxiety had fallen, she was less upset about her difficult parents' behavior toward her and Ralph, and she was feeling far more positive about her marriage.

For the first time in years, the couple began to feel sexual toward each other. This was particularly interesting because a common side effect of Prozac is diminished sexual interest and fulfillment. For this marriage, however, and many others I have seen, an SSRI worked so well to relieve irritability and anxiety that it allowed the couple to get closer and more sexual than they had been in years.

Alice no longer regularly takes Prozac or any other medication, but Ralph has stayed on Prozac for almost a decade; he and Alice want him to stay forever just the way he is right now.

Alice and other patients who have seen the benefit in themselves or in loved ones following the use of medication often express concern that the medication has fundamentally changed the person they married. They see medication as some sort of external, unnatural, threatening artifact—a crutch. I don't see this as the case. I believe that, when used successfully, medication can dampen harmful emotional reactivity and reveal a person's more naturally comfortable and appealing personality.

Most of us don't want to see ourselves as automata responding to biologically driven signals. We wish to believe that we are fully in control of our emotional responses. We don't want to think of our brain as an organ of our body. We want to experience all of our reactions as being totally reasonable to the situation at hand. But sometimes our brains don't function optimally through no fault of our own. My experience with Ralph and Alice and many others like them has taught me to respect and admire the power of biogenetic vulnerabilities and biological treatments for both clinical and *subclinical* emotional difficulties. No pill can ever substitute for clear, honest communication and a genuine desire to change. But if you and your spouse have failed to make changes in your marriage because either of you is excessively irritable, depressed, frightened, anxious, enraged, or in any way very emotionally uncomfortable, I recommend you investigate the use of pharmacological options combined with couple's therapy.

Educator Karen Kaiser Clark wrote, "Life is change. Growth is optional. Choose wisely." All marriages change over time. Many marriages change slowly, imperceptively, with each spouse accommodating the other as they go along. However, unsatisfying or troubled marriages must change to survive. Sometimes there is very little time left in which to do it. Sweeping the need for change under the rug only makes the job bigger when the time finally comes to clean house.

Put the changes that would be helpful to you and your marriage squarely on the table. Make small, calm, nonblaming requests. Fully explain the reasons for your requests. Simply start by explaining how you feel about the issues at hand. Figure out what you could do to improve the atmosphere of the marriage. Take that first step yourself. For a few months break the negative spiral by behaving exceptionally well yourself. Show your spouse the way, leading by example, not command. Trust your spouse to rise to the occasion and join you. At least give your partner and your marriage that chance.

CHAPTER 4

Lie: When You Marry, You Create Your Own Family Legacy

Truth: You Bring Your Family into Your Marriage No Matter How Hard You Fight to Keep It Out

If you don't know [your family's] history, then you don't know anything. You are a leaf that doesn't know it is part of a tree.

—Michael Crichton

I'm going home next week. It's a kind of emergency—my parents are coming here.

—Rita Rudner

Having a family is like having a bowling alley installed in your head.

—Martin Mull

In our first session, Rita and Stanley are the embodiment of marital unhappiness. They sit as far away from each other on the couch as possible, angle their torsos away from each other, and make little eye contact. Rita begins her criticism of Stanley by telling me that he's selfish and thoughtless. He never does anything without her asking for it first, and then he does it either grudgingly or so slowly that she has to nag him endlessly. Stanley responds that whatever he does,

Rita criticizes it; everything has to be done just right—meaning her way and on her timetable—or he won't hear the end of it. Rita can't stop feeling as if she's being taken advantage of, and Stanley won't preempt Rita's criticisms by being a more proactive member of the family because he thinks he's fighting a losing battle.

It emerges that Rita's mother was a frustrated housewife, a very bright woman who raised six children but never seemed happy doing it. Rita recalls her as overwhelmed, irritable, and depressed with her lot in life. Rita's father came home at the end of the day, settled into his easy chair to read his paper and nurse his Scotch, and waited to be served his dinner. He never cooked, cleaned, or even cleared his own dishes, and he rarely played with his kids. Rita's mother resented this behavior but couldn't change it; Rita vowed never to put up with a man like her father.

Stan came from a well-off family. For many years his father was so financially comfortable that he didn't have to work, so he spent most of his time on various hobbies and squired Stanley's mother through an active social whirl. Stan's mother had plenty of help around the house and seemed to get a great deal of pleasure and satisfaction from her children. All the kids went away to boarding schools beginning in seventh grade, but their mom seemed very happy and loving when they came home to visit the family over extended vacations.

I helped Stanley and Rita see how the predominant values and emotional themes of their families of origin had created their individual expectations of marriage and shaped their responses to each other. Rita felt abused by Stanley's automatic assumption that she would be happy doing virtually 100 percent of the child care. She saw his attitude as reminiscent of her father's unwillingness to help her mother, and it infuriated her. Stanley was shocked to find that his wife wasn't always thrilled with her role as mother, since his mother had always seemed so fulfilled. He conveniently over-looked the fact that, unlike his mother, Rita held down a full-time job on top of managing the household. Though he also had to work, Stanley still assumed that, like his father, he was entitled to live a life of leisure when at home. Both Stanley and Rita were reliving the traditions of their families, unconsciously allowing their family legacies to erode their relationship.

If we hope to preserve our loving connections over a longer period of time, we must become more aware of the impact that our family traditions have on our lives. Powerful forces within our family begin to shape our sensibilities and sensitivities from the earliest days of our development and continue to exert enormous control over the way we think, feel, and behave throughout our lifetime. *Human beings are the carriers of all the emotional traditions of their families—the whole assemblage of family values, styles, beliefs, relationship patterns, and behaviors, and their* reactions *to them. Many of these traditions are connected to painful childhood experiences to which we no longer want to feel vulnerable. Paradoxically, we often use these familiar traditions to protect ourselves from further hurt. These internalized patterns of behavior are as fundamental to our character and identity as is our inherited biology. This is true about us whether we like these traditions or not, or even whether we are aware of these traditions or not.*

Clearly the kinds of traditions that cause problems are not the celebratory ones—the Thanksgiving stuffing cherished for generations, the yearly decoration of a Christmas tree, the recollections shared at every family reunion. The kinds of family traditions I'm talking about that interfere with marriage are those that are rarely acknowledged and have more to do with issues such as the sharing of information (being open or more closed off), communication, values, trust, manners, and sexuality. Also, each of us grows up having a certain emotional position in the family. A child can grow up being the family peacemaker, helping wounded parents sort out their differences; the family clown or historian, charged with entertaining the troops or keeping track of the family mythology; the soldier, drafted into one parent's army to fight battles against the other; or myriad other roles. Almost any of the repetitive behaviors, values, feelings, beliefs, or roles played by a family member can become an automatic pattern. Usually, we give little thought to these patterns, if we're aware of them at all. Nonetheless, they are living forces within the family, shaping the future of each member and having particular power to affect the kind and outcome of the relationships we form as adults.

Most of the conflicted spouses I've seen in my practice dismiss the influence of their families of origin; in fact, many of them believe that once they marry, they divorce themselves from any unwelcome influences of their parents. However, I almost always find that they've treated these unwelcome family traditions in one of two ways: either perpetuating an unhealthy pattern, or going so far in the opposite direction that they've created the opposite, equally troublesome pattern. For example, if a child grows up witnessing intense strife between her mother and father, strife that is never settled amicably or without intense residual resentment, that child, when in her own adult relationship, is likely to mimic this interpersonal style or its opposite, conflict avoidance.

Ruffling the Family Feathers

Gabriel, a patient of mine, recalls that the only form of "problem solving" he ever saw in his parents' relationship was "Fuck you, fuck you, and slam the door." And sure enough, even though he hated it and never wanted to have a marriage like his parents', Gabriel brought this basic ingredient of his family's powerful tradition to his own marriage and imposed it on his wife and children without being aware of it. He sees himself as relatively tolerant and mild-mannered by comparison to his tyrannical father, but his wife and children experience him as impatient, curt, and short-tempered. Like his father, he insists on having things the way he wants them and rarely gives his wife's wishes or ideas much credence.

Jeanette, Gabriel's wife, has likewise perpetuated her family traditions. Her parents' habitual manner of dealing with differences was to be completely unyielding in arguments and then to give each other the silent treatment. Conflicts were never resolved, only frozen over by icy stares. Jeanette's mother ignored her husband's opinion and simply did whatever she wanted. In the end, Jeanette's parents went through an angry, child-damaging divorce. Now Jeanette treats requests from Gabriel with the same disdain that characterized her parents' interactions and avoids dealing with him whenever they disagree. This hurts and then infuriates Gabriel. Jeanette, in turn, then feels even less willing to consult with him and more eager to act on her own. Gabriel and Jeanette each blame their own feelings and reactions entirely on their spouse's poor behavior, and neither is aware of how they themselves are maintaining their family's traditional ways of dealing with differences and disagreements. They perceive their own behavior as perfectly justified, especially when they have to contend with someone as difficult as they perceive their spouse to be. Clearly, they are caught in a vicious cycle in which both partners unwittingly serve as representatives of the traditions of their family of origin and, in doing so, are reinforcing in each other a dogged adherence to their own traditions.

It's important to recognize the negative patterns holding sway beneath the surface of your relationship and to make conscious choices about your future. Are you still slavishly playing your childhood roles, enacting the old traditions or their reflexive opposites? All too often, relationships break up because the spouses don't know how to manage conflicts between each other's traditions. This can stifle further emotional development because spouses just assume that the conflict is nothing more than an argument between their own reasonable self and their unnecessarily difficult partner.

Making the Kindest Cut

When a child dramatically changes an openly acknowledged tradition—for example, by leaving the family religion or changing political parties—this departure from the parents' expectations can create significant disruption in the fabric of a family's life. It is a testimony to the flexibility of many families that they can actually absorb major changes in their traditions and make room for growing children to hold different views. On the other hand, there are other, more rigid families that cannot easily tolerate dissension from the previously established family order, which they regard as "true," "right," and necessary. Many people and many families are simply not comfortable with change. In some families change causes severe stress. This is also true when the change is in less consciously acknowledged family traditions.

Clair, a single thirty-eight-year-old woman, came to see me because she very much wanted to be in a relationship with a man. She had only had a few relationships, and all had ended with the man leaving her. Closer inspection of these relationships suggested that they were not that gratifying in the first place. The men were domineering and, fearful of asserting herself lest she threaten the relationship, Clair would capitulate to their demands. Over and over, she ended up first dissatisfied and then alone.

This was particularly remarkable because in her professional life as a lawyer, Clair was assertive and very well respected. How was it that she could make demands on others and be both assertive and effective on the job, but let men roll all over her in her private life? The difference, she explained, was that in her work life she wasn't representing herself but her clients and had no trouble advocating on their behalf. However, she felt terrified of doing this for herself with a man.

Clair was an attractive, good-humored woman. Nonetheless, she was convinced that she would live her life trapped as an "old maid" and was seriously depressed about the prospect. She described herself as very shy and unable to look men in the eye. She felt totally unable to flirt, even a little bit, with an interesting or available man. "I'm just the good little religious girl I was always trained to be," she said. However, while she couldn't shake off her view of the teachings of her religion, she had no difficulty having premarital sex and using birth control. When I pointed out to her that I had many patients of the same religion who did not seem to have her problems with men, she was at a loss to explain what was making it so difficult for her to put her best foot forward.

It emerged that since her parents' divorce twenty years earlier, Clair's mother had never once been on a date with a man. Her parents' marriage had been stormy and unsatisfying. After they divorced, her mother had told Clair on many occasions that she "had no intention of letting another man ruin her life." Nonetheless, Clair's mother always encouraged her daughter to date and find a husband and always seemed interested in the details of Clair's latest relationship, though her romantic advice about men struck Clair as opinionated and prudish, especially now that she was in her late thirties.

It was clear to me that Clair's family had a very strong tradition of poor love relationships. Clair's vision of herself as an "old maid" was really her willingness to accept her mother's role in her life. It was time for her to understand this and to decide whether she wanted to break this tradition. To do so, she would have to risk feeling that she was leaving her mother behind to be the sole "old maid" in the family. She would have less in common with her mother if she were to have a gratifying relationship, and that might make the two of them grow apart. Either way, she would feel more emotionally separated. If she were to start her own family, she might not want her mother around that much because her mother could be critical and domineering. All these concerns made it harder to consider abandoning the traditional single-mother, single-daughter role in which she found herself.

Once Clair understood why change felt like such a betrayal of her mother, who had taken such good care of her as a child and was still very involved in her life, she was able to move on. Once she understood the emotional meaning of her behavior pattern, she could begin to break it. However, it took a while for Clair to believe that she could actually change her life and find the courage to put that belief into action. She eventually realized that if she found her mother difficult to deal with after the change, she would still be much better off negotiating their differences rather than giving up the dream of having her own relationship. Furthermore, maybe her mother would follow her lead if Clair got herself into a good relationship. Who knows, maybe Clair's mother was so loyal to her daughter that she was remaining an "old maid" to be sure that her *daughter* wasn't the only "old maid" left in the family!

Biting the Hand That Fed You

As Clair learned, it is very painful to break unconscious emotional ties to your family of origin, even when it means eliminating unhealthy patterns. These ties are held in place by the twin bonds of love and loyalty and are the expression of deep attachments formed early in childhood. As you grow and develop, these ties become so overlaid and obscured by experiences such as intellectual growth, academic or financial success, maturity, rejection, and rebellion that they can become almost invisible. It's not until you accept that they exist anyway and begin to take the necessary steps to identify, then modify or break them that you begin to appreciate how very powerful these bonds are.

When my patients begin the hard work of changing these negative patterns, which cost them so much grief as children and now cause them so much unhappiness as adults, they expect to feel liberated, even elated. Instead, they are usually shocked to discover how much pain and guilt they feel. Often, when things begin to go well, as the rigid family bonds loosen, the guilt created by these changes is expressed as terrible worry that something awful will happen to oneself or a loved one. Davina comes from a very unhappy family, but she has worked very hard to change her life and escape from the legacy of her parents' troubled marriage. Every time she and her husband begin to do better in their marriage, she starts to imagine that one of them will die of cancer, have a car accident, or succumb to some other tragedy. Without being aware of it, her guilt over breaking her loyalty to her parents' marital style causes her to believe that she'll somehow be punished if she experiences any satisfaction in her own marriage. Interestingly, if she is successful at work, something at which her parents excelled, she experiences no guilt or fear of catastrophic events or losses.

Families always react to change. Some family members will actually go to great lengths to deter an errant family member from pursuing change, which is not seen as progress. Most families will try to get you to change back to the way you used to be, back to the way that is more familiar, comfortable, and acceptable to the family.[1] Some family members actually undermine emotional growth in their children, without realizing this is what they are doing.

Floret, a woman in her thirties whose mother was an alcoholic, worked for years in therapy to overcome her belief that if she were happily married, her mother would be very jealous of her. Her mother had been in a very dissatisfying marriage for most of her life and regularly complained to Floret about her father's inadequacies. When her mother got drunk, her father consistently called Floret, begging her to come home to help. She felt too sorry for her father to turn down his pleas and usually returned home to minister to her inebriated mother.

With the help of therapy, Floret slowly disengaged herself from her parents' conflict. Her mother joined Alcoholics Anonymous and was actually able to stay sober for the first time in Floret's life. Then Floret met and fell in love with a man who treated her well and appeared genuinely to care for her. For many months she postponed telling her mother about her new relationship, fearful that it would cause her mother distress. Finally, she broke the news to her mother in a phone call. That night, for the first time in over a year, her father phoned, begging her to come home to take care of her mother, who'd gotten drunk and collapsed on the kitchen floor.

Stephanie is another example of someone who must betray a

critical family loyalty in order to grow. An attractive, intelligent woman in her early thirties, she suffers from chronic depression, which has gotten worse since the death of her father three years ago. Stephanie wants me to help her figure out why she can never have a gratifying relationship with a man. She's had many lovers, but none has lasted. Either she loses interest in the man or the man loses interest in her. She thinks that her terrible temper has a lot to do with it. Whenever a boyfriend criticizes her, she feels unjustly attacked and verbally lashes back until she feels entirely victorious and safe from further hurt. I was treated to a display of this interpersonal style once when I questioned her view of some financial matter. Stephanie became instantaneously defensive, furious at me for second-guessing her. Her reactive emotional style said, "I won't take crap from anybody, especially men." She says that she knows she shouldn't get so angry but that she cannot help herself.

Stephanie's father and mother had an awful marriage. Her father was a "rageaholic" who regularly lost his temper, screamed, and berated his wife on a daily basis over the smallest perceived transgression. As a child, Stephanie begged her mother to leave the marriage, but her mother was too dependent and frightened to do so. To this day, Stephanie feels she was damaged both by hearing her father's unrelenting verbal abuse of her mother and by witnessing her mother's powerlessness to take the appropriate self-protective action.

Within a year of our working together, Stephanie developed a relationship with a new young man, Carl. After a few blissfully intense romantic months, Carl began to complain about Stephanie's continued relationships with past boyfriends, whom she kept as friends and still saw on occasion. Carl feared she might leave him for one of these old beaus or some other man. When Carl aired his worries or accused her of flirting with other men, Stephanie thought he was acting "crazy" just like her father and became enraged. Often she attacked him until she reduced him to tears. Soon their once-good relationship was on the verge of collapse.

Stephanie realized she was acting like a carbon copy of her

rageaholic father but she couldn't stop herself. I pointed out that she was no longer a defenseless, vulnerable little girl who needed to pump herself up to feel strong enough to stand up to a tyrant. Slowly, Stephanie began to moderate her perceptions of herself and others. Soon, her boyfriend seemed less "crazy" to her, and their relationship began to improve.

As Stephanie became noticeably less prone to angry outbursts, her attitude about her father changed. She began to feel more compassionate toward the man who had suffered from such terrible loss of control of his feelings all his life. She knew that his own father had treated him with contempt and abuse, and she felt sad that her father wasn't able to break this pattern before he died.

As Stephanie's relating style *differentiated* from that of her father, she became increasingly aware of her hidden attachment to him and saw that she'd expressed her loyalty to him by adopting the very characteristics of his that she most hated. The more she worked to give up her (and his) reactive character trait of intimidating anger, the more aware she became of her feelings of connection and love for him, even in the face of her conscious rejection of the way he had lived his life.

Stephanie's attempts to break her family tradition were complicated by her family's vigorous efforts to undermine her relationship with Carl. Under Carl's influence, Stephanie had begun to drink and smoke pot less—activities her family very much enjoyed—and they were working overtime to convince her that Carl was therefore a "bad influence" on her!

Nevertheless, Stephanie's relationship with Carl flourished, and soon the couple was considering marriage. This meant that Stephanie had to bond even more closely with Carl and consistently work harder to solve their conflicts. Doing this was violating another unwritten family tradition—living with unresolvable, constant conflict. Stephanie's emotional choice was either to break with her family's expectations and traditions by having a satisfying relationship with Carl and tolerating the feelings of disloyalty, sadness, guilt, and anxiety this would provoke, or to find some way to disrupt the forward momentum of her life so that she could avoid these frightening emotional consequences. Stephanie unconsciously chose the disruption course; she developed a crush on a man at work and was seriously considering having a fling. Maybe, she thought, monogamy was just too difficult for her. Maybe she wasn't really able to settle down with just one man.

I suggested that she consider this impulse to have an affair as her way of sabotaging her relationship with Carl and wondered what she thought would happen if she just let the relationship with Carl be. Where was it going and what would she feel if she didn't act to destroy it? By her account, things with Carl were wonderful. He was loving, generous, and hardworking. Sex was exceptionally good. So why, if the relationship was so gratifying, did Stephanie want to torpedo it? Because Stephanie's family tradition was that relationships always deteriorated over time. She worried that Carl would get tired of her and leave. It might be better for her to end the relationship now than to risk greater disappointment later. "I feel too scared to trust it," she said.

"Well," I asked, "is Carl a trustworthy person?"

"Yes," she said, "he is very loyal and very attached to me."

"What if he doesn't leave? What if you feel loved by him and he by you and the two of you have children and bring them up in that kind of atmosphere? What if you solve your problems in the future the way you've been solving them for the past few months? If that happened, how would you feel?" I pushed.

After a lengthy silence, Stephanie said, "I'd be the only one in my family, you know. Of my mother, my sister, and my brother, I'd be the only one in my family to have that kind of life, to be happy."

"That would be tough," I said. "Could you do it? Could you allow yourself to be the *only* one to have a sustained loving relationship with a spouse?"

"Yes," she said, "I think I can, but I didn't know it would feel so strange to actually do it."

It's hard to be the first to break a family tradition, especially if those traditions interfere with having successful relationships. It will mean leaving some family members in a less happy state than you are. It will make you feel disloyal and alone, separate in this important way from the people to whom you've always felt so close. It will be hard for you, and perhaps for your family as well, to forgo sharing important unconscious negative traditions, even if the bond is a penchant for failed relationships, unhappiness, or pessimism. However, as I tell many of my patients, there are better ways to show your love for your family than by sacrificing your own life.

Shooting Yourself in the Foot

As Stephanie's office flirtation indicates, there are endless ways to accomplish any self-defeating task, and many of us are veritable masters of this art. Out of the blue, the man or woman to whom we were so attracted months or weeks ago seems strangely less beautiful or handsome to us. We lose our sexual interest in our spouse without warning. We pick fights with our mate or find that those adorable quirks we used to love now unexpectedly irritate and exasperate us. Strangers, surprisingly, seem more remarkable and fascinating to us than our devoted companion. We embarrass our spouse in public or engage in thoughtless or impertinent acts guaranteed to offend. We label the spouse who dares to complain as "too sensitive." *Even though we don't realize this is what is happening, in hundreds of different ways, we can subtly or brazenly undermine and destroy our intimate connections when they threaten to go beyond the limits that our adherence to our family traditions allows.*

Why do we go out of our way to shoot ourselves in the foot? Why are we so masochistic in the relationships that matter most to us? I believe that *masochism, from a family perspective, is the unconscious predisposition to create endless varieties of relationship-destroying thoughts and behaviors for the purpose of remaining bound to the emo-*

tionally limited or negative traditions of our family of origin. For those whose family influences are extremely pernicious, perpetuating destructive family traditions becomes a crippling way of life. They thwart interpersonal development and ensure unstable, unhappy relationships. For others, masochistic acts are more sporadic, alternating with periods of more hopeful progress. Typically, this tendency toward intermittent (self)-sabotage of relationships happens just as the relationship is about to move to a new—and scarily unfamiliar—level of maturity. Feeling *frightened* by new demands and needing to avoid the *guilty feelings* of betraying our family of origin, we do or say something guaranteed to threaten our growing connection. It is a classic case of "the devil you know is better than the devil you don't know." The unconscious need to remain loyal to the family of our youth reaches out and pulls us back from the fearful abyss of emotional maturity and potential happiness. It is a classic "escape from freedom."

Unfortunately, when you engage in a masochistic act that hurts your relationship, your partner generally sees you as being purposely hurtful or mean and will accuse you of being sadistic. Occasionally, this is true. However, it can be very hard to tell whether an action that damages a relationship springs primarily from a desire to harm someone else or the need to stave off emotional growth by hurting yourself. Much of what appears to be heartlessness to others is often fostered by a person's need to impede his or her own progress in relationships.

We are creatures of habit and unconscious loyalties. We tenaciously hold on to family traditions because our sense of identity embodies our ties to our past, our attachments to our families of origin. Letting go of our traditions, changing too much of ourselves, feels like separation and death. Think of how hard it is to give up a long-held *positive* tradition, like being with one's family on Thanksgiving or Christmas Day. Contrary to what most people expect, the sadness of giving up a *negative* tradition can be even worse, especially since it is taking place outside our awareness. Not only do we feel we are separating from our family, but we fear that we are leaving them behind, stuck with all their negative, misery-producing behaviors. Amazingly, we can unconsciously feel sad, anxious, and guilty even if we don't think we like those unhappy parents or sibs very much. Surrendering any deeply held bond feels like losing our identity. When this happens, no matter how old we are, we may temporarily feel like vulnerable orphans cut adrift in a dangerous world. Small wonder our unconscious works overtime to sabotage our marriage and avoid this terrible feeling of separation.

Making the Choice

When I counsel couples on their emotional reactivity and work with them to unravel the negative cycles they've fallen into, I regularly find these transgenerational family traditions at their core. These traditions, and the natural tendency to identify with or blindly reject them, are the spark plugs and fuel that ignite and power a couple's spiral upward or downward. Since these traditions are part of our natural state of being, part of our very identity, they are very hard for us to recognize and give up. We hold on to them usually without even articulating them to ourselves. They make us stubborn. To change, to give them up, often requires the willingness to risk our family's displeasure with our changing and the courage to take a stand for our own growth without attacking them or becoming defensive.

It is probably impossible to remain in a long-term loving relationship without the willingness to accept that some of our "transgenerational traditions" don't work well with those of our partner and, therefore, must be either changed, controlled, or abandoned altogether. If a negative pattern of yours is so detrimental to your marriage that the marriage cannot survive, you face a choice: You can either hold on to the past and give up your marriage, or you can hold on to your marriage and give up something of your past. Unfortunately, because this choice is seldom consciously realized, you may give up on your spouse without understanding how your family traditions have pushed you to that decision. In short, *many of us give up our spouse to remain unconsciously tied to our parents.*

Hugo comes to my office under protest. His wife, Grace, has had to cajole and finally threaten him to get him to consider seeing a therapist. He is a handsome, imposing, self-assured man. He tells me that he doesn't "believe in" therapy and that no one in his family would ever be caught dead in a therapist's office. I ask him how his parents solved problems that occurred between them. "They just worked them out for themselves," he says. "How are you doing at working things out with your wife?" I ask.

"Not too well," he replies.

"Maybe I can help," I say.

"I doubt it," he replies firmly.

Grace wants to discuss a few things that make the relationship very hard for her. Hugo never seems to want to talk with her about important issues, and she's very upset about the frequency with which Hugo tells their five-year-old son that he is "stupid." Hugo tells Grace that there's nothing wrong with telling the boy that he's stupid when he does stupid things; after all, that's the way he was brought up and he turned out all right.

Grace reminds him of the stories he's told her of his awful relationship with his tyrannical father and points out that the only way his "old world" mother could live with his father was just to accept all his demands and abuse. Grace does not plan to live her life that way. Hugo agrees with Grace's description of his father but tells her that, like his father, he's a stubborn man, and she can't very well ask him to change who he is. When I ask him if he just assumes that his wife will stay married to him today like his mother stayed married to his father in the past, he just shrugs his shoulders and doesn't respond. Hugo glances at his watch frequently during our session and is visibly relieved when it ends.

When Grace later informs me that Hugo has come to his one

and only therapy session, and will not be returning, I know that unless something changes, he has chosen to hold on to his family traditions and risk losing his wife. Hugo is counting on his twenty-first-century wife to be as dependent and passive with him as his early-twentieth-century mother was with his father. This is a foolish bet and a marriage with a very poor prognosis.

Identifying Your Branch on the Family Tree

Since we all learn patterns of behavior in our family of origin, it's important to look at your own marriage with this in mind. Consider the role you played in your family and what you learned as a child about communication and conflict.

- What was your family's pattern of dealing with conflict? How did your parents communicate with each other? How did they communicate with you? Consider in particular how they handled conflict, stress, and anxiety. How different are you today?

- What was your primary role in the family, particularly in conflicts? Peacemaker, rebel, or soldier? Family clown or historian? Silent witness? Daddy's girl or momma's boy? Were you spoiled rotten, or were you left feeling hurt and deprived?

- Did you feel abused or cheated as a child? Could this be causing you to overreact to the slightest affront?

- Were you so frightened into submission or so angered as a child that you now have troubling listening to another person's point of view? Are you so eager to make yourself heard that you cannot listen with an open mind?

- Did you grow up feeling that your family was always right?

- Do you feel a sense of entitlement, as though you were raised as a prince or a princess? Were you often told that you were special—more special than anyone else? Are you now too demanding or perfectionistic?

- Did your upbringing leave you with poor self-esteem? Could this be causing you to overreact to your spouse, disrupting your relationship?

- How did your family deal with physical affection and warm feelings? Were they openly loving or more formal? Were they cold and emotionally rejecting or threatening?

- How do you represent your family's traditions? If you're comfortable with the way your family worked, you probably try to live the same way. However, if you hated the interpersonal patterns or values of your family, you may now be trying to be very different. Is your identity built on the idea that you must be the opposite of your parents or very much the same?

- Are you rigid about it, or flexible?

- How would your spouse answer these same questions?

Try to identify those traditions that exist within you—traditions and values that you usually pay very little attention to in your life. They are part of who you are, your identity, very much your own now. Make them more conscious and think of how they influence your relationships with your spouse and your children.

After you and your spouse have determined your family roles and traditions, look at the extent to which they're getting in the way of a better relationship and determine how you'll change *your-*

self and negotiate the differences between you and your spouse. The first step is to acknowledge that each tradition has its value; yours is not necessarily "right" or "better," and your spouse's is not "wrong" or "worse"—they are simply different. I urge you not only to have respect for your spouse's family traditions—even if you think they're negative—but to *speak* respectfully of them, whether or not your spouse speaks that way. Treating the issue with respect acknowledges the terrible power of those family ties. Look for a quid pro quo between your two styles.

Be extremely cautious before you declare that you have changed all the negative patterns that you disliked in your family of origin. This is almost always self-delusion. A patient of mine disagreed with and argued with almost all of his parents' values regarding money, politics, and relationships. He felt sure that he had thoroughly rejected and overcome his parents' intensely opinionated ideas. After all, he held very different views about almost everything in life. What he overlooked in his self-assessment was that he held his new and different beliefs with the same degree of "certainty" that his parents held their old beliefs. Thus, when his wife or children disagreed with him, he reacted to them in exactly the same aggressive, opinionated, self-righteous manner his parents had used with him. He was blind to this similarity because he saw his own beliefs as so much more enlightened than those of his parents. He couldn't fathom how his wife and children could find him such a difficult person. Though he had changed the song, he was still playing on the same instrument. He had changed his values, but he remained wedded to his family's relationship style. Changing that style turned out to be a far more difficult, identity-threatening task than simply changing his values and beliefs. It required him to become far more vulnerable to other people than he ever wanted to be again.

It is very rare to find a family in which everything is uniformly bad. Often hurt and angry adult children wish to reject everything about their upbringing. This can be extremely dangerous because there are positive values in almost every family, and too often the impulse is to throw the baby out with the bathwater. Total rejection of your family is particularly enticing if your spouse's family appears to be much more loving and nurturing than yours. You may be tempted to adopt your spouse's "healthy" patterns whole-sale instead of working together as a couple to create a more bal-anced approach that truly suits you both.

Breaking negative family bonds, ending corrupted, self-harming loyalties, does not require the dissolution of family relationships, even if others in the family go as far as to insist that you are a traitor for having different ideas or living a different life. When you make a real change, be prepared for the probability of family backlash. If you have the courage to change your relationships and challenge your family's behaviors or ideas, you need to anticipate the pressure that your family will put on you to reverse your course. Whatever maneu-vers your family uses, you must never rise to the bait of their threat-ened censure or expulsion by withdrawing emotionally or physically, or expressing rage at their reaction. Most of the time, behind the anger, your family is expressing the fear that they're losing you, or that you are criticizing them. Why else would you want to change? Continue to reassure them of your love and attachment—the tradi-tion you never want to break.

Whenever I work with spouses, I stress how important it is to develop a good relationship with their parents. It is often the key to strengthening a marriage. After all, if you can learn to get along with difficult parents, getting along with your spouse is a breeze. Furthermore, once you've negotiated a better relationship with your parents, once you've resolved some of your hurt and anger with them, your spouse often doesn't look so bad.

However, on occasion, there are times when a family of origin is so toxic that you'll be tempted to break off contact completely. You may be experiencing too much pain or hurt when in their presence or be concerned that their influence will jeopardize your marriage. I urge you not to completely cut family ties. First, truly toxic, irreparable relationships with our parents are quite rare.[2] Many parents *appear* more toxic than they really are because we're so good at setting them off, saying or doing to them the very things guaranteed to push their buttons and bring out the very behavior we most dislike. Believe it or not, adult children can be provocative to their parents in the same way we can be provocative to our spouses. We need to make allowances for how our own behavior influences, even encourages, the difficulties we have with our parents.

Second, it's often true that at the core of what our parents tell us that we most dislike (usually criticism) is a kernel of wisdom we would do well to appreciate. For example, Taisha was furious at her father because he kept offering her what she thought was terrible parenting advice when she was struggling with her rambunctious preschooler, a high-energy fellow who'd taken to hitting other kids at the playground. "Just give him a good smack on the bottom," her father kept urging, "That'll pull him into line right away." Taisha hotly resented his advice; her dad had spanked her for the smallest of infractions when she was a child, and she had always felt humiliated and angry. She would never inflict that on her own son, especially considering that hitting him was unlikely to help him understand why she wanted him to stop hitting other kids. She and her father had several angry fights about this, and finally she wanted simply to cut him out of his grandson's life. She had always found him a bully of a dad, and she didn't want to see herself in any way to be following in his footsteps.

I helped Taisha see that at the heart of her father's advice was an important message about the need to set strict limits for out-of-control kids; she could find another way to set limits that didn't involve physical punishment. She also could acknowledge to her father that he was right about the need for discipline even as she found her own methods of enforcing it.

Rather than make a complete break from your parents when you feel they're a threat, ask for a time-out. You can use self-statements to say something like, "*I* will always love you and *I* want to have a good relationship with you, but *I* don't think we can do that right now. I find that *I* get so upset when we're together that *I* can't handle it. *I* need to take some time to figure out how to deal with you better." You take the responsibility ("*I* can't handle it") and set the timetable for how long you need to be apart before you're willing to try again. The important thing is to keep the door open—the exact model for how you reduce differences in your marriage.

The same thing can happen when your parents or siblings withdraw from you. Your response should reflect your conviction that *family connections are forever*. If your family is angry with you, let them know that you're sorry that your changes are causing them so much difficulty or pain. Remember to speak first to the hurt behind their anger. But keep in touch with them. Do not withdraw. Keep calling or writing to remind them that you still love and care for them, even as they are rejecting you. *Always take the high road.* Over time, if you remain constant and refuse to counterreject them (which, by the way, is what they expect), they will most likely come around.

It is a fundamental fact of family functioning that if you can be yourself and still get along with and be effective with your parents and siblings, you will have a much greater ability to deal successfully with your marital partner. Likewise, if you can learn to appreciate how the past is now interfering with your life, you can try to correct those negative patterns. If you cannot do it alone, if you keep slipping back to the old ways, ask for help in changing them.

We think that when we leave home, we leave home. However, although Thomas Wolfe famously proclaimed, "You can't go home again," quite the opposite is true: No matter where you go as an adult, you carry home—and its traditions—with you, to the betterment or detriment of your marriage. *Your family is forever.*

CHAPTER 5

Lie: Egalitarian Marriage Is Easier Than Traditional Marriage

Truth: Negotiation in Egalitarian Marriage Is Often More Difficult

The road to hell is paved with good intentions.

—Samuel Johnson

If you can live with anything, you can live with anybody.

—Betty Carter

I hate housework! You make the beds, you do the dishes— and six months later you have to start all over again.

—Joan Rivers

Tanya and Kevin have come to see me because they're genuinely baffled about how their marriage went so sour so fast. Married for only two years, they should be living the relatively carefree lives of the quintessential "dinks" (double-income, no kids). Instead, they're constantly sniping at each other and are in my office for what Kevin calls a "tune-up before the engine explodes."

"I don't want to divorce him," Tanya tells me half jokingly, "I just want to kill him."

Tanya and Kevin lived together for a year before they got married. Tanya works in advertising. She travels a lot, conducting focus groups on new products in cities all over the country. Kevin is an art director for a magazine; when he closes an issue at month's end, he has to spend almost a week working late, never getting home before nine P.M. Before the wedding, these two young people led fairly separate lives despite the fact that they lived together. They'd catch dinner on the fly if both happened to be home at a reasonable hour. Tanya did her own laundry, occasionally tossing in a load for Kevin if he was desperate; otherwise, Kevin just dropped off his stuff at the dry cleaner he'd used for years. Kevin, a movie buff, had to see every new flick the weekend it opened. He often left Tanya at home with a book while he stood in line alone most Friday nights. They took some vacations together, but Tanya was really into camping and Kevin wasn't, so she often trooped off with a group of old college buddies while Kevin went antiquing to scout props for his next photo shoot. They prized their independence and individuality. "I really liked that Tanya was her own woman, that she wasn't one of those clingy types who have to check on you every second," Kevin told me. Tanya was glad Kevin appreciated her independent streak. "He really let me do my own thing."

After the wedding, it was a different story. Kevin had a vague sense that they should be, as he put it, "working together more as a couple," but it wasn't happening. Tanya would get home from one of her cross-country trips late at night and be so tired that she'd just go straight to bed. He tried to drag her out to movies so they could have some time together, but she kept begging off. He began to stew about her animated conversations with her college friends about where to take their next camping trip. The apartment went to pot as Kevin threw himself into a launch for a new magazine his company was developing. He found himself feeling more and more resentful when he dragged himself home after work to find that Tanya had just eaten some takeout and gone to bed without him.

They started fighting about household responsibilities. Every time Kevin asked Tanya to do something, she felt he was attacking her. She began to withdraw. The more she withdrew, the more Kevin pressed her for relationship time and the more resentful he felt when she acted put upon instead of pleased.

"I feel like I have a roommate, not a wife," Kevin complained.

"What were you expecting?" I asked him.

"I don't know," Kevin admitted. "It's not like I want Tanya to meet me at the door with a martini, but would it be such a big deal for her to cook dinner once in a while?" "I don't know what he wants from me," Tanya told me. "I just don't get what I'm supposed to be doing. I don't know what marriage is supposed to be. Kevin always says we're equal partners, but he's got some weird Ozzie and Harriet thing going on underneath, and I'm not going for it."

"Welcome to marriage in the twenty-first century," I told them.

Ozzie and Harriet Are Dead, but Their Ghosts Live On

This is a confusing time for married couples. So many partners set out to "remake the rules of marriage," only to find themselves in my office, wondering why it's so hard. Many of the couples in distress who come to my office come from "traditional" families in which their dad worked outside the home and their mom stayed home and raised the kids. If the mom worked, it was more likely to be part-time or volunteer; if she worked full-time, she probably didn't make as much as the dad and she still did most of the housework and child care. Mom's decisions held more sway over the household, and Dad called more of the shots when it came to family finances. If Dad's job moved, Mom and the kids moved with him. Divisions of labor tended to hew to traditional gender lines, with Mom doing more cooking and cleaning, and Dad doing more of the yard work and car maintenance. In the 1970s and 1980s, more women moved into the workforce, and more and more couples began stretching the boundaries of these traditions, but the ghosts of the archetypal 1950s marriage and family life haunted them. They haunt us still.

Here's the truth: Even if you've committed yourself whole-heartedly to creating new traditions for your married life together, to having a truly egalitarian marriage, you will almost certainly be hamstrung by generations of old traditions that hold a surprising power over your marriage. You will be shocked by how often your good intentions to create a fair partnership fall prey to older cultural assumptions about family roles and responsibilities.

In the new model of marriage, men and women want to have equal say in their partnership. They divide household responsibilities evenly and make shared decisions about major purchases and future plans. Both may work outside the home. When they have kids, they usually pledge to divide parenting responsibilities evenly. On paper, this all sounds fine, and is a welcome departure from the less egalitarian marriages of the past. In reality, however, the passage from old paradigm to new paradigm is filled with potholes. Couples often stumble when they try to reconcile their stated goals with the still powerful influence of gender socialization and the practical demands of married life.

For example, many men want their wives to work and contribute to the family finances, but they still expect their wives to take care of them at home. On the other hand, many women want equal power and equal say in their families, but they still wish to be taken care of financially by their husbands. Many couples compromise or neglect the managing of their house or the nurturing of their children because they're too busy, preoccupied by their own professional success, or too conflicted and rebellious about traditional responsibilities to accept them wholeheartedly. Many couples "job out" such responsibilities to third parties like nannies and housekeepers, and then end up feeling unaccountably guilty or dissatisfied with the outcome. Few couples seem really content with all these changes in the marital landscape, but most don't know how to make things better.

The typical response to this disjunction is for the partners to blame each other for their frustrations and discomfort, to get angry, and then to turn away and become cold and distant. Because each spouse is actually caught in his or her own conflict over competing role models, when the relationship is stressed, they no longer have the familiar, time-tested, and useful behavioral prescription to rely on. Often arguments break out over *failed expectations* or which family paradigm is the "correct" one to follow. This confusion and frustration leads to criticism, disappointment, and resentment. Once this negative spiral begins, unless it is interrupted, it can become the source of serious alienation and mutual anger.

Great Expectations, Unspoken Assumptions

Reggie and Mark met as extremely well-educated, successful lawyers in the same large law firm. They shared a mutual interest in the law and had many other similar tastes and interests. Though they came from different economic and ethnic backgrounds—Reggie's family was working-class Irish Catholic; Mark's was upper-middle-class Jewish—neither was deeply religious. Before their children were born, they easily agreed that the kids would be exposed to both religions, and the family would celebrate both Christian and Jewish holidays.

It was only when Reggie stopped work to raise her family that major differences between them showed up. After a typically busy day, Mark would come home at night to find his wife frazzled and irritable. Exhausted from cleaning her home, driving her children around town, helping them with their homework, and planning and cooking dinner, Reggie often turned on her husband and accused him of not helping her enough. They rarely went out alone together, and their sexual life died as Reggie became increasingly overwhelmed, angry, and depressed.

Mark, in turn, felt resentful and annoyed with Reggie. Often he stayed away from home just so that he wouldn't feel put upon by her and the children. The definitive moment of their conflict came one night when Mark returned home after closing a major business deal that had earned them a huge sum of money. Instead of being greeted with congratulations, Reggie retorted, "Just because you made a lot of money today, don't think you're not going to wash the dishes." Mark was furious with her, and for the first time he seriously considered divorce.

I asked Reggie if she'd thought about relieving some of her burden by hiring a housekeeper or someone to help her with her children. She demurred, explaining that it was her responsibility to take care of her home and family, and Mark's responsibility to help her whenever she wanted him to. Mark couldn't understand why Reggie wouldn't be open to my suggestion. As we talked more, it became clear that the spouses had very different internal models of homemaking and family life.

Though Mark had achieved economic security for himself at a relatively young age, his wealth hadn't dramatically changed his lifestyle from what he had been used to as a child. His father had worked hard and provided very well for the family; his mother had stayed at home with full-time help to assist her with cleaning, cooking, and child rearing.

Reggie's father, on the other hand, had struggled financially to eke out a good life for his family. Her mother hadn't worked but, even if she could have afforded it, would never have considered letting anyone in her home to help her with the housework or her children. Reggie's mother considered those "other women" who "let strangers into their home" to cook and baby-sit to be negligent parents and irresponsible homemakers. To Reggie's family, these wealthier women were pampered and weak. Managing child care and homemaking by oneself was a matter of personal pride to Reggie's mother and maternal grandmother. Reggie's father pitched in whenever he could. Her mother, a tough opinionated woman, imparted to her daughter many of her beliefs about the "correct" way for a woman to raise her family. Reggie simply couldn't shake her conviction that being a responsible mother meant doing all the cleaning, cooking, and child rearing without any domestic help. Besides, now that she wasn't working, she felt especially guilty about hiring someone else to do the job that she was brought up to do by herself.

"I'm not bringing in a paycheck anymore," Reggie told me. "How else am I supposed to carry my weight? Sometimes I just really miss my old office. I made good money. I felt like a somebody. I can't stand the idea that just because I have money I could turn into one of those ladies who pack the kids off with the nanny so they can go out and do lunch."

It was extremely difficult for Reggie to admit how ambivalent she felt about staying at home with the kids. When she'd first gotten pregnant, she and Mark had talked about it, and she had eagerly volunteered to give up her job so she could take care of the baby. What she hadn't banked on was feeling so left behind when she read her old firm's newsletter and found herself missing her coworkers and the excitement of a challenging assignment. She dreaded the moment at parties when she'd be asked, "And what do *you* do?" She'd always felt on equal footing with Mark when they were both working; now she felt the balance of power had shifted. She hated thinking of herself as "just" a mom and, while she didn't like to admit it, she felt vaguely superior to the women at the park who had never worked and didn't seem to have "any ambition beyond child rearing."

Without knowing it, Reggie had taken all the drive for excellence and need for approval she'd displayed at her old job and transferred it to raising her kids. For her, hiring a baby-sitter to get some relief was tantamount to admitting that she'd "flunked" her performance review as a mom and a daughter, a prospect she simply couldn't face. Whenever she did fleetingly entertain the notion of getting household help, the specter of her own mother's disapproval chased the thoughts away. And the more dissatisfied and unfulfilled she felt, the more she snapped at Mark, complaining that he never did his fair share of child-care duties.

Mark felt cheated. From his point of view, he was doing his share by being the traditional man, carrying the family financially. He felt he deserved a break when he got home from a long day at work. He felt Reggie should understand if he wanted to sit down with the paper first before launching into the kids' bedtime routine. Instead, Reggie became enraged. Mark didn't know how to soothe her. "If you're so miserable at home, why not go back to work?" he asked her. "We'll take it slow and we'll find a really great baby-sitter." Although Reggie couldn't quite articulate why, Mark's suggestion made her more furious. "It's so easy for you," she told him. "You can go off to work and not feel guilty. If I work, I feel like a bad mom. If I stay home, I feel overwhelmed, get irritable and guilty, and feel I'm a bad mom anyway. I'm damned if I do and damned if I don't."

It took time for Reggie to see how her traditional values and more modern self-concept were conspiring to put her in a terrible bind. While she tried slowly to assimilate new ideas about motherhood, I helped Mark to see that she wasn't just being irritable and difficult, but instead was caught in this uncomfortable conflict, buffeted by her loyalty to her family of origin and the traditional roles of women, her commitment to an egalitarian marriage, and her new dramatically changed economic circumstances. Instead of getting angry with her, Mark did his best to sympathize with her conflict and her burden.

I also had to work with Mark to help him appreciate why Reggie felt so conflicted. Although he and Reggie had always considered themselves equal partners in the marriage, he'd never stopped to think that, just as for him, a lot of her sense of self-worth came from her identity as a successful lawyer. The traditional part of Mark just assumed that Reggie would be totally fulfilled by her new identity as a stay-at-home mom, since he'd seen how much pleasure his own mother had taken from that role.

Reggie slowly began to experiment with the idea of household help. At first she could hire a woman only to help clean the bathrooms and kitchen one half-day every other week. Eventually this expanded to having help for a few hours every day. As she was able to change her assumptions and expectations about what it meant to be a good mother and homemaker, she felt less burdened and began to enjoy being at home. In time, she hired a loving nanny with whom she and the children developed a close relationship. Soon after, she decided to go back to work part-time. Two years later, Reggie and Mark were doing well. Reggie was less depressed and had rekindled her sexual relationship with Mark. Mark was relieved and pleased to find his wife so much more satisfied with her full life. He began to devote more of his nonworking hours to quality time with his family, which in turn made Reggie feel even better.

The solution to Reggie and Mark's problems lay in unraveling many layers of issues. First, the spouses had to calm down the emotional atmosphere of their relationship. Reggie had to understand that simply being angry and critical of Mark wasn't going to make her life any easier or their relationship any better. Mark had to become less emotionally reactive to Reggie's criticism and distress. He had to have more sympathy for the stresses on her life and the shifting paradigms in which she was caught. He had to see past her criticism to her discomfort. Reggie had to adjust to and find a way to make peace with the conflicting roles she was offered as a woman. Finally she had to find a way to be more flexible with her values as she moved from one social economic level to another.

Many modern couples assume that they won't fall prey to traditional gender role assumptions about how to live their lives. They believe that it will be easy to fashion their marriages in a new mold, especially if they have already broken with tradition in other aspects of their lives. It isn't necessarily so. Emily and Jake came to see me because they felt a great tension growing between them that they couldn't ameliorate. They were fighting frequently, and

Jake was becoming verbally abusive when he got angry. The tension between them had gotten so great that they, too, were seriously considering divorce.

Emily was a high-powered, successful businesswoman who left for work every weekday by eight A.M. and returned home usually by six-thirty. Jake was a part-time research librarian who also worked on a novel from home. Jake earned far less than Emily.

Jake took care of all the housecleaning, cooking, and running of errands. When Emily got home, he had dinner on the table for the two of them. Usually he asked Emily to take over some of the tasks he didn't get around to during the day so he could steal upstairs to his study to work on his novel. Emily typically bristled; she wanted more downtime with Jake, time spent just hanging out or maybe going out on a date. She didn't like being "handed a to-do list as soon as I walk in the door." Jake was resentful that Emily wasn't more respectful of his efforts to make something of his writing career. They began to fight more often, and then they withdrew from each other.

As the couple spent less time together and more time alone, each spouse began to feel increasingly alienated from the other. Both felt that the other lacked sufficient respect for their time pressures or work burdens. They each became indignant and reacted irritably when asked to do something for the other. Soon they didn't feel like spending much time together. Emily began to spend most weekends at her parents' house, while Jake buried himself in his novel. Over a period of many weeks, we discussed the underlying gender-role assumptions and expectations that were causing so much confusion and stress. As we did so, their vicious circle of resentment and distance began to unravel. It turned out that both Emily and Jake assumed that because they'd made their respective voluntary choices about careers, each would be completely content with their lives. Furthermore, they assumed that their own and each other's choices implied something about their relationship to household chores and responsibilities. Emily had assumed that Jake would be ready to "play" when she was, and felt hurt when Jake wasn't. She felt insulted when Jake suggested that she wasn't doing enough around the house. Since she was the primary breadwinner and Jake was such an untraditional guy, she figured Jake would want to take over the household chores completely. Also, Emily assumed that this was only fair because she made most of the money for the couple and worked hard all day outside the house.

On the other hand, Jake assumed that, because she was a woman, Emily would eagerly pick up the slack around the house if he wanted to get more writing done. He figured that she knew where the traditional boundary between his duties and hers lay. He believed that Emily "should" do the housework. Their frustrations with each other's choice of marital role were based on mistaken assumptions about each other and the ease with which couples can automatically find the right balance for themselves between traditional and egalitarian models of relationships. As the atmosphere between them improved, they recommitted themselves to working on their relationship by spending more time together and leaving all thought of housework behind. But the bigger work in their relationship was airing and resolving their unspoken assumptions about the clash between traditional and nontraditional roles.

Role Call

In an article published in the *Journal of Marriage and the Family*, sociologist Scott Coltrane reviewed over two hundred studies of how American couples divide up household responsibilities. He found that "although the vast majority of both men and women now agree that family labor should be shared, few men assume equal responsibility for household tasks. On average, women perform two or three times as much housework as men." Coltrane's review concluded that couples who have figured out a satisfactory balance of labor are more likely to have happy marriages and less likely to experience depression.[1] Sociologist Juliana McGene of Penn State University also studied this issue and concluded that squabbling over the division of household duties is more likely to jeopardize a couple's marital bliss than is their romantic baggage from previous relationships.[2]

According to a 1999 study by Chloe E. Bird, a professor of sociology at Brown University,[3] being asked to shoulder a disproportionate amount of the housework can cause anxiety, demoralization, depression, and worry in wives. (Her study also found that in those rare situations where husbands did a disproportionate share of the housework, they, too, were prone to depression.) Bird's analysis showed that couples' perceptions of how much housework each spouse did—the degree to which they shared the burden—had greater effects on their levels of happiness and satisfaction than the actual number of hours each spent on chores. In other words, it was the wife's feeling that the distribution of labor was unfair and inequitable that led to her depression.

Interestingly, Bird found that when couples married, the wife ended up doing more housework than when she was single, even though she now had a partner with whom she could presumably share the chores. On average, a married woman did fourteen more hours of housework a week than her single counterpart, while a married man only did ninety minutes more than his bachelor pals. Bird theorized that the extra burden caused more anxiety and depression because the wives felt their extra labor generally went unrecognized, offered little fulfillment, and didn't offer the satisfaction of paid work outside the home.

It's clear that it is extremely important to find a way to comfortably share family tasks. But in this world of shifting gender roles, how do you work toward a paradigm that satisfies both of you? The only way fully to recognize the pull of tradition is for you and your spouse to spell out what you see as a fair distribution of roles and responsibilities. Experts agree that the best way to dissipate the power of unspoken beliefs and suppositions is to bring them out in the open. Get ready for a long discussion. Remember that neither of you is a mind reader; the cardinal rule for this conversation is that you say what you believe and want, and your partner does the same. Always focus on solving the problem. Neither of you needs to criticize the other for expressing honest opinions or desires.

You may balk at taking the time to talk about daily family responsibilities. After all, you reason, my household is running fairly smoothly. Who needs to spell it all out? You do. If you make a list of family duties, you are very likely to find out that your spouse is taking care of a number tasks that you never thought of, and vice versa. You may find that what you assumed was a trivial responsibility is much more complicated, time-consuming, or psychically burdensome than you realized. For example, choosing the family health-care plan may seem simple, but its ramifications can be huge if you choose the wrong plan and lack critical coverage. Other chores may take longer, be more physically demanding, or more unpleasant than you thought—for example, you both adore your parakeets, but did you know it can take hours to clean the cage? Making a list and discussing it helps avoid the trap of taking for granted what you and your spouse do for each other and your family.[4]

Once you've compiled your master list, divvy up the duties fairly and equitably. Of course, you have to take into account how much time each of you is working outside the home. The goal here is not unyielding similarity but *fairness*. Fairness implies that in the end, when all is understood, both of you feel that the division of labor is reasonable and balanced. You both don't have to do the same number of dishes each week or clean the bathtub equal numbers of times. One of you may gas up the car and mow the lawn and the other may make dinners and go grocery shopping if you both choose it and feel that, overall, the division of labor is fair. This form of fairness of function is often *complementary* in nature. Though for many it may come naturally, it is remarkable how often one person will think that all is going well while the other spouse secretly feels that the responsibilities of life have been unfairly divided. This belief, justified or not, can destroy a couple's ability to enjoy life together. Going over the division of family responsibilities ameliorates this possibility.

What's the best way to establish this complementarity? Here are some time-honored questions from marital therapists and real-life couples to ask yourself.

Who does it better? First think of those tasks in life for which you are better suited. If the wife is a financial whiz and the husband is a terrific cook, it might make sense for each to choose to do those tasks according to his or her ability. Notice that I said "might." Talk this out. Many people don't enjoy getting stuck doing something just because they happen to have a talent for it. If you feel you're being railroaded into something simply because you do it well, but you're tired of the burden, speak up. Even the most talented chef enjoys being cooked for once in a while; is this one of those chores you should trade off? Also, while it might be easier in the short run for one spouse to handle a particular chore, it might benefit the couple in the long run for both to get involved. For example, I see a lot of couples in which the men handle all the finances. Later, if the husband dies or is incapacitated, or if the couple gets divorced, the woman must suddenly take on crucially important financial responsibilities without the background or knowledge to handle them. It often benefits the couple more for both spouses to become adept at handling the family finances.[5]

Who likes doing the task more, or dislikes doing it less? It will feel like less of a chore if you take on responsibilities that you enjoy.

Can you take turns? Let's face it; certain jobs are simply "dogs," such as cleaning out the litter box or swabbing the toilets. You may have to rotate the task or negotiate a quid pro quo.

Who cares more about the task? Maybe you feel it's essential to send out Christmas cards every year, while your spouse doesn't care one way or the other. You might consider taking on the task that means more to you. Also, be careful of the standards and expectations you set for household functioning. For example, your standard for cleaning a bathroom might include going over the grout with a toothbrush and scrubbing down the shower door once a week; your mate might be satisfied with a quick rubdown of the sink and a swish of the toilet brush in the bowl every now and then. When one spouse holds consistently higher standards on what he or she considers a job well done, that partner may end up feeling forced to take care of a disproportionate number of tasks to ensure they're done "properly." This can quickly lead to a sense of unfairness and resentment. The overfunctioner has to be careful not to let the underfunctioner take advantage of him or her. On the other hand, the overfunctioner has to be very aware that he or she has a strong tendency to take over, to devalue the person with lower standards, and to enjoy feeling superior. For example, rather than be critical of the less organized person, the neat freak (the over-functioner) who feels compelled to do more of the cleaning, needs to work out an arrangement that allows him or her to feel that the burdens of family life are fairly balanced. Likewise, a disorganized slob has to take more responsibility for his or her messiness, agree to make personal changes, or craft agreements that also satisfy the needs of the more organized spouse.

Who is least inconvenienced by the task? If one spouse never gets home until after the dry cleaner is closed, then it might make more sense for the spouse with more flexible hours to take charge of this duty. Again, I said "might." I have seen the spouse who works longer hours outside the home beg off on so many duties that the spouse who stays at home or works fewer hours ends up doing much more than seems reasonable even under these circumstances.

Can you fend for yourself? If you simply can't agree on standards, can you each agree to do for yourself, without feeling resentful? You certainly won't want to do this for every chore—there's so much to be gained from learning to share household responsibilities—but if you can't resolve an issue—say laundry and dry cleaning—you may want to handle it separately rather than clash over it constantly.

Can the kids help out? Even small kids can be taught to help around the house. You both might hate dusting, but a younger child may actually be excited at being given such a "grown-up" job, and an older one may be mollified by an allowance. Be careful to assign or require the same work of both your sons and daughters, lest we continue the same gender-role problems into the next generation.

Can you switch sides? According to clinical psychologist Susan Heitler, Ph.D., "In general, people get their role assumptions from who did what in their family of origin. A man whose dad vacuumed will vacuum." So shake things up. Try flipping chores for a week.[6] If you do all the cooking, hand the spatula to your mate. If you've never done the laundry, take a spin with the spin cycle. Find out what's really involved in the chores you steer clear of—how time-consuming are they? Difficult? Unpleasant? You may be surprised to find that your spouse is doing more than you gave credit for. You may find that you don't mind a task you've always assumed you'd hate. After switching jobs, one of my patients discovered that she actually enjoys mowing the lawn. She finds the smell of the freshly cut grass invigorating and says she likes making the straight green stripes.

Can you skip it altogether or lower your standards? Do the windows have to be washed twice a year, or would once do? Is rotating your seasonal wardrobes in the closet worth the effort? Does the whole house need to be vacuumed weekly, or just the heavy-use areas? Discuss whether some of your resentment stems from battles over who will do chores that need not be done so regularly—or even at all.

Does it make sense to hire outside help? If you find yourselves coming to blows regularly over a given task—in my experience, keeping the house clean is a common flashpoint—consider whether bringing in outside help can solve the problem. This is often a tricky suggestion. Actually, some people don't feel comfortable hiring outside help to do those household chores that they would traditionally do themselves. Many find hiring household help financially unfeasible or wasteful. Even so, it is worth another look.

The reason that many of us have negative attitudes about hiring outside help is that we were raised at a time when household help wasn't as necessary, because one member of the couple, usually the wife, stayed at home and saw it as her job to take care of the house and family. This then became an American middle-class tradition. Today, though, 60 percent of married women work outside their homes. This means that housework and child care often get added on to their day when they get home.[7] Though many women still do much of this work themselves and feel that their husbands should also pick up the slack, it isn't so easy for either spouse to add this much "work" time to their already busy lives. And if they do add the time, where does it come from? Certainly it comes from family time, leisure time, or time together as a couple. None of this is necessarily good for a marriage. So I often find myself suggesting to couples, even those for whom it's a financial stretch, that hiring some help to relieve this stress on their marriage might be a good strategy.

Consider it: How would even a small outlay of money affect your long-term financial goals? Would it be worth hiring, say, a one-day-a-week cleaning person to make your life easier and help you have a better relationship with your spouse, even if it meant reaching your savings goals more slowly? Would agreeing to order takeout or eating at a restaurant every so often be worth the bite out of your budget if your squabbles over whose turn it is to get dinner on the table could be lessened? I am not suggesting that if you throw money at a problem it will always go away, but, paradoxically, feeling freer to spend small amounts of money to lessen stresses on your marriage is probably a very good long-term *financial* investment.

There are at least three very important reasons for this. First, I have found that many people easily spend money on things that don't help their marriage, but then foolishly balk at spending money in ways that would bring them greater interpersonal comfort. For example, I have a middle-class client who would rather own a $5,000 home theater than use that same money to hire years of part-time household help to diminish the stress on his relationship with his wife. Second, many couples don't reasonably evaluate their financial situation over the long term. Couples with young children tend to forget that as they get older they will need less help around the house at the same time that their incomes tend to increase. Their *financial anxiety* often drives them to save the most money at the very time when excessive saving may actually jeopardize their marital relationship. It is often a better decision to save a little less for college than to fight endlessly with your spouse over who does more in your mutually overburdened household.

Finally, there is nothing more expensive to a family than divorce, and, for the moment, I am speaking only financially. Wouldn't it be just simply crazy to save $4,000 a year by not getting some household help, but then ending up divorcing, paying lawyers a fortune, and supporting two households, in part, because you and your partner were under so much stress that you couldn't stop fighting or being critical of each other? Yet I see this kind of foolish financial decision making all the time.

Of course, if it interferes too much with your long-term financial goals or is truly economically unfeasible, buying your way out of a bind could be a poor investment. But judicious spending can head off or end a negative emotional spiral if you both think long term and decide it's worth it.

Be scrupulously honest with yourself. Did you sign up for a particular task because you felt you "should" do it, even if you hate the idea? Are you annoyed at your spouse because you think he or she "ought" to do a certain task and didn't take it on? Are you avoiding a particular task because you're afraid you'll look old-fashioned, because you think the task is more properly done by someone of the opposite sex, or because you'd feel a little silly doing it? These aren't legitimate reasons and bear closer scrutiny. I've had a lot of women in my office admit that even though they consider themselves very modern, they really want to do more of the cooking and other traditional "women's work." They feel as if they're selling out the feminist movement if they do what feels right for them. Other women report that they feel happier returning to work and hiring a baby-sitter, but are nagged by the feeling that they're not "proper mothers" because they chose not to stay at home. I point out that the women's movement has always been about giving women greater opportunity and the freedom to choose, not forcing them to choose any one thing. Nevertheless, many women fear that they will be harshly judged by their peers, especially their female colleagues, no matter what path they take.

When my male patients express trepidation because they want to take over a traditionally female task, such as child care, I remind them that there's nothing that makes either sex inherently better as a nurturer and role model. Nevertheless, they believe that others, particularly men, judge them as less "manly" if they don't adhere to strict gender assumptions. It is very important that you acknowledge the stress induced both by trying to depart from these kinds of traditions or by trying to hew to them.

Check for the buried assumptions dictated by the power of ingrained traditions, especially gender stereotypes. Have you assumed that a wife should be the family social director because "women are more gregarious"? Did you assume that the husband would want to be in charge of washing the car and doing the yard work? Did you take it for granted that the wife would stay home with the kids, or that the husband wouldn't want to, or that whoever made less money should give up his or her job? Go down your list item by item and challenge yourselves to tell the truth about what you feel. Negotiate from there. Even if you consider yourself fundamentally traditionalist or egalitarian, there will be choices for which you might not want to tout the "party line." Talk them out.

These discussions typically unearth a lot of surprises and ambivalence. Allison found that she wanted Derek to treat her like an equal, yet she expected he would support them both financially after they started a family, when she planned to quit her job and stay home. This was news to Derek, who was not at all comfortable with the idea of loosing Allison's income. Al expected that Lorraine would continue to work outside the home after they had kids, but he still assumed that she would take care of the lion's share of child care and housework; Lorraine quickly disabused him of this notion. Parker wanted to cook fancy meals and expected that Helene would do all the dishes; Helene floored him by telling him that after working all day and taking care of baby Carlie in the evening, she'd rather have a simple hamburger than have to clean up ten pots and pans after one of his nightly extravaganzas.

No Backseat Driving

Once you've apportioned your duties and responsibilities in a complementary way that both parties understand and agree upon, it's time to do the impossible: Stay quiet while your partner does it his or her way.

Yes, I realize how agonizing it is to watch your spouse do something the "wrong" way, by which I mean not your way. Get used to it. If your idea of grocery shopping is the fifteen-minute "raid on Entebbe" sort, and your spouse prefers a leisurely stroll through the aisles, grin and bear it—or stay home. Let go of your notion that there's just one way to load a dishwasher or do a load of laundry. If your partner's housecleaning means one-part vacuuming and three-parts sitting down with a pile of magazines for one last perusal before the recycle pile, leave it alone. As long as the job gets done, stop caring about whether it was done your way. Remember the 10 percent solution: Just getting your spouse to do something that he or she hasn't done before is a major contribution. You can kill all the good-will behind that gesture with a single complaint or even a "gentle" correction about how to do it better (i.e., your way).

Relationships do not usually break down over the apportioning of responsibility, but instead over the way in which the sharing of responsibilities gets discussed. You and your spouse have to be able to initiate a conversation over differences within your marriage in a manner that supports an exchange of ideas and feelings, and stays focused on solving the problem. Remember, if you start by blaming or devaluing your spouse, all the energy of your discussion will go into proving or defending your point and usually your honor. Very little energy will go into solving the problem. Listen and respond to each other's distress or call for help with empathic support, but without reacting defensively or countercritically. Review chapters 2 and 3 if this continues to be a challenge for you.

Be sure that your division of labor works in practice as well as in theory and that the reshifting of the burden hasn't created more tension. Though this is hard to do, check in with each other regularly to discuss whether the two of you are living up to your agreement. If you spot a problem, don't wait for a formal shareholder's meeting to bring it up; mention it specifically and politely (remember to stay in your zip code) and offer or ask for some suggestions for a solution. It's easier to make a smaller course correction early on than to nurse a grudge and then erupt at a partner with wild exaggeration later.

Express Your Appreciation

Failing to appreciate your spouse's efforts is an express ticket to the negative spiral. Intellectually, you know that saying "thank you" is a good idea; it's free, it's polite, it says you care. So why don't couples do it more often?

- "He's supposed to be doing it anyway. Why should I thank him for doing his job?"
- "I'm just so angry that she waited so long to help; I can't bring myself to tell her I appreciate her efforts."
- "It's a fraction of what he should be doing. You expect me to applaud when he occasionally does the laundry himself while I'm still stuck doing it the rest of the time?"
- "Give me a break. I was out on business all week. I have no idea what she was doing while I was gone."
- "Sorry, I've been so swamped I didn't notice."

If I sound like a broken record when it comes to advising couples to make the effort to express appreciation for each other, it's because I've seen how often this is left out of marriage and the dramatic results that such an added simple gesture can bring. There may be times—years, even—when the two of you will be stuck in a situation where there may be little you can do to improve your life circumstances. Perhaps you're caring for an ailing parent. Or a job puts inordinate stress on one or both of you, even requiring late hours or long trips away from home. Or child rearing or unemployment drains you dry. At these times more than any other, sometimes all you can do is hold on to each other and express *appreciation for whatever is being done in the face of all that can't get done*. Stay on the same side, joining together to oppose the stress. Don't fall into the trap of opposing each other.

For example, if you're trying to encourage change in a spouse who is reluctant to take on a fair share of household responsibilities, the temptation to withhold your appreciation will come at the very time when a well-placed "thank you" for the little that he or she does can make the most difference. Remember, if you want your marriage to move forward, first change yourself to change the emotional atmosphere in your relationship. Taking the time to notice and appreciate what your spouse does makes this happen.

Marriage Is Not a To-Do List

Sometimes it's not until you've written down and discussed all your responsibilities that you realize why you always feel so tired and overwhelmed, and why there is so much tension at home. If you feel too burdened, consider where you can cut back on some of those responsibilities. Perhaps, until your lives are calmer, your marriage cannot feel more successful. Do you go out too often? Could you survive on less money? Is compulsively "doing" interfering with "being?" On weekends, are you both so exhausted running errands that you don't have the time or energy to enjoy each other's company? If some task isn't absolutely essential to your relationship, or if hiring a third party to help won't address the problem, see if you can do without it altogether.

If both of you work, you may have bought into the assumption that those two incomes will make your lives easier. This is not necessarily so. Having more money provides very little marital insurance.[8] If you each focus too much on your careers to the exclusion of your marriage, all the extra income in the world won't undo the damage you can do to your relationship. All you may end up with is more furniture to divide when you get divorced.

Realistically, many of us have to accept the fact that we spend more hours on the job than with our spouse. Take a look at the degree to which your job pervades your home life. How frazzled are you at the end of the day? How much close attention do you pay to your spouse when you're not at work? How much work do you bring home—either in your briefcase or in your mind? Is your marriage really more important than your job? Even if you feel that way, do you act that way?

Egalitarian marriage is a goal worth trying to reach, but it will be achieved only with a great deal of effort. Until new, workable paradigms are forged, the temptation to fall back on traditional models that still offer some practical relief from stress will be huge. Believing that your marriage is *not* the one your parents had won't be enough; you will have to create a marriage of mutual satisfaction based on your own beliefs and values. These beliefs and values will come from many different paradigms and models, some of which may contradict one another at the onset. Don't be afraid to build your own unique marriage on your own terms, and then to put that marriage into action.

Separate, but Equal—Together, but Different

Another major dilemma for modern couples is the challenge of finding common ground when two independent people come together in marriage. In past generations, couples married at a younger age, often right out of high school or college, spent most of their passage into adulthood together, and made most of life's major decisions as a couple. In essence, spouses grew up together. However, more and more people today marry or remarry later in life, after they've become adults or lived on their own for many years. Most of the important decisions in life have already been made, and important choices have been organized around self-interests. Most people marrying in their thirties, forties, and fifties are proud of their individuality and find it hard to give up their hard-won sense of adult separateness or identity. Learning to mesh two separate, fully formed, adult lives, finding the right balance between selfhood and togetherness is a much more common and challenging task today than it was even a generation ago. There's no ready-made template for this experience.

Jennifer and Seth were locked in a struggle that threatened their relationship. Both had been married before. Jen had three daughters from her first marriage; Seth had no children. They both suffered from their earlier divorces when their former spouses had ended their marriages to be with other partners. Both of them had been surprised and deeply hurt. As a result, they were extremely fearful of another failed relationship and wanted to do everything possible to keep that from happening. They greatly admired and loved each other, feeling that they had been extremely fortunate to find each other at this point in their lives.

Jennifer worked in human resources for a large corporation. Her job was important and very demanding. Nonetheless, she managed to get home early every night to see her children and considered herself lucky to have a really good baby-sitter. She had an exceptionally busy life that she barely kept in balance, but she seemed to thrive amid the responsibilities and demands placed on her by herself and others. She was part of a very social network of friends who had been very supportive and helpful to her in both the business world and her private life. She often held parties in her home and was invited out regularly. She loved her social life, which she believed was critical to her well-being.

Seth initially looked like her perfect match. A successful physician with no children of his own, he accepted Jennifer's daughters and quickly developed a strong positive relationship with them. They began spending every weekend at Seth's home in Pennsylvania, a four-and-a-half-hour drive from New York City. At first all seemed ideal, but over time the long drives to and from the country home began to wear on the children. Still young, they became fussy and whiny in the car, irritating Seth and making it hard for him to drive. He thought the children should behave better and was annoyed that Jen didn't take more control of them. On some weekends, Jen wanted to stay in the city instead of making the long drive to Pennsylvania. Seth wanted to go to his home every weekend and couldn't understand how Jennifer could prefer Manhattan to the fresh country air. He refused to stay in the city with her and the kids even when she begged him to. This made them both very sad.

Seth had worked very hard for many years to develop his Pennsylvania property. He was very proud of it and attached to it. He'd come to hate what he saw as crowded and dirty New York City. He dreamed of establishing a more rural practice and of moving permanently to the country with Jennifer and the children.

To add to the problem, Seth felt distant from and uninterested in Jen's social world. He was generally bored by parties and social chitchat and felt that he had very little in common with most of Jennifer's business-oriented friends. Though they were nice enough people, he also felt they weren't especially interested in him. Generally he preferred to be alone hiking, reading, or working on projects at his country home. Though she admired Seth's ability to enjoy a more solitary life, Jennifer found his refusal to be a more "social animal" increasingly grating. By the time they came to see me, this couple had become very critical of each other's lifestyles and preferences, yet they were in love and desperately wanted their relationship to work.

In my office they usually began sessions by trying to get me to choose sides; Jennifer wanted my support for how difficult it was to pack up the kids and spend almost nine hours each weekend in a car; Seth wanted me to get Jen to be more of a disciplinarian with her children when they misbehaved during their long car trips. He was irritated by Jennifer's suggestion that the drive was too much for them. Jen thought Seth was stubborn in his refusal to sell his adored home. Seth thought Jen was a social butterfly who prized New York society above a quiet family life in the country.

Each of them had a perfectly reasonable vision of the way life should be and felt entitled to live that life. Each further believed in the lie of unconditional love; that the other partner should love them enough to want to join them in the life they wanted. They both had good values and sound, understandable agendas for their futures. The only question was, could they figure out how to live their lives together or would they have to separate for each of them to have what was important to them?

Initially, we worked to break the cycle of mutual criticism and antagonism. I pointed out that neither of them had a monopoly on the truth, or on the right way to live. I supported their bond by telling them that it was rather remarkable that Seth was willing to play such an active role in Jennifer's daughters' lives, especially given how much time Jen needed to devote to her children and how little time was left for the two of them to be alone. I encouraged their getting away by themselves when Jen's ex-husband had the girls on alternate weekends.

As they stopped criticizing each other, they began to face the real differences in the way they wished to live their lives and began to worry about whether they could actually find a way to settle their differences and stay together happily. In the old days, differences such as these were usually resolved by the man getting his way and the woman, often begrudgingly, going along. Jennifer would have needed Seth's financial umbrella to protect her and her children, and would have acceded to anything he wanted. But, like so many women today, Jennifer made enough money to support herself. As a result, she had enough power to negotiate with Seth as an equal.

If spouses come to a marriage with a commitment to be equal partners—meaning they have equal power, equal standing, and equal say—there is often no readily available, convenient path to solving the problems caused by significant interpersonal differences. If power cannot be used to cover up a problem or impose a solution, spouses often find that that they have to deal with many more differences and incompatibilities than they expected.

As Jennifer and Seth fought less, they both got more depressed. It became clear that their mutual criticism and bickering had been an attempt to get each other to change enough to avoid the threat of their relationship ending over what appeared to be irreconcilable differences in their lives' agendas. The problem was that their differences were real and important. They were both fully formed, grown people capable of taking care of themselves. Their fighting to a draw made it clear that they both held equal power, were equally in control of their own lives, and could not bully the other into capitulation. Neither could *win* the argument. However, though it helped them avoid their greatest fear—separation—their constant bickering was, nonetheless, ruining their relationship by making them feel unhappy, resentful, and discouraged about each other.

I pointed out to them that if either agreed to make a significant change for the other, it had to be made willingly and without holding on to residual bitterness or resentment. Feeling forced to change something important against your will causes resentment, and this resentment can erode good feelings between people. Agreeing to do something against your will can lead to marital unhappiness, even though it looks like progress has been made in settling a difference. Seth and Jennifer would be better off separated, each free to explore other opportunities, than to make adjustments for the other that they would regret and for which they would always hold the other responsible.

At the end of a very difficult session, they left my office feeling despondent. A line was drawn in the sand and neither would budge. They sadly separated a few days later and agreed to see less of each other. This standoff lasted a few weeks until Seth decided that his desire to be with Jennifer was more important than his attachment to his country home. He chose to sell his beloved country house and look for a place within a two-hour drive of New York City that he, Jen, and the kids could enjoy with less stress.

Jennifer said that if they lived closer to New York, she would want to go to the country more often, perhaps even for day trips. She offered to limit her social calendar and to accept Seth's natural reluctance to be as gregarious as she was. Both agreed that she would go to certain social events alone without feeling that, if Seth didn't attend, it implied something negative about his character or their relationship. Jennifer also decided that she had been too lax with her girls' unruly behavior. It *now* occurred to her that she had been overly lenient with them because she worried endlessly about the negative effects on them of her divorce from their father. She also encouraged their father to spend more time with the children so that she could be alone more often with Seth.

This couple ultimately held it together and thrived because they found the right balance among their prized independence, their personal power, and their desire for a mutually gratifying partnership. But it wasn't easy. First, they had to develop a real tolerance and respect for their individual differences, and then they had to find a way to bridge these differences without fighting, obfuscating them with "communication problems," or using their power to force the issue or intimidate each other. They also had to modify their personal styles, beliefs, and agendas to accommodate the wishes of the other person in the relationship. Finally, given that they were in a relationship of equal power, someone had to be brave enough to go first. And, the response from the other person had to be conciliatory rather than advantage seeking. For too many people today, the thoughtfulness and accommodations required for this kind of egalitarian solution seem to be too difficult. In this case, as great as their differences were, Jennifer and Seth overcame them because the couple deeply cared about each other and didn't want to experience another failed love.

Liberty, Equality, Difficulty

Paradoxically, the acceptance of the idea of equality in marriages has made it more difficult for couples to remember that their partners are, in fact, completely different people.

By marrying, many of us secretly hope to attain the ultimate narcissistic dream of union with someone of the opposite gender who is essentially just like us. In this corollary to the belief in a soul mate, we marry to bind to us the missing "other half" of our self.[9] However, the moment we actually take the leap to being emotionally engaged with another real separate human being, the dream surely begins to unravel. *No matter how similar we are, no matter how much we have in common with our loved one, just as the baby hatches from its mother and eventually finds out that he or she is not the same being as the mother, each of us hatches from the fantasy of perfect union with our idealized lover and discovers that our partner is a separate, distinct, and different person.* In a culture that tries for the sake of fairness and equal opportunity to minimize the discrepancies among people, it comes as a shock to many of us that *different people are, in fact, very different.*

At the heart of almost all marital dissatisfaction is the difficulty of learning to live comfortably with a spouse who thinks, believes, and behaves differently than you do. The essential problem of marriage is not just that we have trouble communicating with each other, but that we come into our relationships with different styles, beliefs, traditions, life agendas, and expectations. We then must struggle to reconcile these differences with our spouse while trying to maintain a comfortable, respectful, and loving relationship. Furthermore, it is commonplace to see marriages in which the partners have initially denied each other's differences in styles, beliefs, and agendas in the service of their desire for togetherness, only to have these differences painfully emerge later, frequently at times of increased stress or anxiety.

Spouses can come to blows over a staggering range of life issues: how to spend money, how to raise and discipline children, how many children to have, how to talk to each other, what to talk about, how to help each other, how much time to spend together, what to do in their spare time, how to have sex, how often to have it, how to relate to each other's families, and so forth. *In your desire to forge an egalitarian marriage, you will be surprised to find that, especially because you have tried to achieve parity, you still will not be able to reconcile many of life's issues. You won't be able to compel your partner to adopt, or even appreciate, all your different goals, attitudes, or styles of behaving and thinking.*

Angela and Steven were very much in love with each other and had a lot in common when they married, even though they knew they had very different personal styles. Though they both agreed they wanted a family and were of the same religious and political persuasion, their ways of thinking about and interacting with the world were very different. Angela was an extremely anxious person and a perfectionist. Like her mother, she lived her life according to a set of principles dictated by what she believed other people expected. In many ways this limited her ability to function freely, but it also made her very sensitive to the feelings of others and made her a paragon of good taste and behavior.

Steven was raised feeling put upon by the demands of his needy, social-climbing family. From the very beginning, he rebelled against many of his family's social preoccupations and instead relied on his own inner values and beliefs to define his actions. Brilliant in his line of work, he set his own course in life. Steven was a "collector" who couldn't throw out old newspapers and magazines and was very disorganized about his affairs. Angela was neat and orderly. Steven didn't concern himself with Angela's discomfort over the mess he made. When Angela complained about it, Steven reminded her that she knew what he was like before they married, so it was unreasonable to expect that he should now change for the better. Steven wanted Angela to stop worrying about other people's opinions, and Angela wanted Steven to be more cognizant of the effect he had on others, including herself.

Steven's lifestyle and limited sensitivity to Angela's feelings began to eat away at Angela's positive regard for him. She responded by becoming distant and critical. She became even more preoccupied with other people's impressions of her and increasingly ineffectual and passive when it came to taking charge of the many tasks Stephen requested of her. His response was to devalue her further and to become more impervious to her criticism. Rather than change for the better, he became more controlling of their life and uncaring of her feelings.

With the birth of their children, their already strained marriage broke. Attempts to get them to negotiate their differences and to treat each other with more dignity failed, and the couple finally divorced.

Use the following questions to open up a discussion about how you and your spouse differ:

- In what ways are you and your spouse different from each other? In what ways are you similar?

- In what important ways do you look at the world, experience things, and have values and goals that are different?

- What are your priorities in life? What are your spouse's priorities? How do the differences cause stress in your relationship?

- Explain to your spouse how these differences affect you. If you don't feel your voice is being heard, ask that your feelings, beliefs, styles, and agendas be taken more into account.

- Do the same for your spouse. Be more aware of the effect that who you are, what you do, and what you want in life is having on your partner.

- Do you or your spouse personalize these divergent priorities? Do you fight over them? Do either of you reject or devalue the other's point of view? Is that necessary or helpful?

- Do you attack, indict, belittle, or devalue your spouse for ways in which he or she is different from you?

- Are you locked into a power struggle over these differences—refusing to give in until your spouse first yields to your point of view?

- Do you feel hurt because what you care about is not as important to your spouse as it is to you?

Ultimately, *your challenge is to acknowledge and accept that the two of you are different people who must live with and reconcile those differences*. Remember that not everything has to change for a relationship to thrive. You can live with many differences. However, if your differences are too great and cause you chronic unhappiness, you may have to face the painful fact that while you may have a marriage of equals, you still may be in a chronically unsatisfying union.

Work 25/8

Our culture of acquisition has made it harder to establish new functional traditions in marriage. More than ever, the material world we live in grades success with a financial yardstick, and, increasingly, both men and women feel they're failing to measure up. Even as women are sharing (and often must share) the financial burden of the family, many men are feeling driven to work harder and to make more money. Even if they wish to participate more as fathers and homemakers, few men are willing to limit their success by working less outside the home so they can take on more responsibility inside. Also, many women who want their husbands to help more around the house aren't willing to have it come at the cost of limiting or decreasing their husbands' incomes or business prestige. In addition, many women now feel the same way about their own careers and income.[10]

Though not all couples struggle with time in the same way, it is an increasingly common predicament. Too often, the couples who come to my office feel enslaved by their jobs, even if they have chosen their own professions and are often their own bosses. Doctors, executives, lawyers, investment bankers, salespeople, and others all seem to work endless hours and/or to regularly travel far from home on long business trips. They live at the office or on the telephone, in airplanes, or in hotels. They spend hours each day answering e-mail. When they're home, they remain psychically tethered to their jobs even without the electronic reins of PDAs, e-mail, and faxes. Alexia, age forty-one, told me, "I remember that when I was a kid, my dad came home at five-thirty sharp. He'd sit down in his chair for a drink and read the paper before dinner. He hardly ever brought work home with him; he was pretty much done for the day before the sun set. I get home at seven, maybe seven-thirty every night, and it's rare that I don't need to put in another hour or two at my computer after I put my kids to bed."

Wives, both those who stay at home and those who work outside the home, complain bitterly about their husbands' lack of availability to them and their children. The men respond that they do what they do for their families, but even under pressure from their wives, they rarely will reduce their devotion to their careers or the income their careers generate. Men are still raised to view money and career success as a primary goal. Wives who are CEOs, lawyers, doctors, and so forth, are able to maintain families only with a great deal of help from child-care workers and/or unusually cooperative husbands, grandparents, or other extended family members. I see a lot of spouses in their mid-thirties who are so busy at work that they barely have time to see each other. When they do, they're often too exhausted to enjoy themselves anyway.

What gets sacrificed on this "altar of acquisition" is free time, downtime, restful time, and restorative time, time to be with other people, children, and each other. Almost every couple I see is suffering from a lack of quality time together even though from all outward appearances they are quite successful. The availability of things to buy has spurred the economy, creating more wealth and further demand for more products for consumers to buy. This, in turn, requires us to work even harder because having more stuff seems so essential to us. We are caught on a materialist treadmill that shows no sign of slowing down. Unfortunately, all this preoccupation with money and consumer success has become a blatant threat to our marriages.

The only way you can make your marriage your priority is to plan for it with as much commitment and forethought as you bring to your work. You need to spell out your responsibilities within your marriage and design an equitable division of labor. But making the trains run on time in your relationship will never be as important as finding the time to enjoy each other's company. Make dates with your spouse—and consider them unbreakable. Limit the amount of time you both talk about work, then pack the discussion away in a bottle until the next day. Feed your interests besides work and home by taking hikes, reading books, going to ball games, playing golf, taking trips to museums, and spending other mutually enjoyable times together.

In a real marriage it is possible to remake the rules of marriage and create a fair division of labor in which you have equal responsibilities, an equal voice, and an equal portion of joy. You'll just have to both work equally hard at it.

CHAPTER 6

Lie: Children Solidify a Marriage
Truth: Your Children Are a Serious Threat to Your Marriage

Children nowadays are tyrants. They contradict their parents, gobble their food, and tyrannize their teachers.

—Socrates

I have known more men destroyed by the desire to have wife and child and to keep them in comfort than I have seen destroyed by drinks and harlots.

—William Butler Yeats

Lee, a woman in her mid-fifties, is seriously contemplating divorce. She tells me that she and her husband, David, have been married since she was twenty-one and he was twenty years old. They have known each other since she was eighteen. In the first years of their marriage, everything was fine. She worked and David went to school to become a civil engineer. Their first child was born when Lee was twenty-five, and their second child came three years later. When I ask Lee if she can tell me when she first began to notice any deterioration in her relationship to David, she pauses and says she isn't sure. "Take your time," I tell her. "Think about it."

After a while she says, "Maybe it was after Chris [their second child] was born. I had my hands full with the kids, and David was beginning his career and working like a madman."

"What happened?" I ask.

"I think we just slowly grew apart," she says.

"How much time did you and David devote to your relationship, to your being adults together?" Lee curves her thumb and forefinger into a zero. "I was taught to devote myself to my children, not to my marriage, and David was taught to focus on work, to be a provider," she says. "David and I did our duty, and now we barely feel connected to each other. When the kids were home, I didn't really notice or care about our lack of connection. Now that they're gone, I realize it was never about the two of us. It was always just the kids, kids, kids. We have no real relationship. I feel all alone."

Of course you always knew that having kids wasn't going to be a picnic all the time. You'd seen your share of exhausted new parents walking around like zombies or bickering over whose turn it was to change the diapers. You'd heard all the jokes about no sex after the baby. You'd rolled your eyes at the litany of after-school activities that parent-friends enumerated: soccer practices, play dates, birthday parties, piano lessons, karate, religious instruction, tutoring. You'd even seen marriages pulled apart at the seams by the stresses of disabled kids. And yet, deep down, you believed that all that physical and emotional hard work wouldn't damage *your* marriage and would be more than compensated for by the pleasures and love that children would bring to your relationship. Or, at least that is what others assured you, and you counted on it as you took the plunge into parenthood.

So why are you having so many pitched battles over whose turn it is to bathe the baby, supervise the homework, or talk to the teacher about little Justin's school problems? You've probably read that most couples fight about sex and money. This is certainly true, but in my experience, the issue of child rearing is just as likely to drain the energy out of a couple and send them into the negative spiral. Unfortunately, children are often the reason that couples end up fighting about sex and money.

The problem is that we want so much to believe in the innate goodness of families and the inherent value of having and raising children that we fail to prepare ourselves adequately for how stressful raising children actually is for marriage. As a result, when trouble starts, too many couples are unprepared and/or too emotionally immature to handle the situation.

Longitudinal studies of marriage consistently show that for the overwhelming majority of couples, marital satisfaction drops precipitously after the birth of the first child.[1] Children are even more problematic for couples in second marriages. It is widely accepted that the high rate of divorce found in remarriages is related to spousal conflicts over children and stepchildren.[2] In my practice, there is no doubt that the number one source of trouble for remarried couples is disagreements over the time spent with and the tolerance for children from previous marriages. The Brady Bunch notwithstanding, remarried families often break down over loyalty conflicts, which create tension between the children of the earlier marriage and the current spouse, with the biological parent caught in the middle.[3]

That children are a seriously destabilizing force in marriage is a very difficult concept to accept in our family-oriented society. *Very few of us are willing to acknowledge fully that the presence of children is perhaps the single greatest stressor in most marriages and a major reason that couples divorce.* We're especially likely to deny this if raising a family is one of the very reasons we've gotten married in the first place. Just as we've bought into the lie of marital bliss, we all want to believe that it is universally and uniformly wonderful to have children, though intellectually we know it is more complicated than that. Of course, having children can be an astonishingly fulfilling experience. But couples are almost always caught flat-footed by how extremely difficult and emotionally and physically taxing it is—and will be, for a good eighteen years or more.

Most divorces take place in families with young children. This creates a terrible irony about family life. It turns out that *the very families we most worry about in terms of the impact of divorce—families with young children—are the very same families that are at high risk, in part because they have children.*

Strictly speaking, of course, children don't directly cause their parents' divorce. However, the stress associated with taking care of children certainly contributes mightily to the demise of many marriages. Having and raising children can work for or against the viability of a marriage. Sometimes it does both simultaneously.

If you want your children to have the best chance to grow up in a secure and intact home, I strongly suggest that you first work to preserve and protect your marriage. *Your children should not come before your marital relationship.* You will *be* a better parent if you *become* a better spouse. Also, by securing your marriage first, there is a better chance that your marriage will survive the difficult years of child rearing and be available to you after your children leave home. Always remember that because we now live longer and have fewer children, the child-rearing years of a couple last a relatively short period of time compared to the many years that spouses will live together with children out of the house. Just a hundred years ago this was not the case; one spouse usually died within two years of their youngest child leaving home.

When Two Become Three

How do things change when you have children? Married spouses without children are focused primarily on themselves and each other. After taking care of themselves, the spouses usually make their "couplehood" a high priority and generally feel closely bonded. The desire for children, in part, grows out of this tight bond between the spouses, and it is assumed by them that having children will further strengthen their union. When the first child is born, a colossal shift takes place in the couple's relationship. Whatever love the spouses felt for each other is usually magnified as they experience a new feeling, the love for a child they made together.

I have heard innumerable times from my patients, most often women, that no matter how much they love their spouses, this love cannot compare to the love they feel for their newborn. Often these confessions are made with both awe and guilt, because many of these new parents feel strange about recognizing and sharing with me that their attachment to their newborn feels more intense than their attachment to their spouse. Many men also report feeling "engrossed" by their newborn children. They knew that they would love their children (though, of course, some had worries about how much), and most had friends who told them that they would experience something altogether extraordinary and new. Even so, many parents are astounded and overcome by just how powerful their love for their babies turns out to be.

In a well-functioning couple, in which both the husband and the wife feel cared for and adequately nourished by the other, the birth of a new child can be one of the most joyous times of their lives, even as they struggle with the new burdens of caring for their infant. The shift in responsibility transforms couples, thrusting them into a new maturing phase of adulthood. Parents are awed by the knowledge that they have undergone this whole miraculous process together. They are like a team that has just prevailed in some great competitive sports event—immensely proud of their feat and full of team spirit. They see themselves and their child as extraordinary. This is why we so often hear people commenting about new parents by saying, "They think they're the first people on earth to have children!" For a while everything is wonderful.

However, as time goes on, the spotlight cast by friends and relatives and their newborn's uniqueness begins to fade. Women move from the starring role of expectant parent and new mother to the far less glamorous role of supporting cast member to a demanding and often irrational child star. "When I was pregnant, I got so much attention," Bethany told me. "Everyone fussed over me constantly. Now I'm just the flabby servant with dirty hair and circles under her eyes who fades into the background while everyone oohs and aahs over the baby." The couple becomes consumed by their newborn's needs. You're all too familiar with this stage: There's little time to sleep, take a shower, read a newspaper, or be alone with each other.

Here's where the lack of a new paradigm for modern couples raises its ugly head yet again. Even if you both promised in advance to coparent equally, to have a truly fifty/fifty parenting arrangement, there's no social framework fully in place to support your intentions. In the majority of couples, men still outearn their wives, so financially it continues to make more sense to have the bigger wage earner return to work. The number of fathers who take paternity leave or quit work altogether to stay home to parent is still vanishingly small. Therefore, for many couples, having a baby induces a shift in the marriage back toward a more traditional gender model of spousal relationship, the consequences of which will reverberate like a sonic boom.

Even contemporary couples that, from the beginning, have chosen this more traditional division of labor don't easily adapt to it. Most modern women, unless they were full-time nannies before they became parents, aren't used to motherhood. And no matter how well prepared they believe they are, few new mothers really appreciate how much work and self-sacrifice is going to be required of them. Also, many new mothers are now older and used to living their adult lives for themselves. For some women, no matter how much they wanted children, this makes the adjustment to motherhood that much more difficult. On top of it all, they're initially asked to metabolize this massive change in their life while coping with the emotional turmoil created by dramatic postpartum hormonal shifts within their body.

In a short time, as the increasingly difficult tasks of child care put pressure on the couple, the spouses inevitably look to each other for more help.[4] Usually it is the mother who turns to her husband for relief from the stresses of prolonged child care. Some mothers are fortunate enough to be able to hire help to spell them or even completely take over large chunks of their child-rearing responsibilities. Others return to work and hire help for that reason. But time away from their babies often inspires guilt, and working mothers still want help when they come home tired from a day out of the house.

Though there are some men who are very dedicated to spending time with and taking care of their infants on a daily basis, most fathers aren't as committed to this task as their wives. More of them still work outside the home and believe that they've fulfilled their obligation to the family by bringing home a paycheck as their fathers did before them. So, when the wife looks for help from her mate, she often doesn't get it, gets it in a limited way, and/or gets it with reluctance.

The difficulty of finding enough time for oneself and the conflicts that develop around the needs of children usually reach their zenith after children become mobile and before they are able to care for themselves, typically between the ages of one and seven years. Although infants require large amounts of attention, they're more manageable because they're more containable. They can be left alone for brief periods, as long as they are in a baby-proofed, safe environment. Once toddlers begin to roam, they must be attended to more or less constantly, except when asleep. This is an exhausting responsibility for a caretaker, and is why getting a child to go to sleep and stay asleep easily and reliably becomes a mission of crucial, almost life-preserving, importance for most parents.

As the child grows, the physical demands on the parents will eventually lessen. However, it is one of life's great ironies that just as the physical demands placed on parents by young children diminish, the emotional burdens of raising querulous adolescents takes over.

The Demotion of Love

This pressure to deal with the demands of infants and young children comes amid the sense that something radical has shifted in the emotional life of the parents. Parents frequently report that their children, not their spouse or their marriage, are the central focus of their lives. Some people actually begin to feel that their children and their marriage are simply one and the same thing. "When Judy and I had Tami, both of us became totally devoted to her. She was the center of our lives. We forgot about ourselves. We only thought about 'the family.' Now Judy and I barely care about each other. We're like two strangers coparenting a seven-year-old." While this can happen to both parents, it is typically the father who feels more of the fall from grace as the mother becomes progressively more deeply immersed in her relationship with her child. "I used to tell Adam that he was the love of my life," Marla confessed. "Then we had Kayla. And I realized who the *real* love of my life was. Adam fell to a distant second." Now the husband has a rival, one whom he cannot beat. Whereas he could easily understand his envy of another man, he can only dimly perceive that he is uncomfortable with his wife's dramatic investment in *his own child*. For most parents, this isn't a serious problem. But if, as the burdens of parenthood mount, the spouses fail to devise a reasonable method of taking care of their children and *each other's* desires, serious tensions can develop. Neither the mother nor the father may end up feeling adequately cared for or *appreciated*, and, in this atmosphere, one may also feel profoundly rejected by the other's intense investment in the children. This is considerably compounded if the couple's sexual life doesn't return to some semblance of its former self.

There is a particularly pernicious, but very common, outcome to this situation. In some couples, the woman transfers virtually all the passion in her life from the roles of wife and lover to the role of mother, relegating her husband to the back burner. Many women describe a seismic shift in their inner life that cannot be solely explained by their husband's limitations or changes in behavior following pregnancy and childbirth. Writing candidly about this in *Talk* magazine, Susan Cheever described her experience this way: "My love for my baby boy had a blinding intensity, as if everything I had called love before had been a shadow of the real thing. . . . In the light of this new passion my love for my husband seemed like old news. . . . The same thing had happened when my daughter was born seven years earlier, and within four years her father and I had divorced. . . . In the *love trance* of mother and child, the father is out of place (italics added)."[5] Women often report that their husbands no longer appear as sexually desirable to them and that they feel less erotic themselves. Their new role as mother seems to eclipse their previous experience of themselves as wife and sexual partner. As one client put it, "I used to get a lot of my self-esteem by feeling that I was attractive to men. It made me feel good about myself, confident and powerful. Now that seems very unimportant to me. My self-esteem comes from being a good mother." Another mother shared this with me: "I used to like to do all kinds of kinky things with my husband. Ever since my daughter was born, that has very little appeal to me."

On the other hand, some men also report finding their wife less sexually alluring as the woman becomes pregnant and takes on the mantle of motherhood. The new identity of "mother" appears to interfere with these men's sexual desire. Many pregnant women find this hurtful, particularly if they themselves are feeling heavy and less attractive. Recently, I asked one troubled couple when they thought their problems had started. The wife said she knew exactly when; it was with her second pregnancy. Her husband hadn't been enthusiastic about the pregnancy and stayed away from her sexually throughout most of it. In her seventh month, while on a vacation, he approached her romantically for the first time since the conception. Somewhat relieved, she began to cry. But her tears put him off. They got into a fight, and he then refused to have sex with her. From that moment, five years earlier, their marriage had continued to deteriorate.

Other men have secretly admitted to me that they were very uncomfortable at the birth of their children when they witnessed the bloody vaginal discharge that accompanied childbirth. They all feared that their wives or friends would be terribly disappointed if they admitted how distasteful the experience had been for them. For many, the experience caused a profound loss of interest in sex with their wives. This emotional reactivity of some men to witnessing childbirth is an underappreciated, but very important, hidden source of sexual tension in some marriages. It needs to be further studied.

Though there are many exceptions, once the child is home, it is more often the man who withdraws from the extra work of child rearing. If he avoids child care, his wife ultimately becomes annoyed with him. If, on top of this, he feels shut out of the mother-child pairing, he often becomes resentful of his wife and even more unhelpful, critical, and angry. His wife gets exasperated by his poor behavior and withdraws further from him, often criticizing him for his lack of help and emotional withdrawal. In this scenario, the wife already feels too pressured by child care, has little patience for her husband's behavior, and sees his complaints and demands as the whining of yet another "baby." Often the husband falls into the "baby" role himself, becoming more and more demanding of his wife and less and less competent as a husband and father. His misguided attempts to get more attention from his wife usually fail, and he ends up unconsciously paying her back for what he perceives as her desertion from their previous life together.

Oh, Grow Up!

When I work with a woman who complains that she finds herself married to another "baby," I first ask if she thought of her husband as a "baby" before the children were born. If the answer is yes, then I wonder what kept her from dealing with her husband's incompetence or dependence before they had children. Was his behavior okay with her then? Did it serve some purpose for her in the relationship? Often, the woman admits that she enjoyed aspects of taking care of her husband before the baby was born. It made her feel he was reliant on her. Others tell me that their husbands' behavior didn't bother them before; they didn't mind it as much. The men didn't seem like babies then, but they do now because of all the new demands on their time and energy. Mothers feel too busy and preoccupied with their new responsibilities as parents to continue taking care of their husbands in the same way. Shouldn't the men understand this and accept the change with more maturity?

I think the answer to that question is "perhaps." If his behavior was acceptable before the birth of the baby, it's not so unreasonable for the husband to assume that things will continue in the same vein. Also, a lot depends on how much modification is being asked of him. I am certainly not saying that husbands shouldn't have to change and grow with the birth of their children; of course they should. However, wives also have to appreciate that their husbands might not experience the need for change as intuitively as they do because men aren't as intimately biologically connected to pregnancy and birth as women are. Women have the nine months of pregnancy to internalize the changes they're undergoing physically and emotionally; men don't have that advantage no matter how eager they are to be full participants in parenting.

If couples are to survive having children, besides asking men to grow up, there needs to be a concern for the father's situation and a greater awareness and sympathy for the primary importance *that wives continue to play in the emotional lives of their husbands.* One patient asked her grandmother what had allowed her to be so successfully married; her grandmother gave her the following advice: "Always remember you are married to your husband, not your children." When I first heard this years ago, I thought it sounded quaint and Victorian, the pronouncement of a woman who didn't work outside the home and had servants to help take care of the children.

Although it's exaggerated, this woman's grandmother was making a useful point. On the other hand, many husbands fail to notice that their wives' lives have radically changed and behave as if everything should be the same as before children.

For the last few decades, in society at large and in many marriages, men's interests and desires have been devalued and thought of as immature. More than ever, we live in a society that appears to put a very high value on the aspects of family life that are traditionally very important to women, such as intimate discussions, emotionality, and family time together. Men's interests, behavior, and traditions, such as nights out with the guys, sports, gadgets, cars, and their common preoccupation with sex are often made fun of in television sitcoms and advertisements. Men are portrayed as stupid, spoiled, demanding, petulant, thoughtless, or foolish. They are seen as adolescent brats, arrogant entitled egoists, whining babies, or sometimes all three at once. One of my female patients regularly opines, "Most men aren't worth the powder it would take to blow them up." This attitude doesn't accept that men have legitimate desires of their own that are typically male. Many wives, once they become mothers, have little patience for those needs and desires, in large part because these needs are perceived as trivial by comparison to the more pressing needs of the children. The women are under enormous stress themselves, taking care of their children, managing outside jobs, and getting insufficient help at home from their husbands. Who has the time for sex, football, or play? "It's his child, too!" is the common refrain. "Why can't he just grow up?"

When men feel chastised and belittled for expressing their desires, they often learn to hide their objections and unhappiness, sometimes for years. However, the unhappiness doesn't always go away and, sooner or later, those unhappy feelings reemerge. Then the men get angry and/or begin to fantasize about life with another, more understanding, sympathetic, and intimately available woman. If no correction is made in the couple's modus vivendi, it is often only a matter of time until the man enacts his fantasy and jeopardizes his marriage. When women ignore male desires, they put their marriage in peril. The dissatisfied, ignored, disappointed, or criticized husband is very susceptible to the interest and devotion of the "other woman." *No matter how strong they look, most men cannot tolerate feeling rejected or unloved by their wives.*

I am *not* blaming overstressed new mothers for their husbands' affairs. I *am* suggesting that parents are in a predicament that requires resolution within the marriage and that women need to acknowledge and appreciate the legitimacy of what their husbands want, even if they cannot fulfill all those wants. Remember, everyone is entitled to want what he wants, whether or not he gets it. The danger is in ignoring or, even worse, belittling those wants.

Also, *the very same warning can be given to men.* When men ignore women's concerns, they also put their marriage at risk. If men don't come to terms with their wives' need for help or companionship, adequately addressing their distress and frustration, they run the risk of leaving their spouse chronically discontent. Many men have little understanding of or sympathy for how difficult it is to stay at home and take care of children, even children who were desperately wanted. Some men act as if they believe child care is easy compared to the "real" work they do in the office. Even if they realize that rearing children is difficult, some men envy the perceived "life of indulgence" that they believe comes to their wives with staying at home—daytime tennis, leisurely lunches. They cannot fathom the complaints of women who are stressed by the responsibilities of housework and child care. Too many men devalue their wives' hard work, often by saying that their mothers took care of them and never complained about it. I often suggest that these adult men ask their mothers if they felt that taking care of children was a difficult or exhausting job. When men do this, they often hear that their mothers felt that child care was, indeed, very hard work, but a job worth the sacrifices they made. Furthermore, previous generations of women usually say that they were raised to become mothers. Many of the mothers of today's grown men say that they felt they had no other choice but to become pregnant and stay home to take care of their kids. Some enjoyed it, but many others have been blunt enough to admit that it was not what they wanted or felt they were meant to do.

When men don't show sufficient sensitivity to the complex issues surrounding modern mothers who either work by staying at home to raise children or work outside their homes and still manage to rear their children, they run the enormous risk of alienating their spouse. Remember, women leave marriages more often than men do. Disappointed, frustrated, overburdened women eventually blame and turn away from their husbands. If they think they can afford to divorce, they eventually may do so.

Though married women are considered about half as likely to have affairs as men are, many do have them, and working women, who have greater opportunity, may be as likely to stray as their male counterparts.[6] A woman who has lost all patience with and sexual interest in her husband can suddenly find herself attracted to a man who initially appears to be solicitous of her and her feelings. "Overnight," as if by "magic," an overtaxed, asexual mother can experience a reawakening of her long-lost romantic desire. This phenomenon suggests to me that the loss of libido that often began with the change in hormones and the physical exhaustion experienced in the weeks after childbirth is frequently maintained by unresolved spousal conflicts and resentful feelings that develop as the couple try to handle the additional burdens of child rearing. I have had many married mothers tell me that for years they assumed they were sexually "dead," only to find out that they were very much alive as soon as they got involved in a new relationship or an affair. Women who for years reported having lost all interest in sex may, with a new lover, find themselves totally preoccupied by sexual fantasies that they never again expected to have. If they are having an affair, these women are then loath to give it up because they feel that they have lived too long without passion. They believe they are deeply in love with a new, extraordinary person.

The affair often becomes the exit strategy from the marriage. Whether it be the husband's or the wife's, this is very unfortunate because, as we discussed in chapter 1, the complexities of marriage cannot compete with the romantic simplicity of an affair. The affair revives the belief in the myths of romantic love and relationship bliss, even though most people who have been married awhile realize that relationships are far more difficult and complex than those myths would have us believe. However, the belief that the problems are mostly the spouse's fault and the hope that a better relationship can easily be had are very strong. As a result, many people leave their stressed marriages through the portal of an affair rather than choosing to stay married and work their way through difficult times.

The Way We Were

It is remarkable how often couples come to see me for help because the issues precipitated by raising children are about to sink them. When I ask these conflicted or distant couples to tell me the story of their marriages, they often become very sad. They wistfully tell accounts of their lives before children. They remember how they used to feel about each other.

If you have children and your love for your spouse has faded, I encourage you to revisit your memories of the time before your children were born to remind yourself of how you used to feel. Let those memories rekindle some of your forgotten amorous fire. Ask yourself when your marriage began to change. Very often you will see that the change came shortly after the birth of one or another of your children. Though every couple has its own story, the similarities are notable. The common themes are (1) exhaustion, (2) mother's feelings of being overwhelmed, (3) her resentment that she doesn't get more help or interest from her husband, (4) father's feeling that he is being unfairly asked to do too much, (5) both spouses feeling personal and emotional deprivation, (6) increasing mutual resentment, (7) the mutual feeling that there is insufficient *appreciation* from the spouse for all that you do, and, finally, (8) the demise of affectionate, romantic, and sexual feelings, which at first may go unnoticed but in the end becomes chronic, making everything worse.

Conflicting Parenting Styles

The added workload of child rearing is taxing enough, but it is even more difficult when spouses' parenting styles don't mesh. Disagreements over how to raise your child can be very intense because parents are very invested in their children, and the conflicts usually represent a clash either of family traditions or of gender-based values. As I explained in chapter 4, most of our child-rearing strategies are forged in the crucible of our original family, either congruent with or in opposition to the way we were raised. When your spouse disagrees with your parenting strategy, it is very hard not to see it as an attack on the bedrock of your most closely held beliefs and traditions.

A common flashpoint for overburdened parents with differing agendas is their child's bedtime. Bedtime is a battleground because children regularly resist going to bed and parents have to get them there for the kids' own good and for their own sanity. It's usually only after the children have gone to sleep that mothers and fathers get some much-needed rest and occasionally even a moment alone together, perhaps briefly remembering what it was like for them before they were parents.

The usual conflict results from the differences in the spouses' desire and ability to set limits on their children and enforce a bedtime. A wife I worked with cannot bear her children crying at bedtime and because of that always ends up sleeping in her children's beds. A husband comes home at night and begins to roughhouse with the children just as the mother is trying to get them in bed. Both of these scenarios lead to bedtime disasters and spousal conflict. Couples who cannot comfortably get their children to *stay in bed* and go to sleep at a reasonable hour become even more stressed and inevitably complain that their spouse is the source of the problem. They say that one spouse is either too strict and, therefore, uncaring, or too lenient and, therefore, is spoiling the children. Often parents become severely *polarized* around issues such as this.

When a spouse disagrees with or even attacks your child-rearing techniques, it's very difficult not to interpret it as an assault on your parenting ability. If you're a stay-at-home parent or if you do the lion's share of child care, a dispute over how to handle the kids can feel like an indictment of your very identity.

Overcoming Overparenting

Sometimes one parent's excessively intense investment in the children causes severe conflict. When one spouse too often puts the children first and the other spouse second, engrossment or involvement with the kids may turn the marriage into a battle between two people, one who feels self-righteous and the other who feels deprived.

Michael and Pilar came to see me because each felt chronically unappreciated and criticized. They didn't know how to get themselves out of their negative spiral. Michael researched and wrote a financial newsletter from home. He did not want the extra expense of renting an outside office. Pilar worked outside the home as a loan officer at a bank. They had a three-year-old daughter, Brett. Since both parents worked, they also had a baby-sitter who came to the house to care for Brett every day. However, even though Michael kept his office door shut, Brett knew that he was at home and frequently burst into his office to see her daddy. Michael didn't love being constantly interrupted, but he did love his daughter, so he generally played with her for a while before asking the baby-sitter to take over again. When Pilar got home from work, after not seeing her daughter all day, she usually took responsibility for making dinner and watching Brett. From the moment Pilar stepped in the front door, Michael considered himself "off duty." It made Pilar feel very pressured and irritable to try to get dinner on the table while being pulled at by her attention-seeking daughter, who was understandably very needy after a whole day without her mom. When Pilar asked Michael to pitch in during this time of day, he thought she was being unfair; after all, he'd already paid a lot of attention to Brett. Now it was his time to catch up on his work. Pilar felt righteously indignant about Michael's refusal to help. How could he not sympathize with her predicament? She had worked all day, too. Both felt the other was being totally unfair. Attempts to discuss the problem at home usually became very nasty and ended with Michael becoming enraged and calling Pilar names. They were deadlocked, and Pilar was seriously contemplating leaving the marriage.

I asked Michael if he could consider keeping Brett out of his home office, leaving her to play only with the baby-sitter during the day so that he could work without interruption. Then he'd be free to play with Brett in the evening and simultaneously help Pilar when she got home from work. At least he'd feel less resentful about her request. Michael felt it would be very hard for him to turn down Brett's many daytime requests for contact. It was extremely important to him to avoid hurting his daughter's feelings. He worried that she would feel that she wasn't very important to him. Meanwhile, of course, those were the very feelings Pilar was having. *She* felt rejected by and unimportant to her husband. I pointed out to Michael that it seemed as if he was more concerned about his daughter's feelings than his wife's.

Michael is guilty of overparenting. While it's true that his daughter needs his nurturing, it is also true that she has two loving parents and a nanny and gets plenty of attention from everybody. Her wonderful baby-sitter is more than capable of taking care of her needs during the day while Michael works. Michael ultimately moved slowly toward supporting his wife rather than gratifying his child's immediate needs; however, it wasn't easy for him. He had been willing to allow his wife to feel rejected, even to risk divorce, to overparent his daughter.

It is remarkable to me how common, though unnecessary and ill advised, this choice is. Often it is not a conscious decision, but one made by parents who got too little or too much nurturance from their own parents. As you may have already guessed, Michael came from a family with two seriously disturbed parents. He felt that he got almost no positive attention as a child and could not tolerate the thought of his daughter having to experience *any* similar feelings. However, his concern for his daughter was threatening his marriage and, therefore, threatening her very future.

Unfortunately, it is not until severe damage has been done to the marriage that some parents understand how their seemingly natural choice of always putting their child before their spouse undermines their marital relationship, actually damaging their children. In the long run, I am convinced that it's more important for your children to see their parents getting along and helping each other out than to get a little extra attention from either one of you. Clearly, I'm not suggesting that children should be neglected, but your spouse also needs to feel cared for. Which do you think is in the long-term best interest of your child: seeing loving parents who cooperate with each other, or having unhappy, angry parents who feel ignored or rejected by each other? If this in any way characterizes your family, it's probably because you've allowed your marriage to get seriously out of balance. You may be caught in a downward spiral, blaming your spouse rather than understanding the stresses of your circumstances and your own choices. Knowing how vulnerable marriages are today, you would be doing something far better even for your children if you remembered regularly to focus attention on your couplehood. Your children cannot always come first.

Overparenting at the expense of your marriage is also a common problem for women. Here's an example. Colin comes to my office complaining that his wife, Irene, has sent him for therapy because he keeps criticizing her for her methods of raising their children, ages four and six. The story he tells is that he and his wife were wonderfully close until they had two daughters twenty-one months apart. Colin loves his children, but he feels that Irene has let them totally control the family. She doesn't believe in setting limits or punishing children for bad behavior. Instead, she believes that everything can be talked out with children in a reasonable way. From Colin's point of view, this doesn't work.

For example, the children insist that Irene stay with them until they fall asleep. Usually too tired to stay awake, Irene lets them fall asleep with her in the marital bed. This means that the couple rarely has the time or privacy to have sex. When Colin wants to go to sleep, he must carry the children from his bed to their own bedrooms. Often one or the other awakens during the night and crawls back into bed with them. When this happens, Colin cannot sleep and feels irritable and angry with Irene, who won't agree to enforce a stay-in-bed rule with the children. More often than not, to get a good night's sleep, he has to leave his own bed and sleep alone in one of the children's rooms.

When Colin complains to Irene that this is no way to live, she tells him that it's common for most very young children to sleep in their parents' bed and, besides, that the kids will outgrow it. From his point of view, things are getting progressively worse. The children never listen to him and do whatever they please around the house. They behave like little tyrants. When Colin tries to set limits or to discipline them, they run to their mother, who contradicts his authority. Whenever he raises objections with Irene about the children's behavior or her lack of support for him, she tells him that he has a problem controlling his anger. He feels hopeless, but he wonders if his wife might be right. Maybe the conflict is entirely his fault because he doesn't seem to be able to communicate with her or the kids in ways that would make them listen.

I asked Colin if he could recall one incident in which his wife agreed with him in the area of child care. He could not. At my request, Irene came to see me and confirmed his story. She readily admitted that she couldn't accept any of his suggestions about handling the children since she felt Colin was too aggressive and didn't understand children or their needs. She believes that parents can always reason with children, even very young ones. She says that this was the way she was raised and she turned out all right. Irene could find no room in the marriage for her husband's opinions about child rearing; he would just have to adjust to her parenting methods because she wasn't going to change the way in which she was raising *her* children. Irene also wanted Colin to stop his irritating attempts to get her to listen to him and to go along with her program. She was adamant that the kids' needs came first. "After all," she told me, "they're only little for a short while, and then they're gone. Colin needs to realize that they've got to be our priority. There'll be plenty of time for us, as a couple, after the kids have grown up." Sadly, *because* many couples think this way, it will not turn out to be true.[7]

I continued to see Colin for a few more years. In spite of his deep frustration, he didn't want to leave the marriage, so we worked on a strategy for tolerating his wife's parenting philosophy, hoping that, in time, it would change. As they grew older in a family without behavioral restrictions, his children became more and more uncontrollable. Two years later Colin reported that Irene had begun to get fed up with their bossy attitudes and frequent misbehavior. She finally agreed that some changes had to be made. She began to refuse the children access to her bed and enforced consequences for their rudeness. As she modified her position, the children's behavior improved. However, to this day, they have attitudes and conduct reflective of their lack of discipline as youngsters. By acknowledging her misjudgment though, Irene helped Colin become less angry. Over time, the marriage settled back down, although Colin had built up a considerable bank of resentment over the way he had been marginalized in the family for years.

The Added Difficulty of Troubled Children

Another significant factor that creates stress on couples is that in certain ways it seems more difficult than ever to raise good children. While all of us tend to hang a golden halo over our own childhoods, conveniently forgetting the risks and dangers we grew up among, the world really does seem like a more dangerous place to raise a child today. If you remember all the ruckus over whether to have a smoking lounge in your high school, you're probably feeling stunned when you read reports about middle-schoolers having easy access to Ecstasy, cocaine, and worse. Kids are having sex younger—and the consequences are higher. You're terrified by reports of school violence and shocked at the idea that your youngsters may be asked to pass through metal detectors on their way to class. You've read reports about escalating rates of teen depression and worry about whether it will claim your kids. If either or both of you work long hours, your children will have less and less connection to you. Inevitably, as your children grow older, they'll increasingly turn to their peers, and the natural influences of their friends will become more seminal than you are to their lives.[8]

Just a generation ago, the really "bad" influence a parent had to worry about was whether their child was "hanging around with the wrong crowd." Today, our kids are bombarded by negative, and often irresponsible, images everywhere they look: movies, television shows, video games, MTV, popular teen magazines, and endless input from the Internet. The sum total of all this is that we live in a world in which parents are less able to supervise their children. The results are that we are losing control of and forfeiting influence over our children at an alarming rate.

Many of the couples who come to my office have seen their

marriages disintegrate under the stress of coping with a troubled child. In the past, some prominent family therapists believed that children with emotional problems actually served as sacrificial saviors of their parents' marriage because their worried parents would focus less on their own marital woes and more on the child's dysfunction. But today, marriages are much less cohesive, and quite the reverse is true. If the marriage isn't satisfying, the parents will eventually divorce anyway, usually blaming each other for their child's problem. Often, if the parents are unhappy, they rationalize that the divorce is necessary to protect the children from the spouse's pernicious influence. Disturbed or problem children unwittingly, and certainly without malice or forethought, add increased stress to their parents' marriage.

Also, it is well known that having a child with any kind of disability, whether emotional, psychological, developmental, or physical, is a major stressor on marriage and that the divorce rate among these couples is much higher than average. It is crucial to acknowledge this additional stress and to seek out professional help early to keep your marriage intact while you cope with this particular burden.

So What's a Parent to Do?

Once you have kids, life and marriage are never the same, for better and for worse. Though some marriages can handle the shift in focus, others are cruelly strained by the transformation and don't survive it. *The most important step you can take is to appreciate, acknowledge, and anticipate that your beloved children can pose a potent threat to your marriage.* We all love our children and want them to feel loved and cared for. However, as we try so hard to be good parents, too many of us neglect our marriages. In the long run, this is a poor choice for our children. The key in negotiating the balance between partnership and parenthood is understanding that you must put your marriage first for the sake of your kids.

Get on the Same Page

It is crucial that the two of you be on the same page as far as child-rearing strategies are concerned. If you can't agree on discipline, bedtimes, and so forth, you will not only confuse your children but also alienate each other. Bringing in an outside parenting expert can help.

When I say "be on the same page," please feel free to take me literally. In my experience, women, even those who work outside the home, do much more of the spadework of figuring out parenthood, not only by spending more time with their kids, but by talking to other parents and by reading books and columns by parenting experts. If this is so in your family, I suggest that the father acknowledge that the mother may be more experienced with the children than he is, at least until he takes the time to read the books or stay at home with the kids. In such a situation, it is useful for the children and the marriage if the father can get comfortable deferring to the mother's opinion on child-rearing issues he has not yet mastered. This doesn't have to be a regular occurrence; it's only that full-time mothers tend to be far more expert on children's issues than busy, out of the house, part-time fathers, and they should be acknowledged as such. However, there is nothing gender-specific about learning how to raise good kids and putting theory into practice. I encourage both of you to share this journey as equally and as practically possible.

Do you and your spouse share the same values? What values do you want to teach your children? Are you and your spouse of the same religion or spiritual persuasion? Have you agreed on your children's religious upbringing? For example, are you both willing to go to religious observances and participate in taking the children to religious school? Talk about these issues and figure out where you stand.

Remember the claims that your families of origin put on you; their influence is enormous when it comes to values, religious upbringing, and child-rearing practices. You and your spouse are very likely to champion different traditions and strategies that mimic the ones by which you were raised or are in direct opposition to them. Talk out your differences and respect that your spouse's methods may not necessarily be wrong if they don't agree with yours.

If you cannot agree on the basics about raising your children, seek out professional help—for the sake of your children and for your own sanity.

Negotiate a Fair Division of Labor

Few people appreciate the sheer number of duties involved in child rearing until they become parents. If you experience tension over the fair division of these jobs, start by making a list together of every child-care responsibility, then decide who is going to take care of what. It's best to put it in writing so that both of you can review it together and discuss any points of disagreement. Unspoken frustrated assumptions about child rearing create conflict or resentment. Don't assume that mothers are always responsible, that if one parent stays home, he or she will be responsible for every child-care duty, or that if one parent works outside the home, he or she is exempt. Here are a few basic questions to start the discussion.

- Will one of you be the primary caretaker of the children, or will you try to share child care fifty/fifty, or somewhere in between?

- If you plan on sharing child care, where will the time come from to meet your increased commitment? What will you have to give up, and how do you both feel about it? If you work outside the home, will you be able to get up at night to care for children and manage your career responsibilities the next day?

- Who in your family will be able to help you with the children? Where will your support come from?

- Can you afford professional child care? How much help do you each want to have? Can you tolerate someone being in your home, living in or helping part-time?

- Does your family tradition lead you to negative judgments of mothers who hire help to assist them in raising their children?

- Who will leave work at a moment's notice to pick up a sick child from school?

- Who will stay home with a sick child? Who will miss work to take the child to the doctor?

- Can you tolerate the involvement of your parents or your spouse's parents with your child? Will you feel comfortable with their more frequent visits? What role do you want family members (grandparents, uncles, aunts, older siblings, half siblings) and friends to play in your child's life?

Balance the Psychic Burden

With some effort, it's not difficult for parents to figure out how to quantify and fairly divide child-rearing tasks. However, it's common for some spouses to forget to factor in more intangible efforts and divide those fairly as well. For example, infants require a steady stream of diapers, clothing changes, bottle paraphernalia, toys, transitional objects, and so forth. The diaper bag needs to be stocked and ready. It's not rocket science to figure out whose turn it is to go shopping for those items. But who makes up the shopping list in the first place? Who will plan ahead for the next change of clothing or shoe size, the new wardrobe necessitated by the changing seasons, or the addition of new foods to the child's menu? Maybe you've already figured out who has to pack up the kids for school or camp—but did you consider who has to do all the work involved in researching the appropriate school or camp in the first place? Who gets on the phone to arrange play dates, soccer pickups, and sleepovers? In addition to maintaining your own schedule, who keeps all the children's appointments in mind and makes them happen smoothly?

In my experience, these more intangible burdens fall mostly to women, even women who work outside the home, logging as many hours at their jobs as their husbands. Once again, modern couples who give lip service to throwing over fusty tradition find themselves hewing to old-fashioned gender roles when it comes time to take care of children. More and more women come to my practice complaining about their husbands' failure to pick up the slack of child rearing and assume their rightful share of the everyday burden.

"Not fair," Neal protests. "I'd be happy to run out to the drugstore and get new diapers. All Rebecca has to do is ask."

"I'm more than willing to take Alexander for new shoes," says Bruce. "Arielle should just tell me what size shoes he's wearing and I'll pick up some new ones."

"What is so magical about looking in the closet and seeing how many diapers we have left?" Rebecca says. "Neal and I are in exactly the same boat. Neither of us ever had a baby before Tamar. I went out and bought Dr. Spock and all the other books. They're there for Neal to read whenever he wants to. I don't have any special skill in figuring this stuff out. I just consider it my responsibility to get in there and do it. Why can't Neal pitch in the same way? Why is it up to me to have to tell him when we're running low on the stuff Tamar needs?"

Arielle has the same grievance and says so with only slight condescension. "First you look inside the kid's shoes to check the shoe size. Then you take the kid to the shoe store and see if the same size fits or if you need to go up a half size or whole size. Then you have to see if Alex likes the style or if he's going to throw a fit because it makes his feet itch. It can take a couple of visits to a couple of stores to get the pair Alex can live with. But Bruce acts like all you have to do is just toss any pair into your cart and you're done. He doesn't get what a big deal it is to do it right. But he'd get it right away, if he just did it for a change!"

When I ask women what bothers them most about what they perceive as an unfair division of labor, they commonly say something like, "It's not enough for my spouse to say he'll do something if I just ask. Why do I have to be the one *asking* all the time? Why is it up to me to have to remember all this stuff and then ask him to do part of it? Why can't we *both* be responsible for figuring it out and dealing with it?"

These women are raising legitimate complaints. Anticipating and planning for the needs of children can be as time-consuming and as wearing on the psyche as the child-rearing chores themselves. *Many mothers will tell you that they maintain an exhausting constant mental awareness of their children's needs, relieved only when they lie down to sleep.* Why wouldn't they feel that sex was the last thing on their minds? It simply isn't fair to expect one spouse to assume all these duties.

On the other hand, it is not uncommon in my practice to meet women who want to be the primary caregiver. They take enormous pleasure and pride in their role as mother, whether they also have full-time jobs outside of the house or not. Even those who work outside of the home and hire help to manage their children see themselves as being in charge of their households. They are aware of the greater opportunity offered woman in the past thirty years, but they continue to find meaning and self-esteem in maintaining the traditional gender roles of wife, mother, and homemaker. A generation ago this was a woman's *only* source of power.

Today, many of these very busy women often don't actually ask for a lot of additional help from their husbands, but they do expect some help and they do expect more appreciation for what they are doing, how hard they work, and how well they do it. In my experience, this complaint often comes from women whose husbands take their enormous outlay of energy and competence for granted or, worse, tend to devalue it and the traditional work of women.

This courts marital disaster. Among the worst marital scenarios I commonly see are the painfully polarized spirals in which women complain that they are overburdened by their child-rearing and homemaking choices, while their husbands respond that these responsibilities are easy to perform and that the complaints are indicative of spoiled, entitled, or lazy women. This, of course, leaves the women feeling unheard and unappreciated, forcing them to complain more, which makes the husbands believe that their wives are "whiners" who have little about which to complain. *Men, beware. Never minimize or devalue the contributions of your wife's role as mother or homemaker, for in doing so, you will create more bitterness than the bonds of most marriages can handle.*

Remember, there is absolutely nothing gender-specific about figuring out what supplies a child needs, calling up a baby-sitter, making a play date, scheduling a pediatrician's visit (and making sure your child is kept current on whatever shots he or she needs for school), or performing any of the hundreds of other largely invisible tasks that raising kids requires. If you feel you're being asked to assume too many of these chores, you must call it to your spouse's attention and ask for a fairer division of labor. It makes no sense to stew and become resentful because your spouse has once again failed to be a perfect mind reader. And if you're the one who has overlooked these psychic burdens, it's your responsibility to dive in—without waiting to be asked.

Again, No Back Car-Seat Driving

Another common complaint I hear from spouses (mostly men) is that whenever they do try to help with child care, the other spouse criticizes their methods. "She sees me diapering Sandy, then marches right over and tells me I'm doing it wrong. So I've just stopped doing it." "Why do we have to do clean up her way? My way is just as good. But she gets on my case if we don't do it exactly the way she planned." "I'd help out a lot more if I didn't have Catherine looking over my shoulder, waiting for me to screw up."

This is a legitimate gripe. Spouses—mostly women—need to realize that if they allocate a child-rearing task, they have to allow the other spouse the freedom to do it a different way or on a different schedule. If they don't, they set up the situation in which one spouse, usually the woman, becomes vastly more expert at a given function, making it more likely that the other spouse won't have an opportunity to learn how to do it or practice it sufficiently to gain the same amount of confidence and expertise. This usually ends up reinforcing the traditional gender-bound roles that the couple was trying to get away from in the first place. (This dynamic and its dangers are beautifully described in Rhona Mahony's *Kidding Ourselves: Breadwinning, Babies, and Bargaining Power*, which offers lots of helpful advice in achieving balanced parenting.)

Another problem is that the more expert caregiver often assumes that there will be big trouble if things aren't done his or her way. More often than not, this turns out to be a signal of underlying anxiety, which the more controlling person has been able to minimize by being very organized and prepared. Often, when faced with giving up some control, the more anxious person begins to worry excessively about terrible consequences happening to a loved one, in this case the child. This tendency to "catastrophize" causes friction in couples when the less anxious person tries to take over the management of the children from the more anxious person. The more anxious parent inevitably becomes fearful, worrying about the potentially disastrous consequences of poor decisions, and then blames the spouse for creating the situations that stir up this terrible anxiety. In this cycle, the more anxious, usually more organized, parent needs to learn to tolerate this anxiety and the less anxious parent needs to respect the other spouse's tendency to worry, trying to more directly help allay the fears.

Vera and Rob have decided that Vera will take care of all the school stuff for their two kids and Rob will handle all the summer camp duties. "The first time Rob was in charge of camp was really hard for me," Vera confessed. "I told him, 'We've agreed that we want to do camp for the kids. You need to appreciate that there are strict deadlines for registration, and that if we miss them, the kids won't get to go. So you have to research everything way ahead of time, and you have to understand that I'm really neurotic about this, so you have to promise me you'll stay on top of it. You talk to the kids, get their feedback, and decide where they should go.' So Rob took care of it completely. And I freaked out because he decided to send our nine-year-old to eight weeks of sleep-away camp. Can you believe it? But Andy said he really wanted to do it, and Rob had always done the same thing as a kid and loved it." Vera was really apprehensive; Andy had never been away from home for more than a few days, and she was convinced that *he'd* be miserable being separated from the family for an extended period of time. But she accepted that, as she had asked, Rob and Andy had discussed the matter and that Rob had made the decision. She forced herself to back off and hope for the best. Happily, Andy adored sleep-away camp, and Vera began the process of learning to trust Rob's judgment.

So, after you've divvied up all the child-care chores, step back and let your spouse handle his or her share. Let your partner make the mistakes necessary in learning any task and try not to criticize or step in to take over.

Say Thank You

If you haven't discovered this already, you'll find that much of your time as a parent is consumed with teaching your children good manners. You'll drill them over and over to say "please" when requesting something and to acknowledge someone else's effort with a "thank you." (If you're not already doing this, now would be a good time to start.) But how often do you actually apply this etiquette to your own marriage? In troubled marriages, spouses generally don't ask for things with a "please" and rarely say "thank you." Often they report that they felt *unappreciated* for long periods of time before their conflict broke out in the open. Have you regularly told your working spouse how much you admire the way she helps support your family and how grateful you are for the income that she brings in? Have you told the homemaker and child-care giver what a great job he is doing maintaining the house and taking care of the children? Or do you just comment when you're disappointed or something's wrong or missing? Often, I find that people are very complimentary of their spouse to other people, but not directly to the spouse themselves. Why is it easier to say something nice about our spouse to a friend than directly to him or her?

A common refrain I hear in my office is, "I just want him/her to *notice* what I do." Not do it, not change it—just notice it. Kelly told me, "I was feeding the kids for the billionth time, and I remember thinking that I was just so sick of the whole thing. No one really gets how fundamentally boring it is to have to make meals for kids over and over. One day, I thought I was just going to lose it. And it just happened then that Barry walked in the door, gave me a big hug, and said, 'I just want to tell you how much I appreciate what an incredible job you do making such great family dinners for us all the time.' It was amazing how much that single comment jazzed me up. It meant so much. Making dinner no longer seemed like such a terrible chore." The smallest gesture of appreciation—a simple thank-you or compliment—is sometimes all your spouse needs to make the world right.

Remember, it is much easier to get someone to listen to what you would like to change if that person feels that you essentially *love*, *admire*, and *appreciate* him or her.

Got a Date?

Make your couplehood a priority as you're coping with parenthood. If you wait until after the kids are grown and gone to resume being "just the two of you," it may be too late. Put your spouse first by committing to regular time alone as a couple. I tell my patients that they must go on dates—just the two of them, no kids and no friends allowed. Ideally, you should do this once a week, but at least once every two weeks. I also encourage you to go away for weekends together without your kids. It is remarkable how quickly couples can (re)find joy in each other by simply getting away from their children for a night or two. Even a rewarding relationship with kids is attention- and time-consuming, making it difficult for parents to be with and available to each other. Find someone—perhaps a family member or child-care worker—with whom you can leave your kids for a weekend and go away together. It doesn't have to be far away or grand, just peaceful and comfortable. Imagine sleeping until you naturally wake up. When our children were young, my wife and I would occasionally just check into a modest hotel less than two miles from our apartment in New York City for an adults-only weekend. We'd go to movies, have dinner, sleep late, and go shopping leisurely without worrying about or being interrupted by our children.

Though some children may protest your leaving them at home, it is crucial for their development, as well, that they learn to tolerate minimal separations like these. It is equally important that your children are given the opportunity to internalize a vision of their parents as a bonded couple. So, whatever the benefit for you of getting away for a weekend, always remember that you are also doing your kids a favor, whether they realize it or not. Try it.

I am often shocked by how many parents of young children admit to me that they actually never go out just by themselves. Even when strongly advised to do it, some parents can't. These people no longer know themselves as a couple. Why does this happen? Often, it's because the chore of finding a reliable baby-sitter and negotiating the acceptable time frame falls to one person, usually the wife, and it can fall so far down on the list of things to do that it slides right off the bottom. You may be understandably nervous about leaving your child with a stranger; you may not feel the pool of available teenagers is responsible enough; you may hate the hassle of begging some adolescent for a few hours of her precious time; you may feel you cannot afford the money to go out. These are obstacles you must overcome; *you absolutely must have time together to revitalize your commitment to yourselves as a couple.*

If you can't find a reliable baby-sitter through referrals from friends, local postings, and so on, you may have to cast your net more widely. Local colleges often have baby-sitting services. Many areas have premium nanny services (which naturally come at a premium price) that offer well-screened, reliable baby-sitters. If you have no grandparents available, consider a baby-sitting swap with another couple. Ideally, you'll develop a relationship with a baby-sitter with whom you have a standing order for service on a regular schedule. If not, trade off the responsibility for hiring the sitter, or negotiate a quid pro quo if it's truly difficult for one person to make all the arrangements. Trade off the responsibility for making the evening plans. Consider a movie, dinner, a play, a trip to a museum or lecture, a ball game or evening of tennis, a window-shopping walk downtown. You might want to make a wish list of things you'd like to do, then see if you can tick them off one by one.

However, if you still find that you cannot regularly leave your child at home and go out as a couple, you will probably have to accept that one or both of you is far too anxious about your child's welfare or has serious separation problems of your own. If this is so, you should probably consult a local professional to get your marriage more balanced before real trouble starts.

Many couples balk at the expense of a regular outing. Depending on where you live, the costs of the baby-sitter, dinner, and movie can easily mount to over $100 for an ordinary night on the town. However, it is less expensive to go out with your spouse than to risk letting your couplehood deteriorate to the point that it ends up in divorce litigation. Also, allocating your money to an evening together actually reinforces your commitment to it. Once you're out the door, try not to talk about the kids. Challenge yourself to talk about the kinds of things that absorbed you before the children.

Remember Sex?

A survey from *Parents* magazine once asked new mothers how they felt about sex after the baby. One woman responded, "Fine. Just don't wake me." There, in a nutshell, is the problem just about every couple brings to me. After two have become three, and the two of you find yourselves coping with exhaustion, loss of libido, the new mother's hormonal changes, lack of privacy, and no free time, it's difficult to believe that you'll ever rekindle the flames that made you a couple in the first place. I'll address this issue in the next chapter.

CHAPTER 7

Lie: The Sexual Revolution Has Made Great Sex Easier Than Ever

Truth: A Media Circus Is in Bed with You, and It's Sabotaging Your Marriage

Love is a dirty trick played on us to achieve the continuation of the species.

—Somerset Maugham

I know nothing about sex because I was always married.

—Zsa Zsa Gabor

Joanne had been married to Robert for seven years. In therapy together, Joanne complained bitterly about their inadequate sexual life. Robert showed so little desire for her that she wondered if maybe he was secretly homosexual. The more she criticized him for his lack of sexual interest, the more he kept his distance. In a couple's session, she spoke of how, all her adult life, she had envied the sexual life of her married friends. "Everywhere I go, I see my married friends and think of what a great time they're having in bed and what I'm missing," she said. Robert, who was sitting next to her, began to squirm uncomfortably.

I asked her which of her many women friends she envied the most for her sexual life. She seemed surprised by the question and told me that she had no idea because she had never discussed sex with any of these women. She just *assumed* that they were all having great sex with their husbands. "Why," I asked, "wouldn't they assume the same about *you*?" She said that she had never thought of that, and then, after some thought, voiced a common concern. "But aren't there some married people who really do have good sex lives?" she asked.

Of course, many married couples have fulfilling sex, but there are also many committed couples who struggle with sex and rarely speak of it to their friends. Joanne's mistaken idea that all her married friends were having better sex than she was adding to her resentment of her husband and making them both feel worse than they needed to. It was skewing their relationship, making it impossible for them to improve their situation.

Over a period of a few months in therapy, after years of frustration and bad feelings, this woman and her husband went on to develop a more satisfying sexual life together. At the end of their work with me, they wondered why they had waited so long to get help and felt badly that they had wasted so many years stuck in a condition that they didn't know how to improve. The key to their success was accepting that they had bought in to a lie, a lie that suggests it should be easy to have great sex during a long marriage and that everyone else is having it. A corollary assumption is that if you're faltering in the bedroom, your marriage is doomed. This belief made it impossible for Joanne and Robert to openly address their problems. Understanding the forces that made it so difficult to be sexually comfortable together helped them repair their sex life.

When you're in bed with your spouse, the two of you are never alone. Between the sheets with you are a thousand voices and images telling you how great sex is supposed to be, how ripe for the picking your most luscious fantasies are. Yet you're in bed wearing boxers and old T-shirts instead of Victoria's Secret loungewear, going over paperwork from your briefcase, checking your e-mail from work, trying to read a few pages of *People* magazine or poring over bills before the baby starts crying again. Suddenly, it's all too clear. You can never have the sex you're always fantasizing about and can rarely enjoy the sex you get. You think you are an intelligent person, part of an intelligent couple, able to make the separation between the fantasy of sex and the reality that is your life. However, the turning of sex into a commodity has made such deep inroads into every aspect of our lives that mental control over our sexual expectations is almost impossible. Our bombardment with sexual images and the fantasies they excite are now influencing our feelings about our spouses.

The Sexual Revolution Will Be Televised

Beginning in the 1960s, America underwent a "sexual revolution." In essence, sex came out of the closet. The idea that sex should be fun, available, and enjoyable to everyone was, more or less, a new concept. In the previous century, sex was something "nice" people allegedly didn't think too much about and "nice" women weren't supposed to be interested in it at all. This has all changed. Now the expectation is that everyone is supposed to be interested in sex and to be good at it as well. Today, if you aren't very interested in sex, or not particularly skilled at it, you and others will wonder what is wrong with you.

At the same historical time that men and women are trying to cope with their changing gender roles and responsibilities within marriage, they're also being torn between competing media- and culture-driven visions of who they're supposed to be sexually. In the dating game, women feel whipsawed between the *The Rules*[1] paradigm, which suggests that they return to the strategy of their great grandmothers, manipulating men by tricking them into the pursuing position, and the *Sex and the City* paradigm, which makes it chic to be sexually proactive without being accused of being "slutty" or overly aggressive. Men tell me they want their wives to be more sexually aggressive, and then find themselves haunted by the traditional paradigm that says that men are "supposed" to take the initiative. Even when couples do a remarkable job of negotiating these tectonic shifts in sexual roles, it's noteworthy how many of them feel that someone is looking over their shoulder, judging them on their sexual performance. Often, the voice criticizing them turns out to be their own.

Increased expectations about sexual fulfillment are putting a strain on almost all marriages, but particularly on those marriages in which sexual pleasure is difficult to achieve or sustain. I can tell you with absolute assurance that sexual problems are common in marriage. But, for the general population, this is still a big secret. It is not the subject of your average dinner-party conversation. In many couples, one or both partners experience difficulties with sexual desire or performance. Often these difficulties are by-products of interpersonal tension between the spouses. However, just as often, they are the result of one partner being *temperamentally* less sexually driven, or the consequence of changes in desire and function that accompany childbirth, parenthood, and aging.

If a couple is having trouble with the sexual aspects of their relationship, if either spouse in dissatisfied, and the partners are unwilling or unable to fix it, there is a very good chance these days that one or the other is either going to have an affair[2] or leave the marriage to experience a more fulfilling sexual life. This is another example of how the institution of marriage has changed and become more fragile. This would rarely have happened prior to the sexual revolution. We now consider it our God-given right to have fulfilling sex lives and are incredibly intolerant of anything less. I've found this to be equally true of women and men. We have no template for how to work harder to be sexually compatible if we're disappointed with this aspect of our marriage.

Porn Goes Public

The sexual preoccupation of the media industry has changed dramatically in the last fifty years and is having a powerful influence on our image and attitudes toward marriage. For example, when I was growing up, there were no overtly sexual scenes in American movies. Today, explicit sexuality is not only a part of many movies, but is particularly designed to appeal to adolescent audiences. Almost all of us have seen pornography or overtly sexual pictures. *Playboy* and pornography existed forty years ago, of course, but they weren't as explicit or readily accessible. We are inundated with images of endless sexual activity in ways that were never feasible or imaginable even in the recent past. These ubiquitous scenes influence us and set up standards in our mind. We long to experience the same excitement for ourselves, and, when we don't, we're easily disappointed.

The pornography trade floods magazine racks, video shelves, and the Internet with images of women who are willing to engage sexually in whatever men wish. In a porno movie, the woman never says no. She's always available and always interested in sex. She always seems to love it, never gets enough of it, and will do whatever the man wants. If she's not pleasing, all you need to do is double click on another site or eject the tape and put on a new one. Eventually every man can find the video woman who looks exactly right and does exactly what he desires—just not to him. In pornography produced especially for women, the men all have great bodies; they behave sensuously, have unfailing erections that last until the woman is completely satisfied, and never leave the bed or fall asleep before the woman wants them to. They are experienced, perfect lovers.

You don't need to be a porn connoisseur to see all this sexual imagery; it's on display everywhere you look. Consider how much of it comes into your life practically unbidden. Turn on your TV to catch a harmless sitcom and you'll discover that we've come a long way since Ricky and Lucy's twin beds were chastely separated by a nightstand. Virtually every sitcom—even those broadcast during what used to be quaintly called "the family hour"—features characters jumping into bed with one another after a courtship that lasts for about the time it takes to drink a grande latte. Sex sells virtually every product, from cars and perfume to electronics and pet food. Women's magazines run earnest articles on balancing work and family life next to how-tos on giving better oral sex.

"Sometimes I watch *Friends* with my kids," Joy tells me, "And I have to remember to say to them afterward, 'You do know, don't you, that not everyone jumps into bed with everyone else after the first date?' And then I realize that we've all come to expect the characters to do that, and we like them so much that we don't think it's a weird thing for them to do. I find myself wondering what kind of subtle messages TV shows are sending my kids, and then I realize I'm getting those same messages myself."

However, when the TV is turned off, real life awaits. Then we have to go home and get into bed with our real spouse—familiar, tired, frazzled, angry, fed up with the children or with work or with us for acting so badly that day. It's a far cry from the movies, whether pornographic or "Hollywood." We have some control over the images we see on the screen, but little control of the person to whom we are married. In order to get that *real* person to make love to us, we have to behave in a way that fosters and maintains his or her fondness and sexual interest.

Of course, we know that real relationships aren't the same as those we see in the movies, that real sex isn't a porno flick, and that real men and women aren't staring out at us from the pages of the magazines. Nonetheless, no matter how hard we try, in most of us there is this alternative image of life eating away at our willingness to live within reality. When you flip through a magazine, it's very hard to remember that the hand-picked model has been artfully posed, painstakingly made up, and airbrushed to within an inch of her life. Though you can watch a porn video and picture the director asking the actors to simulate desire on cue, have you never compared yourself or your spouse to that centerfold or porn star and found reality disappointing? These images excite our fantasies of having a perfect sex life. If only our life could be more like what we see in the movies, or sex more like the kind viewed on our favorite steamy video, perhaps then we could feel better about what we have.

This is not to say that pornography should be illegal, or for that matter, kept from adults. It's just that we need to be much more aware of how its pervasive availability in our lives has changed our expectations about sexual behavior and sexual functioning within marriage. What we see displayed in the media frequently reflects and, in turn, influences our attitudes about sexuality.

Many married couples are able to sustain an excellent sexual life for many years, and many well-functioning couples use explicitly sexual materials to enhance their sexual experiences. However, for others, romantic life is not as fulfilling. Many people have difficulty functioning sexually and many in our culture are still very uncomfortable with sexual matters. Though sexual advice and help are widely available, most couples who struggle over sex don't avail themselves of that help and wait far too long to work on their problems and dissatisfactions.

One patient told me that throughout her thirty-five years of marriage, whenever she and her husband had sex, she felt like "a whore" because her husband was never tender toward her or interested in her feelings. She felt he just "used" her for his sexual gratification. Yet she could never bring herself to voice her unhappiness, so her husband never knew she craved a change. Countless people choose to live with their sexual frustrations or unfulfilled fantasies if they have a generally satisfying relationship otherwise. However, if other aspects of the relationship are frustrating or, worse, demoralizing, the lack of sexual gratification will often drive us to seek out relationships that look more like the ones we have seen projected on screen.

The media images flooding our senses do not *cause* us to leave our relationships and go looking for something more gratifying, but they do help *entice* us into believing that there is something more explicitly wonderful out there, that someone else has it, and that we, too, must be free to get it. Therefore, *people in unsatisfying relationships should be aware of their particular vulnerability. There is always a seductive image of a better sexual life as close by as the nearest television set.*[3]

The Death of Desire

At the same time that we're told that great sex is our birthright, many of us have heard that if we're lucky enough to stumble onto great sex, once we're married it won't last. It is a testament to our mental agility that we can simultaneously subscribe to these two competing lies about marriage. On the one hand, we cherish the lie of romantic love and marital bliss. On the other hand, we also believe that sexual attraction to that very soul mate doesn't last forever. Many of us have come to believe that the way we're biologically hard-wired makes us incapable of maintaining sexual passion with the same partner indefinitely. We worry that between spouses, "familiarity breeds contempt"; that sexual excitement requires novelty in the form of endless new partners.

I can't lay all of this at the feet of the cultural bath we bob in, even though it contributes significantly. The bad news is that there seems to be some justification for these beliefs. Just as we seem to have a built-in biological capacity for attraction and attachment, there is reason to believe that there is a limit to our capacity to remain intensely sexually excited and preoccupied with one lover. The emotion of intense romantic passion requires but also creates, in a reinforcing loop, the release of biochemical substances in the brain known as excitatory neurotransmitters. These substances also influence portions of the brain that control perceptions, thoughts, feelings, and moods, which in turn drive our actions. In the process of falling in love, the power of these chemical responses is usually so overwhelming that the whole body gets involved in the process. Responding to and driven by the release of "love" hormones and neurotransmitters, our pulse quickens, we get flushed, our perceptions become narrowly focused on the loved one, and, often, when we are near the exciting person, or just think about him or her, we become sexually aroused. Being "in love," in short, is a powerful physiological, biochemical, neurohormonal state. In this sense, when we fall in love, we fall out of control. We no longer respond rationally to our experience.

In this intense irrational state, which is both tremendously exciting and dangerous, most of us fiercely idolize the object of our affection. We are unaware of how little we actually know about the person in question, and often we don't care. And yet, falling in love is biologically one of the most pleasurable experiences available to us as human beings.

The fact that we don't seem to be biologically programmed to maintain this intensely elevated state of arousal for extended periods of time is probably a good thing. Imagine a world in which all men and women who fell in love were biologically driven to remain in that highly aroused state forever. A lovesick man or woman floating around in the haze of infatuation is seldom a paragon of focus or productivity. Social progress would come to a standstill. Work would be impossible.

From an evolutionary standpoint, it makes sense for humans to experience intense physical attraction; that's how babies get made. It further makes sense that passion must ebb so that a couple can focus on raising those children without the dangerous distraction of intense infatuation. In our distant past, those who were more gripped by passion than survival would be less likely to repel a real threat. Even today, we see what happens to people who become permanently excited by what they call "love." They're not able to gain control over their emotional lives when they fall in love and frequently fall to pieces when disappointed by a lover. Though they experience love as euphoria, it can rob them of the ability to function. In psychological terms, it often represents extreme dependency or the need for emotional fusion. We're meant to soar with love, but we must be able to gently fall back to earth afterward.

Even though it makes evolutionary sense, let's admit that losing the ability to sustain that peak intensity is very disappointing. It's part of the endless conflict we have about marriage. As Richard Rodgers and Lorenz Hart put it, we are always "falling in love with love," but feeling uneasy when it wears off. Many of us assume (incorrectly) that it means that we're no longer *in* love; we've lost the spark. We feel disillusioned, saddened, and cheated when we experience the loss. Many relationships break up at this point, or sometime soon after, because one or both members of the couple cannot tolerate living without the intense flame-throwing conflagration of new love.

The truth is that long-term relationships require the transformation of the intense excitement of "falling" in love into a more sustainable, somewhat less intense, experience of loving. *Loving* over time *takes patience*. It requires really getting to know your lover as a person and as a friend. Many couples don't realize this and cannot or don't know how to make this crucial transformation. Others who try to make the change don't know how to make it fulfilling. Spouses with either of these problems will find that their marriages are exceptionally vulnerable to disappointment and to fracture, especially at times of increased stress. Those who are disappointed with their love life will find it very easy to fall in love with a new partner and to stray from their marriage. Today, with the relaxation of our traditional religious and social taboos against sexuality and affairs, and the increasing acceptance—even expectation—of divorce, more and more couples separate because one or both spouses seek to reexperience the familiar psychobiological "high" of *falling* in love.

Fortunately, though most humans are not biologically or culturally programmed to *sustain* intense feelings of *infatuation* for their spouse, it appears that we are able to reexperience very passionate loving states for that partner intermittently. *Passion can regularly reemerge in an ongoing relationship, and this resurfacing of passion on a recurrent basis deepens and expands the emotional connection between two people, making an enduring commitment to another person exhilarating and fulfilling.* Couples in long-lived marriages don't have to settle for a passionless love life. You don't have to live feeling emotionally or sexually bored. Mature love is more than comfortable; it can be exciting and enticing. Your spouse can be your lover. I promise you that if you had those sexual sparks at the beginning of your relationship, there is every reason to believe that you can reignite them now.

On Golden Puddle

The problem of love's labors lost is further compounded by enormous confusion about the nature of love itself. There are many types of love, and they are all very hard to define. We use the term *love* to describe the intense, highly sexually charged attraction that two people can have for each other shortly after they meet, as well as the satisfying companionship and intimate caring that can develop between two people who have lived together for half a century.

However, the mass media tends to recognize only the whiz-bang fireworks of instant attraction. In our culture, there is a ceaseless glorification of young love and only rare validation of mature love. When we think about great, heroic love, the adolescent longings and anguish of Romeo and Juliet come to mind much more easily than the connection and caring of the couple in *On Golden Pond*. Primed by ubiquitous romantic comedies, TV shows, magazines, and other mass entertainment, most of us want to experience love the way we did in our youth. Our expectations of what "real love" is are constantly being raised even as our tolerance for accepting what we have is lowered. Even my middle-aged clients complain that they don't feel they're in love because their feelings aren't the same as those they remember having when they were teenagers, when the mere brush of a hand could set them on fire. Though they've learned a great deal about love and relationships since then, they're still yearning for the naiveté of adolescent love.

The problem in long-term marriage is that in order for passion to be sustainable over time, the spouses have to remain positively connected. And this is not always easy to do. Passion and sexuality die when resentment and conflict grow in the wake of disappointment and criticism. Passion and sexuality die when emotional distance creates a loss of interest and involvement in the marriage. And what is most amazing is that no matter what the emotional cause is, it always manifests itself in the same way. It always feels as if you just don't find your spouse sexually attractive anymore. It simply feels as if your sexual interest has worn off—you've gotten bored.

Many of us experience this common occurrence of loss of passion as so disappointing that we forgo our relationship entirely. We are unaware of the emotional process involved and are therefore unwilling to work on the removal of the common impediments to renewable love. What's more, in our highly sexualized culture, when we're already vulnerable we're lured away from our marriages by ubiquitous images of fulfillment elsewhere. Too many of us give up the hope of passion with our spouses without knowing that we can revitalize our relationships and our sexual lives.

Sex Isn't Just About Sex

At the beginning of a relationship, most couples consider themselves sexually compatible because the flames of infatuation help them overlook most of their partner's sexual flaws or differences. In time, many couples become sexually more distant, first, because their sexual differences become more apparent to them, and second, because their inability to manage conflict inevitably causes some alienation in the relationship. Hidden resentments transmute into inhibition, detachment, and loss of interest in sex. Resentment and/or anxiety can transform the image of a loved one from sexually exciting to revolting. If you're not having sex, or have lost your interest in sex with your spouse, chances are it's because your marriage is involved in some kind of negative emotional spiral. Improving your communication skills, resetting the emotional atmosphere of your relationship, and getting emotionally closer and more vulnerable to your spouse will usually allow your libido to find its way back into your marriage. The feeling that your spouse likes, cherishes, admires, and appreciates you generates and constantly renews love, passion, and heightened sexuality. These feelings "turn on" mature couples. Many long-term relationships suffer because we don't associate "best friend" feelings such as admiration and appreciation with the exciting feelings of sexual desire. However, over time, without the former the latter cannot exist.

By the time Bonnie came to see me, she'd been complaining for years about the frustrations of her marriage to Sam. Very unhappy with the way she was treated, she portrayed Sam as a difficult person, "obstinate, opinionated, and thoughtless—the epitome of male self-absorption." Though she regularly pleaded with him to do so, he refused to see a therapist. This finally brought Bonnie to the end of her rope.

In our sessions I tried to help Bonnie see that Sam's thoughtlessness precipitated old feelings about her own similarly frustrating and difficult family, making it especially hard for her to cope with his admittedly problematic behaviors and attitudes. Nevertheless, as time went by, Bonnie's feelings for Sam continued to deteriorate. One day, she reported that she no longer found Sam physically attractive and that for months she'd felt revulsion at the thought of his touching her. Feeling sexually dead in her marriage was the last straw; Bonnie wanted a divorce.

Again, I proposed a joint session as a last resort. Amazingly, probably because he sensed that it was either show up or go through a divorce, Sam accompanied Bonnie to my office.

Although he plunked himself down in one of my chairs, Sam made it very clear that he was in every other way having an out-of-body experience. He didn't believe in therapy, but he had no alternative suggestions for how to help Bonnie with her dissatisfactions or to preserve his marriage. He believed that Bonnie needed psychiatric help because she was chronically dissatisfied with her life. He assumed that something was seriously wrong with her.

We engaged in a long discussion about Bonnie's family, and I agreed with many of Sam's criticisms of their influence on her. Bonnie openly acknowledged the truth of what he was saying about her parents, and Sam, seeing that he was not the subject of attack, gradually began to warm to the session. He listed all the things he did to be helpful to Bonnie, like doing the couple's laundry and fixing things around the house. I then asked Bonnie and Sam to do one of the exercises mentioned in chapter 1 of this book. I asked each of them to write down the three most important ways they show their love to their partner, and then the three ways they would most like to have their partner show love to them. Without doing it, Sam immediately grasped the point of the assignment: "You're trying to tell me that though I feel like I'm doing a great job with my wife, I may not be doing the things that Bonnie needs me to do for her." "And," I added, "she may think she's doing a great job for you, but she may not be giving you what you most want from her."

Bonnie explained that what she wanted most from Sam was the feeling that he would take what she said and felt into account. When she felt he was discounting her feelings, she was too hurt to appreciate anything else he did. Bonnie told Sam that he was correct when he noticed that she was acting angry and abrupt like others in her family of origin. As a little girl, she'd always felt that no one cared about her feelings. (As far as Sam could see, this was still the way it was with her family.) This childhood experience made it very hard for her to live with his abrupt, uncompromising style, which so reminded her of the way she was treated by her parents. She felt she had to protest.

Immediately, Sam exclaimed, "But that's just the way I am. My whole family is like that! It's not about you. Where I come from, we fight for everything!" Sam then told us that his parents were incredibly anxious people. Immigrants to this country, his father was perpetually frightened that there wouldn't be enough money to live on, and his mother was simply "a nervous wreck" who couldn't drive or even leave the house alone. She still called him long distance to make sure that he was safe if she heard it was raining in New York City.

"In my family," Sam said, "you learned early that everything you wanted was going to be a fight. And even then, you probably were not going to get it. If you don't take care of yourself, you just get walked over."

"Well," I asked, "what if fighting from the start, automatically saying no to everything first, actually makes you sound to Bonnie the way your father sounded to you. It then makes her want to give you less because it makes her feel hurt and angry, just the way both of you used to feel as children?" That had never occurred to Sam.

There were several powerful forces at work here. First, Sam and Bonnie had bought into the lie that they'd easily be able to pick and choose the traditions and behaviors they desired to emulate from their families of origin; they didn't realize how they were unconsciously reenacting the very dynamics that had plagued them when they were growing up. Second, their growing *emotional distance had created physical distance*. Then, without the intimacy of a sexual life, their emotional distance widened further. When Bonnie felt repelled by the thought of sex with Sam, what she was really feeling was resentment and hopelessness, which she transformed into revulsion and distaste, the complete repudiation of her sexual interest in her husband. In the end, Bonnie's intolerance for living with a man to whom she was not attracted made leaving the relationship more appealing than trying to salvage it.

I explained to this couple how they'd become emotional tuning forks for each other: Sam's belief that he always had to be strong and fight for everything, even for his independence, interacted with Bonnie's sensitivity to feeling ignored, dismissed, and attacked. Her angry reaction to feeling ignored then reinforced his belief that he had to fight for everything in life, which further exacerbated Bonnie's feelings of being attacked, killing her attraction and her sexual desire.

As the spouses gained some insight into the influence that their conflicts within their families of origin were having on their marriage and began to practice better communication skills (outlined in chapter 2), the emotional climate between them lightened.

A few weeks later, after their session, I went to the waiting room to get my next patients. There I found Bonnie and Sam holding hands, giggling and looking into each other's eyes, clearly flirting. They looked like two young lovers on a first date. During her next session, Bonnie confirmed that she once again found Sam to be sexually attractive and wanted to resume their love life.

"I Love You More Today Than Yesterday"

Couples who successfully handle or resolve their emotional issues, and stay out of or get out of downward emotional spirals, regularly report that they feel *more* in love with each other over time than when they first married. How is this possible? Since resentment and bitterness create the loss of passion, by reversing the emotional atmosphere of your marriage, by solving problems as a team rather than blaming each other for them, genuine, intensely loving and sexual feelings lying dormant can once again come alive. Furthermore, the capacity of spouses to learn to work closely together successfully in facing life's difficulties and challenges promotes optimism, hope, ever-greater closeness, love, and intimacy. The pleasures of shared experiences, companionship, and teamwork engender trust, comfort, and shared joy. All of this leads couples who have successfully worked to improve their marriage to feel more in love "as time goes by."

The End of the Affair

It may seem obvious to you that when people feel hurt or angry, they lose interest in sex or actively withhold it. However, when I counsel couples shattered by an affair, they're often shocked and surprised to discover how much they have avoided acknowledging these feelings and working on the emotional dissatisfactions that led to one or both partners straying. Going outside a marriage for sex may, in the end, have less to do with the sex itself than the quality of the spouses' emotional relationship.

John, forty-five years old, had been having an affair for eleven months with a woman he met at work. Married with children, she had just left her husband and wanted him to commit to a life with her or, alternatively, agree to stop seeing her so she could let go and look for another relationship.

Sitting across from me, John appeared the paragon of self-control. He didn't know what had led up to his having the affair. He was aware that he and his wife had been through some rough times and had different opinions about many things, but until the past year he'd always been a faithful spouse. Only on questioning did he admit that for the past six or seven *years*, his sex life with his wife had been poor. Maria had lost almost all interest in lovemaking and had told him more than once that sex no longer mattered to her. Nonetheless, he kept asking her for sex, and she'd occasionally agree, although sometimes she'd make him wait for hours, wondering whether she would actually participate or not. When they did make love, he felt she was just counting the minutes until he ejaculated so she could end the ordeal. She never moved or made a sound, but instead just lay passively beneath him.

After hearing this sad story, I looked at him and said, "That must have been terrible for you. When a man feels that his wife is no longer physically attracted to him, it's very sad. It sounds like it was very humiliating for you to have to beg for sex in that way." At this point, John began to sob.

Surprisingly, John was unaware that his feelings about his wife's sexual rejection of him had anything to do with his decision to begin the affair. John was one of many people I see (men and women alike) who take actions without making connections to the underlying feelings that compel them. This is particularly dangerous in marriage because it prevents the possibility of finding a resolution of the interpersonal difficulties before serious damage is done to the relationship.

Nonetheless, John described what it felt like to be with a new woman who loved to be with him physically, what a difference it had made to him, and the way he felt about himself and life in general. He didn't know if he could ever give that up. Yet, he still thought his wife was a beautiful, desirable woman. He felt wildly conflicted. On the one hand, he felt entitled to a fulfilling sex life; on the other, he didn't want to leave his wife and break up his family. He said that for years Maria had been preoccupied with and embarrassed by the minor changes in her physical appearance brought about by pregnancy and childbirth. She was constantly complaining that she felt fat, no matter how many times he reassured her to the contrary. He felt sure that her feelings about her body had a lot to do with her loss of interest in sex. Now he was considering divorce, but his wife was adamantly against it. In fact, she was begging him not to leave. "Now that I might be out the door," he said, "she seems to want to have sex with me all the time."

John explained that he used to feel hurt when he had to work late in his nearby office, and Maria never accepted his invitation to come and visit him. He'd felt lonely and unappreciated. However, after he'd brought up divorce as a realistic possibility, she'd arrived at his office one night dressed in a trench coat, wearing nothing but panties underneath. He cried as he told me that he had been unable to feel even slightly sexually aroused when she exposed herself to him.

I said that this was understandable because he had been very angry with Maria for a long time and apparently remained unaware of just how angry he was. I guessed that he had experienced her attempt at sexual reconciliation as being "too little, too late." He nodded his agreement. I then suggested that he now had a very big decision to make about his life. He had to decide whether or not he loved Maria enough to begin to forgive her for the hurts he felt she had inflicted on him and to give her and their marriage another chance. I was sure that if he could truly forgive her for those hurts, he would soon find her sexually desirable again. However, he wouldn't be able to forgive her until he told her how deeply hurt (not angry) he'd been by her years of sexual rejection. (Remember, to communicate most effectively, it is crucial to always speak of *your hurts* and anxieties before you discuss your anger. This automatically diminishes your spouse's need to defend him or herself from your attack.) John also had to tell Maria that he was still afraid that if he did forgive her and allowed himself to love her and be vulnerable to her again, she would revert to being the same asexual person she had been for the past seven years. For things to get better, Maria had to assure him that she wouldn't reject his attempts at intimacy the moment she again felt secure in the marriage.

I continued to see John alone. He also had a lot of atoning to do. He had to apologize for the affair and tolerate a prolonged state of suspiciousness and insecurity from his wife. He had to acknowledge and accept that *his* choice to have the affair, rather than to face his marital problems head on, had badly damaged his wife's trust in him and the marriage. He had to take Maria's complaints about his workaholism seriously and directly redress them; ignoring his wife's pleas for him to do something about this probably had contributed to her hurt feelings and sexual withdrawal. I doubted that it was simply Maria's concerns about her body image that prompted her sexual withdrawal. Perhaps her annoyance with his work habits was why she hadn't accepted his invitations to visit his office at night before; she might have been worried that he would take such visits as her tacit approval of his being away from home for so many hours. I thought that John's need to work so hard, make so much money, and achieve such prominence was his way of compensating for his underlying unhappiness and insecurity. He had bought into the lie that he who has the most toys wins. Actually, it is he (she) who has the most fulfilling marriage who truly wins.

Later, when I met Maria for a joint session, she told me that she never worried about her loss of sexual desire. Amazingly, neither had she considered how sexually rejecting her husband for years might have dire consequences for his feelings toward her and, therefore, their marriage. She had been living the lie of marital bliss and unconditional love, the belief that once she and John were married, she'd be able to count on his faithfulness, love, and support no matter how she behaved. It never occurred to her that John would take his life in his own hands and fashion a romantic and sexual life without her.

Over a two-year period this couple worked very hard to resolve the pain of Maria's sexual withdrawal and John's affair. In time, they were able to reconstruct their marriage and are now doing very well.

Sex on the Scale

Do you remember that classic scene from Woody Allen's movie *Annie Hall*, when Diane Keaton's character complains to her psychoanalyst, "We have sex practically all the time—three times a week," while in split screen Woody Allen's character is simultaneously bemoaning to his psychoanalyst, "We practically never have sex—only three times a week"? It reinforces a popular stereotype: Men are constantly sexually hungry and have to beg or cajole their mates for a crumb of intimacy, while women are sexually uninterested, pleading exhaustion or headaches. In truth, gender is much less relevant here than most people might expect. In my practice there are as many women complaining that they have married men with constitutionally less sexual drive, creativity, and sense of adventure as the other way around. It doesn't matter whether you conform to or defy the stereotypes; what matters is how satisfied you are right now with your sex life and how this affects your marriage.

If you have sex once a day, once a week, once a month, or once a year, and you're both honestly fine with it and your relationship, you don't have a problem. However, if you're far apart in terms of your sexual desire and interests, whether or not your partner raises it as an issue, you need to reevaluate and take action.

My experience tells me that all aspects of sexuality exist on a continuum encompassing an enormous range of diversity. Some people of both sexes seem to have very little interest in sex, while others tell me that sex is their constant preoccupation.

There's an enormous variation in what we do and don't find attractive, and in what turns us on. If we take into account all this variation and accept the complexity of sexual reality, what does that mean for marriage? Simply put, *you have the best chance for a satisfying marriage if your partner naturally has similar or complementary sexual interests and a comparable intensity of desire.*

Ask your partner to rate his or her *sustained* sexual drive on a scale from 0 to 10, with 1 or 2 representing very little interest in sex ("Generally it's not a big part of my life." Or, "I can usually take it or leave it.") and 10 representing an intense desire for sex multiple times each day ("I think about sex all the time." Or, "I can't live a day without it."). Also, rate yourself. Be honest. You are not asking for a snapshot here, but a real candid assessment of the ongoing, baseline importance of sex in your life. If more than three numbers separate you and your partner, there is a good chance that this difference is causing some stress in your relationship. You need to find a way to achieve greater satisfaction in your marital bed.

In my practice, one of the most vexing problems I see is when two people marry who have very different sexual drives and/or very different sexual wishes and fantasies. This is often a huge mistake. It is very difficult to have a happy life in our modern highly sexualized world with a partner who *always* wants much more or much less sex than you do. I've referred many such couples to sex therapists, and I'm sorry to report that many of them have difficulty overcoming this kind of hurdle. So, let's not mince words here; everything else being equal, you will have it easier if you have been careful and thoughtful enough to marry someone with whom you are sexually compatible.

However, this may not happen for many complex reasons. At different times of their lives, some men and women will choose to marry even if their partner is not a compatible lover. Often we marry assuming that sex will improve over time. Then we are disappointed if it doesn't happen or when it actually gets worse. Here's another very common scenario. In my practice, many women in their late thirties make decisions on their choice of mate based more on their ticking biological clock than on something as "frivolous" as sex. They date men they love very much, men they envision—perhaps for the first time in their romantic life—as the very sort of decent, caring man they want as the father of their children. The sex may be ho-hum or downright bad, but the woman chooses to overlook that fact in favor of more important considerations and characteristics.

The couple gets married. Several years and two kids later, she now reports that she finds life unbearable. Her husband is indeed that wonderful dad to her children that she expected, but for her, he's more like a friend than a lover. Now that the shrill alarm of her biological clock has been stilled, even though her husband may be her best friend, she hears the muffled cries of her sexual self crying out in frustration. Now she wants a lover.

If you are married to someone with whom you have *never* had a fulfilling sexual life, you have some very tough decisions to make and some very hard work ahead of you. What can you do in these circumstances?

Basically you have three options. First, you can accept that sex won't be the most fulfilling part of your marriage. This choice flies in the face of the current marital paradigm that assumes that a good marriage must have good sex. This is not necessarily so. If you can draw satisfaction from the other aspects of your marriage—companionship, kindness, partnership in parenting, intellectual stimulation, emotional support, and so forth—a marital paradigm that has served previous generations of couples very well, you may find that you can be very happy in a marriage where your sexual life is not your primary focus. But remember, your partner has to feel satisfied with this arrangement, too. It will help you to manage this choice if you stay very aware of and ignore just how hard a sell you're getting on hot sex from our culture. Your second option is to see a sex therapist. I've referred many couples to qualified sex therapists, and some report real improvement. But if you and your partner were *never* sexually compatible, or one of you has never been terribly interested in sex, you will have some very difficult work ahead of you. Be reassured, though, that if you want to explore this route, you'll have plenty of company.

Your third option, sadly, is to consider divorce. Hard as it is to admit, if you're feeling too sexually pressured or too sexually frustrated, if you are too sexually incompatible with your spouse, you may never be able to feel comfortably married. Hidden sexual frustrations and disappointments are often expressed indirectly in marriage as irritability, wide-ranging criticism, and devaluation. All these expressions of frustration tend to demoralize the marriage anyway, even if their real source is never directly addressed. Unfortunately, marriages with major sexual issues frequently end in divorce without ever tackling the sexual problem directly.

Dry Spells

On the other hand, what if you and your spouse started out feeling that your sexual life was fine or fulfilling, but no longer can find any pleasure, interest, or time for sex? You have to consider whether you are just having a dry spell or whether you are in the midst of a severe, prolonged drought. Let's say you just had a baby or work is overwhelming. A beloved friend or relative has died and one of you is grieving. You're a stressed-out caregiver or are ill yourself. Whatever the cause, sex has gotten lost in the shuffle. Not only do you find yourself having sex less and less, you find yourself thinking about it less and less. You start to wonder whether your libido is permanently AWOL or just temporarily misplaced.

You're not alone. Among the spouses I counsel, men and

women alike, exhaustion, stress, and loss of libido are very common. Also, check to be sure that you and your spouse are not taking a medication, such as some antidepressants or blood pressure medications, that can interfere with your interest in sex.

Often, dry spells are an inevitable result of situations we cannot control. However, surprisingly, I have found that they are frequently a side effect of our increasingly consumer-driven society. As the poet William Wordsworth put it, "Getting and spending, we lay waste our powers." Many of us put in excessively long hours at work to make more money, gain more prestige and self-esteem, and buy more things—often at the expense of our marriage. Workaholism becomes a default way of life. By the time we drag ourselves home, we're too tired or preoccupied to enjoy the lovely life for which we've worked so hard. Many of us are just too tired or anxious to have any interest in sex.

If the only problem in your sex life is the inhibition caused by chronic stress or exhaustion, you can usually make the diagnosis yourself. You'll know this is your problem when you begin to think of how much effort or time sex takes and you feel that the expenditure of energy required is just more than you have left to give. Often masturbation seems easier and simpler. The initial treatment is for both you and your spouse to take a vacation alone together, one long enough to give you some relaxation and rest. If your interest in sex returns or at least begins to return, this is a very good prognostic sign. You can stop blaming each other for the problem and do everything possible to diminish the stress and pressure in your everyday lives.

Back home, it is more of a challenge to carve out the mental and physical space needed to continue to enjoy your romantic life. But at least you'll know what is required. Think about creating boundaries at home. Set some limit on how long you can check e-mail, phone messages, or catch up on the work you didn't get done during the day. Make plans to meet for lunch. Think outside the box.

Sex or Sleep? No Contest

Parents of infants and young children deserve special sympathy. Infant care duties are famously exhausting. Mothers of newborns are physiologically drained, pummeled by lack of sleep and hormonal flux, recovering from the physical trauma of birth. "The doctor gave us the go-ahead to have sex six weeks after the baby was born," Margo told me, "but every time Phil wanted to have sex with me, I just felt like one of those Victorian women who lies back and thinks, If you must. I was so tired all the time that I didn't feel like having sex for a year after Helen was born."

A number of women have told me how they feel tyrannized by media portrayals of "sexy supermoms"—famous actresses and supermodels who looked unfailingly chic throughout their pregnancies, gained about ten pounds, and were back in their size two Dolce & Gabbana slacks and Jimmy Choos a week after the baby was born. These women are never portrayed as having any problem reconciling their sexual selves with their new experience of motherhood, and they certainly don't seem to be knocked off their feet by a demanding newborn, the crazed search for good child care, and so forth. Sexy supermoms are a relatively recent media invention, but they've already become deeply entrenched in our collective psyche as the new standard-bearers for motherhood—another reason for typical mothers to feel bad about themselves. Nadine said, "It just makes me feel even worse that I'm still wearing my husband's sweatpants, and Nathan is six months old. If I have time to take a shower, it's a miracle. The last thing I feel is sexy. Then I have to look at photos of Elizabeth Hurley in low-cut Versace when her kid is about a minute old."

The welter of confusing new feelings, combined with constant sleep deprivation, can wreak havoc on your sex life. You can and should spell yourselves with baby-sitting help if you're able, so you can have a brief break from the relentless pressure of attending to a newborn's needs. However, even with help, you have to be very creative to prevent your sex life from dwindling. There are no easy solutions. I suggest that you try to uncouple the normal sense of utter exhaustion from the experience of sex. Don't let sex become just another thing to do on your to-do list. *Don't wait until the end of the day*, after you've done everything else you can possibly do, when you're sure to be exhausted, to consider whether you're ready for romance. You won't be, and you'll find yourself unable to view sex as anything but another obligation instead of the joyful loving release it should be.

Resign yourself to an imperfect world. Throw out the rules that say that you always have to wait for the baby to be asleep, the sheets freshly laundered, your hair just so. If the baby is safe and happy in a crib or playpen in another room, and you're both awake and alert, go for it. You and your marriage need this physical intimacy, even if at times it's the last thing on your mind. Satisfying sex isn't just personally pleasurable; it promotes cohesion in marriage by releasing a cascade of feelings that soothe you and repair the emotional bonds frayed by the stresses of parenthood. Knowing that you and your spouse can have loving sexual time alone together can actually make all the sacrifices of family life feel easier.

I've counseled many couples whose libidos went into deep hibernation with the birth of their kids. If either of you find yourself constantly too tired for sex, don't beat yourself up about it. Talk about it with your spouse. Acknowledge the love you feel, even if the lust has temporarily fled. If you're really just too tired for romance, be *absolutely sure* that your spouse is reassured that you find him or her attractive and desirable. Sometimes it isn't actually the absence of sex that causes marital friction, but the rejected partner's accompanying hurt feelings and loss of self-esteem that cause the conflict. Spouses whose partners avoid sex eventually feel that they are no longer physically attractive—not loved or desired. Even if this is untrue and irrational, it is a very natural painful assumption that cannot be left to fester. If you're really too exhausted to make love, at least find some way to reassure your partner of your love and physical attraction. Find other ways to remain physically close.

Karen always pushed Roger away when he snuggled up to her after they'd turned the lights out. "That's his signal that he wants sex, and I was just too wiped out to think about it. So I'd roll over the other way." When they finally talked about it, what Karen really wanted was to enjoy Roger's physical closeness without feeling that it had to proceed to sex, which felt like too much for her. What mattered to Roger was that he got to hold his wife and know that she found him desirable; yes, he wanted sex more often than she did, but he was willing to bide his time until they both felt more relaxed.

Take care not to let "too tired" become your typical response to sex. Test it out. Are you willing to try some foreplay with the understanding that if you're really not up for it, you can forgo intercourse without either partner feeling let down or resentful? Many people of both sexes find that once they get past the initiation stage of sex, they can actually get so excited that desire overcomes their fatigue or inhibition.

When it comes to the rigors of raising a family, you've heard it before, but it bears repeating: *This, too, shall pass.* Your libidos will live to fight another day when your kids get older. However, it is critically important and a real challenge to stay happily married until that day comes around.

Marriage requires the acceptance of some frustration and sacrifice. No one ever has everything he or she wants in a partner, certainly not over any significant length of time. Successful marriage is built on the notion that you can live well without having everything; that a good life requires some trade-offs, the acceptance of some disappointment, and some sacrifice. However, the sacrifice cannot ask more of us than we can tolerate and it must provide us on balance with feelings of significant satisfaction and gratification. In today's world, marriage cannot demand that we give up so much of ourselves and our dreams that we are left feeling seriously unfulfilled. Marriage must feel generally satisfying and pleasurable, and sex usually has a big role to play in that equation.

227

Uncorking Fine Wine

Media images are particularly tyrannical when it comes to considering sex for folks whose age exceeds their hip measurements. Women especially get the short end of the stick. *People* magazine will happily declare Sean Connery or Harrison Ford the "Sexiest Man Alive," but when was the last time you saw a woman of the same age glorified as the sexiest woman alive? The few that do, typically, single out actresses who can afford major cosmetic surgery and round-the-clock personal trainers; there are few role models who embody ordinary women over forty as vital and sexy.

Katrina, in her mid-forties, told me, "I used to get so depressed. When I hit forty, my metabolism ground to a halt, and I put on a permanent fifteen pounds. I just didn't feel sexy anymore—no more flat abs, and now I have this droopy butt. The funny thing was that my husband, Evan, never stopped telling me how beautiful he thought I was, how sexy." It didn't help; Katrina couldn't shake the feeling that she wasn't attractive anymore, no matter how ardently Evan reassured her to the contrary. "Then one day I found myself wondering why I was wasting so much energy wishing I looked the way I did when I was twenty. I certainly didn't expect to look that way when I was sixty, or seventy, or eighty. At a certain point my body was going to go to pot no matter what I did. So what did that mean? That I wasn't going to have sex or feel sexy when I got older just because I didn't have the body of a teenager anymore? It just seemed so ridiculous to let a flabby belly get in the way of feeling good about myself. I decided to believe my husband. I still get depressed sometimes when I look in the mirror, but I work harder to shake myself out of it. I deserve to feel sexy no matter what I look like."

With the relentlessness of all those other voices and images in bed with us, we all have to work harder to remember that the most important organ of sexual feeling is in between the ears. We have to use our brains to talk back to those media images and the fantasies they unleash so that we can nurture our own realistic sexuality for ourselves.

I see plenty of couples for whom sex has become an all-too-familiar rut. If this has happened to you, it's time to take action. Speak to your spouse about it. Discuss what would make it better for you and listen to what would make it better for your partner. You have this information about yourself in your head, but you're probably too anxious, too discouraged, and/or too inhibited to share it with your partner. If you can't do it without help, seek professional advice. Remember, sexual intimacy is of critical importance to the long-term viability of most marriages.

Relighting the Fire

If your sexual dry spell has expanded to look like the Mojave Desert, it is almost certainly a symptom that you are stuck in some kind of negative emotional interaction. Review the advice on communication and change in chapters 2 and 3. Work to reverse the negative spiral and renew your positive regard for your spouse. If you can reset the emotional atmosphere of your relationship, most of the time your passion for your sexual partner will reignite.

When this happens, you may be faced with the incontrovertibly awkward fact that you haven't had sex in a while and you just don't know how to begin again. Start by reminding yourselves of the beginning of your romance, the time when you were caught in the grip of infatuation and you knew how to make the sparks fly. When couples come to my office for help on how to restart their love life, I lead them step by step through the initial stages of their courtship. I ask them questions like, How did you meet? What was the first thing that attracted you to her? What did you first find sexy about him? How soon before you got into bed together? What was that like? What did you fantasize about each other?

What did it feel like to be so in love and to feel so close and hopeful about the future? Try to remember these feelings. Talk about the good times. Allow yourself to get really nostalgic. Ask each other these questions. Really get into detail: Did you wear a particular outfit? Did her hair smell a certain way? Did you take a particularly romantic road trip? Take yourselves back to that more carefree time, before the complexities of married life and family intruded, reminding yourselves that no matter what has come between you, you have a shared romantic history, and you know that history can repeat itself. Let go of the layers of old hurts, anger, and resentment, and move beyond them. Forgive each other for past transgressions and mistakes and then move forward.

It's important to acknowledge that you may both feel awkward or weird or frightened if it's been a long time since you last had sex. To a certain extent, you're just going to have to hold your breath and jump into the deep end of the pool. Try to normalize the occasion. Instead of thinking that you've got to make it an award-winning performance, think about regular sex the same way you would think of going out to dinner or a movie. Don't make it such a big deal. If the movie's a thumbs-down, it doesn't mean that you'll never go to another movie again. Don't give up and don't obsess about it, just do it again until it feels comfortable and familiar. If you feel it's still a fiasco the fifth time, I might be more concerned. However, remember that the important thing is to give yourselves permission to be human, imperfect, and get on with it.

The best thing you can do for your sex life is to be aware of how relentlessly our culture tries to tell you what your sexual life *should* be. It is very hard to find your own way and to make your own rules. It is harder still to do this as a functional, sexual couple. You may not ever be able to kick out every one of the uninvited guest images in your bed, but you can starve them of attention by turning off your TV set and turning to each other.

Afterword
Real Marriage for Real People

Marriage isn't about falling in love; it's about staying in love.
—Anonymous

The single greatest weapon *in the battle to improve your marriage and ensure its survival is maintaining your awareness of the fragility of the marital bond.* Never take your spouse or your marriage for granted. Recently, I asked a friend what he thought made his marriage so fulfilling. He replied that it was simple; he constantly reminded himself that his marriage was the most important thing in his life. Many of us would say the same thing, but few of us regularly put this thought into action. If more of us had the willingness and ability to put our marital relationship first, there would be much less marital conflict and divorce. A wise patient, speaking of marriage, once told me, "You know, if you don't work hard at your job, you get fired."

Social conventions and cultural traditions have allowed most of us to grow up believing that marriage is a much stronger interpersonal bond than it actually is. Today, there aren't enough external social forces holding couples together to permit most *unsatisfying* relationships to last a lifetime. The marital glue supplied by religious dogma is gone. The glue of the financial and emotional dependence of women is gone. The glue supplied by prevailing social attitudes and legal constraints is gone. The glue of the primacy of higher-order values like self-sacrifice is gone. The glue of the community's and parental disapproval of divorce is mostly gone and, anyway, more or less irrelevant. The glue of believing that no one else out there has it any better than you is gone. The glue of thinking that you have to live with this person only for a little while longer is gone. The glue of believing that happiness is rare and unnecessary is gone. The result is that *the only glue left to hold couples together is the glue created by the two of you—the glue of mutual satisfaction, gratification, appreciation, and respect—the glue of mature love.* If you don't have this, or if you're deluding yourself into thinking you have it, then your marriage is in serious jeopardy.

We live in an increasingly affluent society, philosophically and politically grounded in the ideals of personal freedom, human rights, and the pursuit of happiness. These conditions and ideals have eroded our tolerance for severe or chronic marital frustration or unhappiness. Less bound by community or social obligation, we are focused on developing our individual potential, often at a cost to our marriage. We expect more of marriage even as we give less to it.

The stresses produced by our intense work ethic and our enormous desire for material success profoundly drain our physical reserves and further endanger our emotional relationships. Men and women who work too hard, and have increasingly little spare time, have limited patience for the demands of children and even less patience for the real needs of their spouses. The pressure to perform, excel, or take care of others creates an ethos in which the marital relationship itself becomes a secondary priority in a spouse's harried life. As a result, many couples are seriously neglecting their marriages at a time when the marital bond requires more attention than it ever needed in the past.

We can't reverse these historical and sociocultural developments and remake marriage in its old mold. Attempts to curtail divorce by simply making it more difficult to achieve or by making people feel guilty if they pursue that course only pressures people to remain in unhappy marriages for longer periods of time. Making divorce harder or more painful only generates more bad press for the institution of marriage, which, in turn, will make it look less appealing to those who still want to consider it. In any case, there's no evidence that remaining in an unhappy marriage helps anyone, including the children of such couples.

We can't hope to fix the institution of marriage by simply shifting from a male-dominated paradigm to a female-dominated one. For all their similarities, men and women are different and often have different agendas for life. They don't always share the same interests, and they certainly don't always share the same communication styles.[1] Intolerance by either gender for the general interests or desires of the other will only make the situation worse. One of the most powerful modern relationship myths is the idea that women are good at relationships and men are not. Actually, neither gender is particularly wise when it comes to choosing a mate or developing satisfying relationships, and neither gender is particularly skilled at solving relationship problems. Women assume that they are better at this process because they are generally more practiced at discussing feelings, but this very attitude makes it more difficult for many women to recognize their part of the problem and to accept the need for change. Men feel that they are pragmatic about relationships. However, men generally do not understand that sharing feelings and becoming vulnerable increases intimacy. Also, they have a propensity to be either too passive or too stubborn.

If you really want your marriage to thrive, if you really want your family to remain intact, you will need to be very brave and honest about the realities of married life. Each one of us must take *personal responsibility* for understanding these pressures on modern marriage and our emotional and behavioral responses to them. Each spouse must recognize and accept how much thoughtfulness and effort it takes to maintain a warm, nurturing relationship over many years. If you want your marriage to survive, you must *actively* cherish your spouse and protect your relationship. One of the greatest dangers to marriage is *complacency*, which is fostered by foolishly maintaining a belief in the excessively romantic lies of soul mates and marital bliss. Your real capacity to love will never be truly tested as long as you naively idealize your lover. It's only after you experience some significant disappointment and learn how to love your spouse in spite of, and in full awareness of, his or her flaws that you pass this test of adulthood.

All marriages undergo significant periods of frustration and struggle. There will never be just one kind of good marriage. On some level, every marriage requires the willingness to give up the romantic dream that your partner will be able to provide everything you yearn for from a mate, both physically and emotionally. Even the most motivated and mature adults will find that successful marriage requires the ability to accept disappointments and diminished expectations.

Long-term marital relationships aren't a part of the natural order. Until the last century, lengthy marital unions rarely existed because of shorter life spans, and they certainly didn't require advanced interpersonal skills to guarantee their stability. As a result, these interpersonal skills have not been passed down from generation to generation and are not hard-wired into our psyches. Many of us have not had adequate parental models to show us how to carefully negotiate long-lasting, intimate loving relationships. Nonetheless, because of the power that romantic myths have over us, we all believe that we naturally have the skills necessary to maintain durable intimate relationships. We assume that we are doing a terrific job. Then, when there's trouble, we are taken by surprise. Usually we feel that it is our spouse who is failing. I hope you will reconsider that position now.

If you can acknowledge that your marriage is no longer held together by traditional social and cultural mores, you will accept that the only force left that can truly hold a marriage together is the positive quality and mutual gratification of the marriage itself. Ultimately, the cohesive core of any marriage is the favorable regard that the spouses have for each other and the capacity to experience and express mutual appreciation and pleasure in the relationship.

When all is said and done, the critical, controllable factors in achieving a lasting, satisfying marriage will still be: (1) the careful and wise initial choice of mate; (2) a more realistic understanding of the stresses impinging on marriage from the outside (historical, social, and cultural) and from within (life-cycle changes, family traditions, communication cycles); and (3) the ongoing willingness to thoughtfully, openly, fairly, and skillfully address both your and your spouse's concerns, dissatisfactions, and differences.

The unique challenge of marriage is for two people to share their complicated lives and remain emotionally connected, while respectfully discussing their many differences. Essential to this dialogue is the capacity to acknowledge your differences and admit when you're not getting what you hoped for or expected from your spouse. Recognizing this fact and having the willingness to hear and respond positively to similar disappointments from your partner are an exquisitely painful, but necessarily productive part of marriage. *It is in the acceptance of our differences that we mature as a couple.* It marks the conversion of the marital relationship from lies to truths, from fantasy to reality, from adolescent longing to adult connection, and from infatuation to mature love. Your marriage, every marriage, must go through this painful transformation during which you learn to love someone in spite of his or her imperfections. That's where real courage comes in. Do you give up and walk away? Is it too much for you? Is your spouse really too different from you ever to make a go of it, or are you just too disappointed, too angry, too resentful, too stubborn, or too prideful to work it out? Can you take a risk? Can you *stop fighting* and start realistically talking about and solving the problems? *Couples who are*

*able successfully to control their emotional reactivity and stay out of nega-
tive spirals have the best chance to do so.*

Because most couples haven't been made aware of and don't
want to accept the fragility of the marital bond, and because marriages tend to function and dysfunction in isolation, I recommend
that you seek out larger groups of couples with which to share the
joys and difficulties of married life in an atmosphere of mutual
inquiry and support. The more we openly talk of our common
concerns and difficulties, the easier it is to accept them as inevitable
and "normal." That's what this book is all about.

My work over twenty years as a marriage therapist has taught
me that a good marriage, a marriage that supports and gratifies
both spouses, is more difficult to achieve and sustain than most
people are willing to believe. Nonetheless, if you're willing to work
conscientiously and continually to have a loving relationship, you
can attain it, and you'll find it among the most fulfilling achieve-
ments of your adult life.

My experience with hundreds of couples tells me that almost
every marriage can be improved, even if only one partner is willing
to put in the work initially. However, if you've tried unsuccessfully
to resolve your differences and decide that you can't live with your
spouse, it's not a sign of mental illness, moral corruption, or a limited capacity to love. Many healthy, reasonable people cannot live
with the spouses they love because the differences between them
make their lives too unsatisfying. Being aware of this is very different than leaving a marriage because you fight all the time, hate
your spouse, and think you're fine just the way you are. Repetitive
fighting is a symptom of the uncontrolled negative emotional spiral. Fighting and/or coldly distancing yourself are not problem-
solving skills. They divert your attention from finding solutions to
your marital problems. They are emotional reactions that interfere
with doing the work of marriage. They are actually the "nonskills"
that have been handed down to us by generations upon generations
of spouses who knew that they could behave badly toward each

other and still count on external social forces to hold their marriage together. Today, fighting usually masks the problems and the potentials of your marriage, and recurring, unresolved conflict poisons the atmosphere of your relationship while it impedes personal and marital growth.

The single biggest problem I see in my practice is that couples who could have made it together come in too late for help. They ignore the problems and the negative feelings they create until one of them is discovered having an affair or until they have become so emotionally conflicted or disengaged that they are on the verge of separation. Then they come for help hoping that all the terrible corrosive feelings that they've allowed to build up over the years can be miraculously, quickly reversed before the last act of their drama comes to a close. I, like other couples therapists, have many ways to help unravel and overcome the conflicts between battling spouses. There are many different useful techniques and strategies for improving relationships in addition to the ones I've discussed in these pages. But all this knowledge is completely useless if one or the other partner no longer cares—is over the cliff.

Creatures of habit, often bad habits, marital spouses locked in frustrating conflict can continue the same destructive cyclic behavior for years, even though they know it's ineffective and hurtful. We refuse to believe that our partner cannot hear what we are trying to say and that he or she cannot change his or her ideas, beliefs, or behaviors even when we offer them obvious proof that they are wrong. So we play out the same negative, painful interaction over and over again until rage or apathy set in and someone finally quits. And tragically, long before this quitting is announced openly, it has taken place in the heart. Once this resignation has occurred, once one partner no longer really wants the relationship with the other, the relationship is over.

If there is anything I hope this book accomplishes, it is that I want fewer people to end up surprised by the end of their marriage. Imagine telling your spouse that there's nothing to work on because a long time ago you actually lost interest in being with him or her. Imagine hearing that same painful message yourself. When the spouse caught in this position asks, "Well, why didn't you tell me earlier?" the other spouse usually responds, "I did. You just weren't listening." Though this is usually metaphorically true, it is not really fair. Very often spouses never directly address the problems in their marriage. If one partner wasn't listening, it's frequently because the channels of communication were blocked in both directions. And now that the partner is willing to listen, desperate to listen, it's too late.

I hope this book has opened your eyes to the vulnerability of relationships. If you see what has happened, the way the world has changed and how this affects your marriage, you will have a good chance to strengthen your relationship before it is too late. However, if the strategies in this book aren't enough to put your marriage back on track, don't hesitate to go for professional help. Therapists may follow different clinical theories and use different techniques, so if one person or one therapy isn't helping you, try another. But don't procrastinate and don't give up easily.

Have the courage and the humility to fight for your marriage. "Love seems the swiftest, but it is the slowest of all growths. No man or woman really knows what perfect love is until they have been married a quarter of a century," wrote Mark Twain. By perfect love, I believe he meant the love that endures between two imperfect people, a love that requires skillful hard work to overcome many differences and misunderstandings. That's the love that real people find in real marriage. May you enjoy that kind of perfect love.

Endnotes

Preface

1. Matthew D. Bramlett and William D. Mosher, *First Marriage Dissolution, Divorce, and Remarriage: United States*, Advance Data from Vital and Health statistics no. 323 (Hyattsville, Md.: National Center for Health Statistics, 2001).
2. Kim K. Hyoun and Patrick C. McKenry, "Relationship Transitions as Seen in the National Survey of Families and Households," *Journal of Divorce and Remarriage*, 34:163–67.
3. Bramlett and Mosher, *First Marriage Dissolution*, 11.

Introduction

1. William Manchester, *A World Lit Only by Fire: The Medieval Mind and the Renaissance: Portrait of an Age* (Boston: Little, Brown and Company, 1992), 55.
2. Stephanie Coontz, "The American Family," *Life Magazine*, November 1999, 79–94. Also, Stephanie Coontz, *The Way We Never Were: American Families and the Nostalgia Trap* (New York: Basic Books, 1992).
3. Another striking example of this limited life span is that in the first American census of 1790, 50 percent of the American population of 3.9 million was sixteen years old or *younger*.
4. Recently, a patient reported being told by his father, "Marriage is essentially a business deal. If you understand that, you'll be fine." Maybe things have not changed all that much in the minds of some.

5. M. B. Keller, G. L. Klerman, P. W. Lavori et.al., "Long-term Outcome of Episodes of Major Depression: Clinical and Public Health Significance, *JAMA* 252, no. 6 (1984): 788–92.

6. For a wonderful example of this all-consuming need, read or watch the videotape of Jane Austin's 1811 novel *Sense and Sensibility*. It is about two sisters, left with little money after the death of their father, whose very existence requires them to meet and marry men who will protect them economically. It is fascinating to watch how this need for economic security interplays with and is transformed into the women's experience of love.

7. It should not be inferred here that I believe that the struggle for women's economic opportunity or equality is over. Only that the process has progressed far enough to dramatically change the historical *absolute* economic dependence of most women on their husbands.

8. For an example of how one can work on a marriage, i. e., do couples therapy with only one member of the couple, see Michelle Weiner-Davis's book *Divorce Busting* (Fireside, 1992).

9. Betty Carter and Joan K. Peters, *Love, Honor and Negotiate* (New York: Pocket Books, 1996), chapter 4.

10. Arlie Russell Hochschild, *The Second Shift* (New York: Avon Books, 1989).

11. John M. Gottman and Nan Silver make the same point in *The Seven Principles for Making Marriage Work* (New York: Three Rivers Press, 1999).

Chapter 2

1. For a further example of receptive listening, see the discussion of the couple's dialogue in Rick Brown's *Imago Relationship Therapy: An Introduction to Theory and Practice* (New York: John Wiley and Sons, 1999).

Chapter 3

1. For an extraordinarily useful explanation of how people engage in emotional dances with each other and what can be done to learn new, relieving steps, see the works of Harriet Lerner, *The Dance of Anger* (New York: HarperPerennial, 1985) and *The Dance of Intimacy* (New York: HarperPerennial, 1989).

2. Michael E. Kerr and Murray Bowen, *Family Evaluation* (New York: W. W. Norton and Company, 1988).
3. Betty Carter. Personal communication.
4. For a fuller discussion of the effects of depression on marriage, see the works of Ann Sheffield, *Depression Fallout: The Impact of Depression on Couples and What You Can Do to Preserve the Bond*, (New York: Quill, HarperCollins, 2003) and *How You Can Survive When They're Depressed: Living and Coping with Depression Fallout* (New York: Three Rivers Press, 1998).
5. *Clinical Psychiatry News* 29, no. 1 (January 2001): 2.

Chapter 4

1. Murray Bowen called this the "two-step."
2. Of course there are some families that are so disturbed that communication with them is almost impossible. When dealing with drug-addicted, alcoholic, or mentally ill parents, special strategies have to be employed.

Chapter 5

1. Scott Coltrane, "Research on Household Labor: Modeling and Measuring the Social Embeddedness of Routine Family Work," *Journal of Marriage and the Family* 62, 1208–33.
2. From Melissa Schorr, "Division of Household Chores Affects Marital Bliss," Available from PreventDisease.com Excerpted from Reuters Health.
3. "Unequal Share of Housework Causes Depression in Women, Study Says." Reported by the Brown University News Bureau, March 15, 1999. Available from www.brown.edu.
4. For more information on assessing marital roles and responsibilities and following up after a fair division of labor, I recommend M. Gary Neuman's excellent *Emotional Infidelity: How to Affair-Proof Your Marriage and 10 Other Secrets to a Great Relationship* (New York: Three Rivers Press, 2001).
5. Far too often in my practice I have seen couples in which the woman, following traditional gender prescriptions, actually avoids any involvement in investment or financial matters until there is a crisis like the husband's ill health, mismanagement, or divorce.

6. From Denise Mann's article, "Division of Labor: Women Still Do Twice as Much Housework as Men." Available from WebMD.com. This article also offers additional suggestions for divvying up housework.

7. See Arlie Russell Hochschild's *The Second Shift* (New York: Avon Books, 1989).

8. Of course poverty or real problems paying bills can also lead to terrible marital tensions.

9. This is a central idea in many Eastern philosophies, the yin-yang of relationships. Unfortunately, this romantic vision of relationships developed in a world in which women had, and still have, very little power. When this eventually changes, the self-determination of women may make the belief that men and women are different halves of the same self sound outdated and quaint.

10. In the 1990's, Americans added nearly a full week of work to their lives each year, working, on average, about 137 hours a year more than their nearest competitors, the Japanese. Americans feel more economically pressured and regularly take less vacation than workers take in any other Western country. The average white-collar worker spends over sixty hours a week at his/her job. "Americans' International Lead in Hours Worked Grew in '90s, Report Shows," *New York Times*, September 1, 2001, p. A8.

Chapter 6

1. John M. Gottman and Clifford I. Notarius, "Marital Research in the 20th Century and a Research Agenda for the 21st Century," *Family Process* 41, no. 2 (summer 2002): 172.

2. Lynn K. White and Alan Booth, "The Quality and Stability of Remarriages: The Role of Stepchildren," *American Sociological Review* 50, no. 5 (1985): 689–98.

3. The difficult problems of stepfamilies are beyond the scope of this book. Suffice it to say that stepfamilies are another example of how children inadvertently contribute to marital instability.

4. For more information on what happens to couples when they become parents you can read Carolyn Pape Cowan and Philip A. Cowan's *When Partners Become Parents: The Big Life Change For Couples* (Mahwah, N.J.: Lawrence Erlbaum Associates, 1992).

5. Susan Cheever, "The Forgotten Husband," *Talk*, June/July 2001, 73–75.

6. E. Mavis Hetherington and John Kelly, *For Better or for Worse: Divorce Reconsidered* (New York: W. W. Norton and Company, 2003), 248.

7. For a good book on how to set reasonable limits for children, read Thomas W. Phalan's *1-2-3 Magic: Effective Discipline for Children* (Glen Ellyn, Ill.: Child Management Inc, 1995).

8. For more on this read the books of Ron Taffel and Melinda Blau: *Parenting by Heart: How to Stay Connected to Your Child in a Disconnected World*, 2d edition (Cambridge, Mass.: Perseus Publishing, 2002) and *Nurturing Good Children Now: 10 Basic Skills to Protect and Strengthen Your Child's Core Self* (New York: Golden Books, 1999).

Chapter 7

1. Ellen Fein and Sherrie Schneider, *The Rules: Time-Tested Secrets for Capturing the Heart of Mr. Right* (New York: Warner Books, 1995).

2. It is estimated that today in America, 60+ percent of married men and 30+ percent of married women have engaged in extramarital sex. In certain cultures it is assumed that almost all men have affairs, partially as a way to avoid divorce.

3. There are, of course, many movies and television shows that portray people in uncomfortable, if not downright miserable, relationships, just as there are movies and television shows that show families in trouble.

Afterword

1. Deborah Tannen, *You Just Don't Understand: Women and Men in Conversation* (New York: Ballantine Books, 1990).

Index